ALTERED
STATES

ALTERED STATES

Creativity Under the Influence

James Hughes

WATSON-GUPTILL
PUBLICATIONS
New York

First published in the United States in
1999 by Watson-Guptill Publications, a
division of BPI Communications, Inc.,
1515 Broadway, New York, NY 10036

Library of Congress Catalog
Card Number: 99-62580

ISBN 0-8230-0163-6

This book was conceived, designed,
and produced by THE IVY PRESS
LIMITED, 2/3 St Andrews Place,
Lewes, East Sussex, BN7 1UP

Art Director: PETER BRIDGEWATER
Editorial Director: SOPHIE COLLINS
Designer: GLYN BRIDGEWATER
Illustrations: IVAN HISSEY, CATHERINE
MCINTYRE, MARK PRESTON
Picture Researcher: VANESSA FLETCHER

Printed and bound in Singapore by
Star Standard Industries (Pte) Ltd.

1 2 3 4 5 6 7 8 9 10/
99 08 07 06 05 04 03 02 01 00

This book is typeset in Caslon and Univers

Dedication—To Mahalakshmi

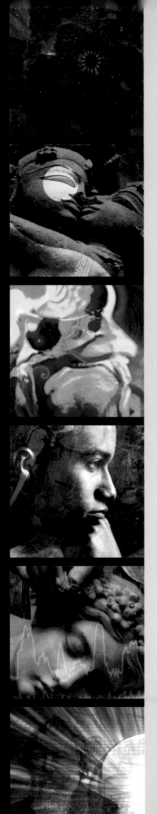

CONTENTS

1
INTRODUCTION

2
POWER AND POSSESSION

3
STRUCTURES OF THE MIND

4
DREAMS AND THE UNCONSCIOUS

5
THE CREATIVE PROCESS

INTRODUCTION

The poet makes himself a seer by
a long, prodigious, and rational
disordering of all the senses.

ARTHUR RIMBAUD

CREATIVITY AND ALTERED STATES

Creativity runs like a thread through all human nature. The paradox of creativity is that it contains ingredients that are both extraordinary and everyday. To bring something—an idea, an object—into external reality out of "nowhere" is associated with a whole range of "abnormal" states of consciousness, from daydreaming and fantasy to trances and drug-induced hallucinations. But it is also part of everyone's evolutionary equipment, a means of producing original solutions to problems, a basic ability.

LEFT **Creativity, to some extent, involves accessing the penumbra of ideas, sensations, and images that hover at the edges of our consciousness.**

The creative act is not "normal" since it involves using unconscious processes in unifying opposites in a new synthesis. The uniting of disparate elements may impose stresses and conditions on the creative personality that seem, and often are, pathological. Dryden observed that "great wits are sure to madness near allied," and contemporary research has identified correlations between various kinds of mental illness, notably hypomania, with prominent creatives. It would appear that the creative process requires, at least in some of its operations, a state of consciousness that is dramatically, sometimes dangerously, "altered," in the sense defined by the American psychologist Charles Tart.

In his classic symposium *Altered States of Consciousness* (1969), Tart published studies of a number of mental states such as hypnosis, dreaming, meditation, and drug-induced conditions that, in his words, revealed "a qualitative shift in the pattern of mental functioning." These he named altered states of consciousness (ASCs), and saw them as challenges to a materialistic explanation of consciousness and the mind. Since the publication of this work, Tart and other investigators have fought to counteract the dominant view that physical matter and physical energies are the only fundamental realities of the universe. Consciousness, in the materialist view, is reducible to physical interactions within the body, brain, and nervous system, and all experience comes down to some pattern of electrochemical firing within the brain. Tart believes that "high-quality scientific investigation has shown there is excellent evidence for a nonmaterial quality to the human mind, evidence that provides general support for the reality of our spiritual natures."

TRANSPERSONAL PSYCHOLOGY

Tart's comparatively new field of study, called transpersonal psychology, is devoted to the scientific study of what may be called the "spiritual core" of human beings, and implies a much broader view of the human psychoperceptual range than that proposed in conventional Western psychology. Transpersonal experiences, in which a person seems to go beyond the limits of his body and mind, and experiences phenomena inconsistent with ordinary possibility, are exceptionally important to their experiencers. They can even form the basis of religions and philosophies. Yet the current scientific position, which equates consciousness with brain functioning, automatically views the content of these vital experiences as illusions and delusions.

It is only natural that conventional psychologists have concentrated on "ordinary" consciousness, which in the West is generally perceived to cover transactions with the external, objective world. Ordinary consciousness is what we use to adapt to life and events as they impact on us at an everyday level. Transpersonal psychologists have identified a large number of experiences, however, which seem to imply that consciousness may not always be restricted to the body and brain, and that there is good scientific evidence for a less narrow theory. At the heart of transpersonal psychology is the proposal that there is a "mind" or "life" component to consciousness that is qualitatively different from known physical systems, and that some transpersonal experiences are not to be dismissed as merely interesting illusions, unusual patterns of neural firing, and so on, but actually tell us something about the potential for transcending our ordinary physical limits, as for example in out-of-body experiences.

THE PARANORMAL

Despite the statements of uncompromisingly materialist scientists such as Richard Dawkins that there is "no evidence whatsoever" for paranormal events, it would seem that such events are perceived to happen frequently in everyday life. In 1975 a representative survey of the American population found that more than half of the sample questioned believed they had experienced telepathic, mind-to-mind contact with someone at least once in their life. Many other kinds of extrasensory perception such as precognition, clairvoyance, and telekinesis are widely believed to occur, and to a significant number of people.

ABOVE The sense of being in telepathic contact is common between twins, particularly at times of crisis when the limited capacities of normal consciousness might be perceived as inadequate.

Popular interest in the occult may merely reflect a generalized sense of powerlessness in the face of the institutions and organizations that control us. Abduction by aliens may seem a good metaphor for the destructive transformation of one's home, life, and work as a result of remote global processes, unmediated by local effects. However, there does also seem to be solid scientific evidence for paranormal phenomena, as for instance in the investigation of dream telepathy by Ullman, Krippner, and Vaughan, carried out at the Maimonides Dream Laboratory as long ago as 1947. In the last 40 years it has been estimated that more than 600 high-quality experiments have been published, most of which show statistically significant evidence for various kinds of paranormal processes.

RIGHT **The fact that paranormal phenomena, such as poltergeists and telekinesis, are frequently associated with younger, more "impressionable" people may account for the lack of interest from the conventional scientific establishment.**

The paranormal is itself defined negatively—it covers all those phenomena not susceptible to the current laws of science; post-Newtonian physics, for instance, embodies many features that would have been described as paranormal before the discoveries of Einstein and Planck. It seems puzzling that such an obvious subject for scientific investigation should have received such obloquy from mainstream scientists. This hostility may be due to impatience at the layman's unscientific interest in paranormal phenomena and extrasensory perception (as witness the success of the TV series *The X-Files*). This fascination may itself be an irrational reaction to the apparently irresistible progress of scientific materialism, or scientism. The many-sided nature of the mind enables it to hold conflicting opinions, and there is little doubt that many people intellectually accept the materialistic worldview of our age while retaining an allegiance to the personal, subjective world of the imagination.

WHAT IS CREATIVITY?

Creative thought involves two different reasoning processes, divergent and convergent. Divergent reasoning, which is a mental operating system rarely found in ordinary consciousness, is the intellectual ability to bring together two quite different sets of facts or ideas so as to form a new and meaningful synthesis. It has been described as a doubleminded, transitory state of unstable equilibrium where the balance of both emotion and thought is disturbed. The resultant creative instability takes different forms in science and art. Convergent thinking is the intellectual ability to logically evaluate, analyze, and choose the best idea from a selection, and to work it into external reality. Both abilities are required for creative output: divergent thinking is essential to the novelty of creative products, while convergent thinking is fundamental to their appropriateness.

Since novelty is the defining characteristic of the creative act, it is the ability to hold simultaneously a number of different perceptions in the mind that marks out the creative personality. As the writer Vladimir Nabokov (1899–1977) put it, "A person hoping to become a poet must have the capacity to think of several things at a time." Nabokov records in his autobiography how, in the course of writing his first poem, he found himself chatting with the village schoolmaster, and simultaneously registering the posy of wild flowers in his hands, the "blackheads on the fleshy volutes of his nostrils, the dull little voice of a cuckoo coming from afar, the flash of a Queen of Spain [butterfly] settling on the road, the remembered impression of the pictures in the village school, the throb of some utterly irrelevant recollection (a pedometer I had lost), the savor of the grass stalk I was chewing... and all the while I was richly, serenely aware of my own manifold awareness."

Creativity is about the use of imagination to transmute the inner world into external reality, and has both an objective, material component and a subjective, invisible component. It begins as an imaginative construct and ends as an external object. Since creativity has, so to speak, a foot in both camps, perhaps it can be the bridge between the worlds of reality and imagination. Moreover "high" creativity—artistic production of a high cultural order—today receives the kind of veneration once reserved for religious phenomena; neurally fired or not, there is something intrinsically amazing about creation, since something emerges from nothing. As a complex mental process bringing together disparate elements to form a new and valuable synthesis, creativity extends beyond the arts, sciences, and philosophy. For it involves the organization of everyday subjective experience as well as of imaginative material, and thus includes the whole of life.

ABOVE **New York subway graffiti artist, lionized during the art boom of the 1980s, dead at age 26 from an overdose: Jean-Michel Basquiat exemplified a common idea of the creative artist.**

Creativity includes not only the working out of an idea into external reality, but also its acceptance and validation by others. This complicates the situation, since all such validation is subject to cultural, historical, social, and even economic constraints. Many signatures have to go on the documentation before a product can be passed as creative, that is, new, original, and valuable in the opinion of the relevant authorities. Since the creative process by definition brings together unreconciled and opposing elements to form a new synthesis, it very often poses a challenge to established values. Successful creativity carries out a transformative role in society, changing the world in some small or large particular. And, although transformation is mysterious and "wonderful," it is also unsettling.

While creativity in modern society enjoys the cultural status that in a previous age would be accorded to religious faith, artistic products are often more valued than their creators—the relationship between a creative artist and his or her society is often uneasy, sometimes hostile and vindictive. All creativity has a destructive component, since the mold has to be broken in order to make something new. As a free spirit who does not observe existing rules, the creative may be envied and feared as well as admired by the normality.

LEFT **Van Gogh's self-mutilation, the result of a quarrel with Gauguin, is a vivid example of the dangerous otherness of the artist.**

CONNECTIONS

Is there a connection, or at least an affinity, between the creative process and such states as dream, hypnosis, psychosis, or psychotropic trance? Clearly there is a connection insofar as all these states exist outside ordinary consciousness. There is also the issue of "automotive" creation, as reported by many creative artists such as William Blake and Samuel Taylor Coleridge. Some literary critics have questioned the latter's account of the genesis of "Kubla Khan," featuring the "person from Porlock" who disrupted the emergence of the poem from dream into external reality, but who may have been a figment of the poet's imagination, a way of excusing his inability to complete his poem. But it is undeniable that automotive creation, involving the ability to produce works of art without conscious mediation—an altered state if ever there was one—has featured in the work of many artists.

Many artists mythologize their activities and their ways of working for numerous and often conflicting

RIGHT *The Ancient of Days* by William Blake (1793). An image of superhuman power and energy, it was inspired by a vision that Blake observed hovering over his head.

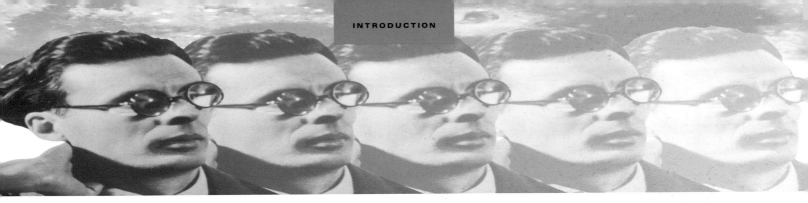

reasons, emphasizing the mysterious, otherworldly nature of their vocation. However, some psychologists who specialize in the study of creativity draw a sharp distinction between the unresolved nature of dream imagery and psychotic art, and "real" art, which is presented in a finished and communicable form. In classic Freudian terms, the dream uses symbolism to disguise its real content, which is too painful for the subject to confront. The artist, in contrast, uses imagery to reveal a hitherto unseen vision. In working toward an external form, the artist may use the same preconscious or unconscious material available in psychosis or dream, but the artist's purpose is to produce revelation rather than concealment, lucidity rather than obscurity. According to Freud's disciple Ernst Kris (1900–1957), the artist finds his material when unconscious processes erupt into consciousness through "an act of regression in the service of the ego," and having achieved consciousness these processes are controlled by the ego for creative purposes.

An important aspect of the creative personality is a readiness to open oneself up to psychic states unobtainable by ordinary means. Students of altered states of consciousness, from Aldous Huxley to Timothy Leary, from Baudelaire to Allen Ginsberg, have seen such states as gateways to a higher reality through the paranormal and spiritual. Other artists may value such states more as a means of achieving a creative product

ABOVE **Aldous Huxley was famous for experimenting with the drug mescaline to explore the nature of its hallucinogenic effects; he recounted his findings in** *The Doors of Perception,* **published in 1954.**

rather than a visionary experience. Art for art's sake is a historically dubious concept—art is nearly always in the service of something else, even if that something is the artist's own ego. Creativity differs in an important respect from the experience of altered states for visionary or spiritual, let alone recreational experience, for it is concerned with form, a finished product or a realized idea.

SELF-CREATION

The development of one's own creativity has come to be seen as a desirable pursuit, an end in itself. Creativity, to a large extent, is a comparatively recent Western construct, closely related to the idea of individuality, while in the East the creative is seen as a collective expression of divine forces. A whole industry has grown up around the idea that we can all be creative if we recognize our unique talents and develop mastery in certain areas.

Many researchers believe that self-creation, the reconciling of disparate elements of the individual's personality in order to form an integrated whole, is the highest form of creativity. But creativity is also advocated as a way of life. Here the object is not so much to achieve public recognition as "the soul satisfaction that comes with living a creative life." The development of creativity as a means of improving one's quality of life has become an article of faith in Western society in the late twentieth century.

ABOVE **The Hindu Creator God Brahma emerges from the navel of the Preserver, Vishnu. In Eastern thought, creativity is part of the divine order and its maintenance.**

POWER AND POSSESSION

All art is magic.

PABLO PICASSO

THE POWER

The power of nature and human power over nature have been principal concerns of humanity since the emergence of *Homo sapiens sapiens* some 50,000 years ago. Natural religion proposes the interpenetration of nature and spirit, the existence of a soul inherent in nature, specifically in animals, plants, elements, rocks, and natural phenomena. Human survival and good fortune depended on successful communication with these entities. The earliest representative art, concealed within deep cave complexes in southwestern Europe, stands witness to an early understanding of the interfusion of spirit and nature, and the use of creative techniques to give form to imagination in the service of religion. It seems probable that the most ancient figurative art concerns human interaction with the spirit world of animals and nature, a world reached through ritual and trance.

CAVE SECRETS

In 1995 a richly decorated cave in the Ardèche Valley, southeastern France, revealed artistic methods that were still being practiced 20,000 years later at the celebrated sites of Lascaux (France) and Altamira (Spain). Carbon dating of charcoal pigment gave a date of about 31,000 years BCE. The Ardèche paintings and engravings of bears, rhinoceroses, lions, owls, and mammoths differ in subject matter from those at the sites at Lascaux and Altamira: there are no depictions of predatory animals, upsetting current scholarly theories about the purpose of the art.

But all these works reveal what seems to be a common inspiration in their concentration on animal forms to the virtual exclusion of plant and human species, the power and grace of the images, the underground locations, and the portrayal of strange, nightmarish spirit forms. The basic impulse, the depiction of supernature in nature, is surely evident in all. Furthermore, these works may be seen as a single "movement," so similar are they in terms of technique and subject matter. Yet the "movement" covers an enormously long period, perhaps the longest movement in the history of art—if art is what it is.

The intensity of the images, the inward realization of animal life, and the massive energy of the paintings all indicate a level of artistic achievement that has seldom been surpassed. Yet their purpose is clearly not aesthetic. Many are hidden in deep recesses of limestone caves, accessible only by means of difficult and sometimes dangerous routes, far from the sun, mysterious, otherworldly. Several feature composite figures—half-human, half-animal, masked and antlered figures—which reach across the millennia, anticipating practices and beliefs found in nomadic, preliterate societies of fairly recent times.

LEFT **Vivid leaping creatures on cave walls: acute realism, yet reaching beyond that, reaching for the spirit world—"the depiction of supernature in nature."**

PAINTING THE UNPAINTABLE

Although the galleries of leaping beasts are the most eye-catching aspect of the cave paintings, nonfigurative marks are far more abundant than figurative depictions. They include a wide range of motifs, from a single dot or line to complex constructions, some isolated in a cave, others closely associated with figurative images. The Freudian analyst Ernst Kris has pointed out that a magic image embodies the subject rather than represents it. A magic image need not, perhaps cannot, represent an object that has its being in the spirit world, but it can affect the onlookers' consciousness, prompting them to see in it the vision of the object. Representative art, in contrast, needs to provide information about the object, to show what it looks like, so that the onlooker will comprehend rather than see directly with the eye of the imagination.

Despite the extraordinarily lifelike representation of much cave art, stylizations and superimpositions impart a

ABOVE **Concentric patterns, as seen in these rock paintings discovered at Tassili N'Ajjer in the Sahara, are common in cave art and have been linked to the visual phenomena experienced during trance.**

dreamlike quality, an indication that the life that is depicted here goes beyond the natural sphere. Many of the nonfigurative marks resemble marks found at sites in North America where rituals have traditionally taken place. These marks—such as red dots and radiating spheres—are believed by some ethnographers to indicate "visions from within," or phosphenes (the sensation of light caused by pressure on the eyelid), which are often reported by subjects during experiments on altered states of perception.

The presence of masked, half-animal figures further supports the view that our earliest ancestors used ritual and trance similar to the shamanistic practices of historical nomadic societies (see page 20) to merge the human with the animal spirit. In the Ardèche cave stands the earliest known compound representation, half-man, half-bison. The cathedral-like size and resonance of some of the caves suggest that sound played an important part in whatever ceremonies accompanied the production of cave art.

SHAMANS

The hunting peoples of the Palaeolithic Ice Age, like their nomadic descendants in Siberia and North America, shared their world not only with the animal creation but also with a vast population of spirits. Their lives, like those of many preliterate societies until recent times, were shot through with spirit consciousness. Although families and individuals in these societies may have had their own spirit familiars, with whom they communicated in dreams and visions, on the whole the people relied, like their descendants, on the services of shamans.

The shaman is a "specialist of the soul," an intermediary between the visible and invisible worlds, a traveler to upper and underworlds in the service of their community. The Siberian Tungus people, from whose language the word "shaman" derives, form part of a spread of peoples extending in a wide band across the Northern Hemisphere, all of whom practice, or once practiced, the art. However, shamanism is not confined to these groups but has been observed in widely distributed nonliterate societies elsewhere, from the !Kung Bushmen of southern Africa to the Aborigines of Australia, as well as in Eastern Asia, South America, and Oceania. Shamanistic phenomena are also sometimes apparent in the religions of more highly organized cultures, such as Japanese Shintoism. The anthropologist Mircea Eliade has shown that shamanism is a stage in the development of almost all human societies; it is universal, the old Earth religion.

ABOVE **An Alaskan Inuit festival mask representing a supernatural creature whose spirit enters the wearer during participation in the festival. Wild dancing and ritual drumming create the ecstatic trance through which contact with the spirit world is made.**

HARNESSING THE SPIRIT FORCE

A belief in the spirit force is the fundamental assumption of shamanizing societies. The whole world is saturated with spirits; everything is influenced for good or ill by their activity. Shamanism involves traveling to the other worlds, making contact with the spirits, and using them for the benefit of the community. This is its principal task, achieved through ectstatic trance. Shamans are "healers, seers, visionaries who have mastered death." They are poets and singers, dancers, artists. They are psychologists, entertainers, and food finders. Above all, shamans are "technicians of the sacred and masters of ecstasy."

LEFT **Masks bring us closer to the spirits through a paradoxical blend of concealment and display. This Inuit mask wonderfully turns the physical world upside down, and perhaps inside out.**

A focus on ecstatic trance is the distinguishing characteristic of shamanism. The condition is induced by ritual drumming, dancing, and ingestion of psychotropic power plants, and it is the means used by the shamans to retrace their interworld journeys. A particular plant or fungus, such as fly agaric (*Amanita muscaria*) or the psilocybe mushroom (*Psilocybe mexicana*) is often the personal ally of the shaman.

ABOVE **The distinctive fly agaric toadstool (*Amanita muscaria*) produces hallucinogens, and can be fatal if eaten. Its extract, muscarine, was used as a fly-killing agent.**

Today, not only the hallucinogenic drugs used by shamans but also their methods of working with dreams, and their ability to be conscious and in control while dreaming, are becoming the focus of increased attention—part of a widening interest in the post-Newtonian, postindustrial societies of the developed world in the applications of nonordinary reality. There is extensive ethnographic documentation of the shamanic, of so-called lucid dreaming and out-of-body traveling, which matches experiences of altered states of consciousness recorded in many experiments. Trances entered through yogic meditation may also yield these experiences, but the wild and wonderful voyages of these shamans, recorded by numerous ethnographers, have caught the imagination of many who resist the more formal approach of yoga and Zen.

ABOVE ***Psilocybe mexicana* was used by the Aztecs in religious ceremonies; they called it "God's flesh." It is still eaten by Mexican Indians for its hallucinogenic effects.**

LEFT **A sketch for**
Yermak Conquers
Siberia by Vasisli
Surikov, featuring a
shaman dressed in
motley with ritual
drum and bells.

A SIBERIAN SHAMAN

Kyzlasov was a famous Siberian shaman from the Sagay village of Kyzlan. He was a very old man when the Hungarian ethnologist Vilmos Diószegi visited his isolated yurt in the 1960s. Kyzlasov gave Diószegi details of his experiences.

◎ It was not the talent I inherited, but the shaman spirits of my clan. . . I had been sick and I had been dreaming. In my dreams I had been taken to the ancestor and cut to pieces on a black table. They chopped me up and then threw me into the kettle and I was boiled. . . While the pieces of my body were boiled, they found a bone around the ribs, which had a hole in the middle. This was the excess-bone. This brought about my becoming a shaman. Because only those men can become shamans in whose body such a bone can be found. One looks across the hole of this bone and begins to see all, to know all, and that is when one becomes a shaman. . . When I came to from this state, I woke up. This meant that my soul had returned. Then the shamans declared, "You should become a shaman, you must begin to shamanize!"

. . . I picked up a white drum and a garment from the other side. . . I went to the chief shaman, the ancestor. When I got there, he measured my drum, its circumference, its length, and its height. He counted the pendants hanging from it. When he was ready, he gave me the "men" [the shamans called their spirits men]. They are my friends. Sometimes they come upon me unexpectedly, then they disappear again. It is to them I owe my well-being, it is through them, when I hold the pulse of a sick person, it becomes clear to me what is wrong with him. ◎

FROM *TRACING SHAMANS IN SIBERIA*,
BY VILMOS DIÓSZEGI (1968)

THE HEALING TRANCE

Shamans have some of the attributes of priests and also of sorcerers, but their role is largely healing. The medical diagnoses, and the cures achieved, are made possible by entering the other worlds and finding the supernatural causes of the illness. Common techniques found in different cultures include catching and breathing in a power animal, and sucking to remove a supernatural dart. Shamans have special skills such as magical flight, control over the elements, super-human strength and endurance, and powers over animals, especially those of the spirit ally. The vocation may be hereditary; it may be revealed in dreams or other visionary states; or it may arise in the course of a traditional vision quest associated with rites of passage, as in the case of the Sioux shamans Lame Deer or Black Elk.

Most potential shamans have suffered a near-death experience in childhood or early youth, either through accident or illness. During this experience the future shaman lies as if dead while his spirit body enters the underworld where the potential shaman meets assorted spirits, including the ones that will eventually be personal allies. But first he or she undergoes violent and terrifying ordeals resulting in dismemberment and reduction to a skeleton. When this is all that remains, the shaman is transformed and reconstituted, and confirms his or her relationship with the animal allies. From these the shaman receives special knowledge, as well as powers of healing, prediction, and dream interpretation, and may acquire the power of magical flight. He or she ascends to the upper world by means of the world tree (which passes through the three worlds). Returning to his or her body on earth,

LEFT **The Sioux Indian shaman Black Elk. The origins of the Native-American population are thought to lie in Asia, following migrations during the last Ice Age, more than 14,000 years ago, so there may be a link between Siberian and Native-American shamanic beliefs.**

the new shaman is ready to become the community's priest, magician, and healer.

First, however, new shamans are usually apprenticed to a master shaman who helps them to develop the powers acquired in the initial trance experience. This senior figure assists his pupils to develop their ability to enter and reenter the other world; to acquire techniques of survival in under-world journeys and in flights to the upper realms; and to develop expertise in hallucinogenic and trance-inducing drugs. However, it is the personal experience of the future shaman, the knowledge gained from that first near-death experience, that enables him or her to return repeatedly to the worlds where the spirit contacts were formed, animal allies found, spirit ancestors consulted, and cosmology and mythology revealed.

Personal experience is the prime determinant of the shaman status. Knowledge of other realms of being and consciousness, and the cosmology of those regions, is the basis of the shamanic perspective and power. With this knowledge, the shaman is able to serve as a bridge between the worlds. The shaman not only lives at the edge of reality but also at the edge of his or her society. Like the artist in today's conception of the role, the shaman is simultaneously an outsider and a key figure in his or her world. And before being accepted as the community's official shaman, the would-be shaman must give a display of shamanic powers that will satisfy the people.

THE ANIMAL ALLY

In shamanic societies, humans exist within a continuum that includes nature and supernature. The ability to use the supernatural powers inherent in nature is the key to the shaman's success. Joe Green, a North American Paviotso shaman who went through conventional medical school, makes this clear.

◎ **Indians were put here on this Earth with trees, plants, animals, and water, and the shaman gets his power from them. One shaman might get his power from the hawk that lives in the mountains. Another may get his power from the eagle, the otter, or the bear. A long time ago, all the animals were Indians (they could talk). I think that is why animals help people to be shamans. When a shaman gets his power from the otter it means that the spirit is many otters. This chief otter spirit tells the man how to be a good doctor. It is this main otter who makes a man a shaman. He lives in a certain place in the water. Only the shaman can see him there. ◎**

Green used his otter-spirit power in the course of his medical practice, but then he lost his animal ally, his power, and almost his life when he mutilated the otter skin he wore. He was saved from death by another shaman who told him, "You will never see the otter again. You cut the head off and now you don't know anything."

ABOVE **Native-American societies, from the Arctic to the Amazon Basin, are marked by their closeness to the animal world. In the shaman it becomes explicit: there is a merging of identity.**

Since trance-induced forms of knowledge and experience run sharply counter to Western practice, it is hard to evaluate the genuineness of the shaman's achievement. Some shamans were charlatans, able to overawe their audience with conjurers' tricks. Others seem to have been seers and mystics of a high order.

For us Indians, there is just the pipe, the earth we sit on, and the sky. The spirit is everywhere. Sometimes it shows itself through an animal, a bird, some trees and hills. Sometimes it speaks from the Badlands, a stone, or even from the water. That smoke from the peace pipe, it goes straight up to the spirit world. . . Power flows down to us through that smoke, through the pipe stem. You feel the power as you hold your pipe; it moves from the pipe right into your body. It makes your hair stand up.

LAME DEER, LAKOTA SHAMAN

In the course of the shaman's career, he or she may bring back beautiful songs, dances, drawings, and paintings from the other world; but the shaman's creativity is valued according to the benefits he or she brings the people: healing, prediction, and knowledge. A practicing shaman must always keep the support of the community, and has to perform in order to move and impress them. The shaman's routine is part séance, part spectacle, and wholly performance.

JOSEPH BEUYS:
THE ARTIST AND THE SHAMAN

The influential performance artist Joseph Beuys (1921–1986) underwent a strangely shamanistic ordeal in his youth, according to his own account. As a German pilot, he was shot down over Russia in 1943, and lay unconscious in deep snow for days before being rescued by a band of nomadic Tatars (themselves inheritors of a shamanistic tradition). They resuscitated him, covering him in fat to regenerate body heat, and wrapping him in felt for insulation.

These materials came to have great importance for Beuys' work, although he did not always stress their autobiographical content. He used fat to illustrate his "theory of sculpture," a universal process whereby everything passes from an undetermined, chaotic state (warm) to an ordered, defined, formed state (cold)—when warm, fat is a formless and flowing liquid; when cold, it is transformed into a defined and ordered solid.

Beuys attempted to apply the transformative concepts of physical matter to the social and psychological spheres. "The concept of sculpting," he wrote, "can be extended to the invisible materials used by everyone: thinking forms—how we mold our thoughts; spoken forms—how we shape our thoughts into words; social sculpture—how we mold and shape the world in which we live. Sculpture is an evolutionary process, everyone is an artist."

Beuys had a shamanistic understanding of the interrelation of matter and energy, but he was not a shaman in the received meaning of the word. His concerns were global and sociopolitical rather than clan-oriented or concerned with healing in any medical sense. But Beuys used many of the traditional accoutrements of shamanism, and came to be perceived as a shaman, particularly after his week-long coexistence and "dialogue" with a coyote in New York in 1974.

PERFORMANCE
IN FAT AND FELT

Arriving at Kennedy Airport, Beuys was wrapped in felt and moved to the gallery in an ambulance. During the ensuing week he lived in close proximity with the coyote, sharing the same space and developing a rapport that expressed itself in a rhythmic cycle of interactivity. Beuys believed that the energies and the traumas of a continent are deeply connected, and their crossing point in Europe and Eurasia had been a constant theme in his work. With *Coyote* he concentrated on an American equivalent. "I believe I made contact with the psychological trauma point of the United States' energy constellation," he claimed: "the whole American trauma with the Indian, the Red Man." This is where the figure of the coyote appears, respected and venerated by the Red Man, despised and persecuted by the White Man: a polarity and a gulf. Somehow the trauma has to be reversed and amends made: "You can say that a reckoning has to be made with the coyote, and only then can this trauma be lifted." The idea of transformation is the key to *Coyote*, particularly transformation of verbal dialogue to energy dialogue.

RIGHT **Joseph Beuys' shamanism challenges the conventions and self-satisfaction of modern "civilization"— a reaction to Hitler, but also to the materialism of postwar Germany and North America. Beuys saw himself as a shamanistic "helping spirit," an "enchanter."**

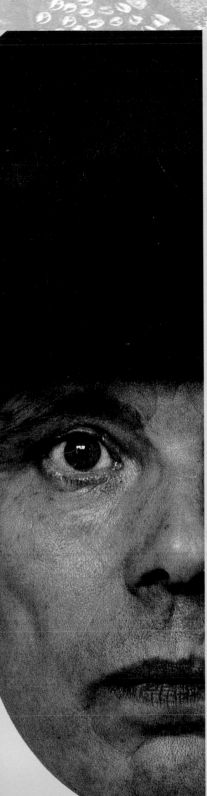
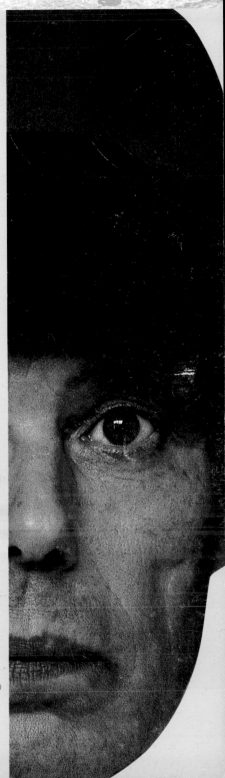

INTERACTIVE DIALOGUE WITH A COYOTE

The conceptual artist Joseph Beuys installed and performed this exhibit at the Rene Gallery, New York in 1974.

For the Indians, the coyote was an image of transformation, and, like the hare and the stag in Eurasian myths, he could change his state at will from the physical to the spiritual and vice versa. . . Then came the White Man, and the transition in the coyote's status. . . His ingenuity and adaptability were now interpreted as low and common cunning: he became the "mean coyote." And having classed him as an antisocial menace, white society could take its legalized revenge on him. . .

The man [Beuys] brought objects and elements from his world to place in this space, silent representatives of his ideas and beliefs. He introduced them to the coyote. The coyote responded coyote-style by claiming them with his gesture of possession. One by one as they were presented he pissed on them slowly and deliberately: felt, walking stick, gloves, flashlight, and *Wall Street Journal,* but above all the *Wall Street Journal.* . .

The man had also brought a repertoire of movements with him and a notion of time. These two were then subject to the coyote's responses, and were modulated and conditioned by them. The man never took his eyes off the animal. The line of sight between them became like the hands of a spiritual clockface measuring the timing of the movements and setting the pace for the dialogue through time. The man carried out his sequence of movements, a choreography directed toward the coyote, the timing and the mood regulated by the animal. Generally the sequence lasted about an hour and a quarter, sometimes much longer. In all it was repeated well over thirty times, but the mood and the tone were never the same. . .

The man swathed himself in the felt. . . The coyote's usual dozing place was the other pile of felt. But when at the end of each sequence Beuys would go to the far corner for a quiet smoke in the coyote's straw he joined him, and that interlude always had the atmosphere of a farmyard: long moments of far-away filtered sunlight.

FROM *COYOTE,* BY CAROLINE TISDALL (1976)

CASTANEDA AND THE COYOTE

It is interesting that the coyote trickster should also have been the spirit familiar of the late Carlos Castaneda (1925–1998), whose vivid accounts of Don Juan, a Mexican Toltec shaman, caught the imagination of an entire generation in the 1960s and 1970s, and still form part of the baggage of many an aging ex-hippie. Castaneda's books have been criticized for apparently borrowing material from other, more academically established researchers, such as Gordon Wasson and Joan Halifax, but it has been pointed out that this trickery is in the nature of the subject itself, a legitimate and traditional ploy of the shaman. Don Juan plays tricks all the time as an essential way of undermining the perceptions of ordinary reality and allowing his pupil to become more receptive to the invisible world that can only be perceived through an altered state. Castaneda's coyote familiar would have been acting out of character if it had behaved any other way.

The shaman's tricks help others to "see" what Don Juan calls the "Nagual," the "part of us which we do not deal with at all." The Nagual is the complement to the "Tonal," "everything we know. . . not only us persons but everything in our world. . ." This is done in the first instance by shaking the pupil's faith in so-called objective reality, by trickery if necessary. And trickery is the coyote's special attribute.

But perhaps the coyote's cleverest trick has been to confuse the excitement and subversive pleasures of drug experimentation with a search for inner truth, for the Castaneda books came out at a time when the psychotropic tools of the shaman had just become available in synthetic form to anyone who cared to use them. Supernatural experience through drugs is, of course, a means rather than an end for the working shaman, whose main business is healing and useful prophecy. The psychotropic, trance-inducing ingredients of traditional power plants that enabled non-Western shamans to leave their bodies and travel to other worlds became the psychedelic fuel that enabled Western users to trip, perhaps even to fly, but not to heal. Castaneda's books created a whole generation of psychic tourists, weekend trancers, part-time gurus.

It is the shaman's art to enter the world of the Nagual by the narrowest of bridges, as illustrated by Castaneda's account of an apparently impossible crossing of a waterfall by Don Juan's fellow sorcerer Don Gennaro. As Castaneda watches the old man leaping from one almost invisible foothold to the next, across apparently unbridgeable distances, he experiences "an extraordinary and mysterious terror," but is unaware of its meaning. According to the Huichol shaman Ramon Medina Silva, whose identical exploit has been captured on film, what the shaman is doing in such a performance is displaying "balance," that special, ineffable capacity to "venture without fear onto the narrow bridge across the great chasm separating the ordinary world from the world beyond."

ABOVE **A Huichol shaman from Mexico displays his special balance within and beyond the physical world. He can leap, or fly, between the rocks.**

THE SHAMAN AND THE CIRCUS

The traditional shaman practices ecstatic communion with the spirits as a means to an end. The shaman's vocation is to use his or her powers for the benefit of the community. But these powers need to be made available through performance. According to Black Elk, "a man who has a vision is not able to use the power of it until after he has performed the vision on Earth for his people to see." Performance is the end product of the ecstatic vision, just as the created product is the end result of the creative process. As the English writer Rogan Taylor has persuasively argued, the performance art of our Eurasian shaman ancestors has a place in the modern world, albeit stripped of meaning: it is to be found in the circus.

LEFT **Apparently innocent family entertainment, but with a heritage and undercurrent of mysterious power:** *The Circus*, **seen through the filter of Georges Seurat's pointillism (1891).**

Taylor suggests that circus clowns embody the trickster elements of the spirit world, while the ringmaster is identified with the master shaman who seeks to bring disparate elements under control. The performing animals reflect the shaman's power over wild beasts, and perhaps also the spirit familiars themselves. Particularly important to shamanizing societies was the bear, the first of all performing animals, and perhaps among the first animals depicted in Palaeolithic cave art. Flying acrobats recall the shaman's powers of magical flight, and the high wire too has reference to the "balance" demonstrated by shamans such as Ramon Medina Silva—the mastery required for crossing the narrow bridge between the worlds. Rope tricks suggest supernatural ascents and descents by means of the world tree that interpenetrates the three realms of experience. The strong man's act recalls the feats of strength and endurance recorded in many Eurasian traditions; and tricks with knives and fire reflect the kinds of ordeal awaiting initiates to the underworld. Tumblers repeat with their somersaults a technique found in many shamanizing societies indicating transformation: shamans of the Tucana in Bolivia perform somersaults in one direction to turn themselves into jaguars (their alter egos) and in the opposite direction to reassume a human form.

In short, the circus is "shot through with magical references and powerful allegories of the extraordinary experiences involved in ecstatic initiation. The show is the living remnant of an ancient and prodigious oral library that took to the road, along with nomadic shamans and their apprentices, when their tribal cultures collapsed and died."

IS IT ONLY ROCK'N'ROLL?

The worlds of the circus performer and the traveling player have almost disappeared, but the shamanistic performance has seen a revival with the emergence of rock music. The importance of sound and rhythm in shamanistic rituals has frequently been noted by ethnographers, with special emphasis on the hypnotic quality of the shaman's mystic drumming, and his extraordinary voice effects. The American rock-and-roll pianist and singer Little Richard (Richard Penniman, b. 1932), regarded as one of the pioneers of rock music, was famous for his extraordinary performances on stage and his scalp-tingling falsetto scream. Little Richard was very active in the 1950s, but retired in 1958 to take a theological degree and be ordained. He began performing again in 1963, touring with the Beatles and the Rolling Stones (who had been heavily influenced by his records), but returned to the religious life in 1977. Little Richard's performances (with costumes, makeup, and on-stage acrobatics) influenced Elvis Presley, Jimi Hendrix, and James Brown. His singing left its mark on the Beatles and Otis Redding, and several of his songs became rock-and-roll standards. Little Richard's profoundly contradictory personality (fundamentalist preacher and high-living sexually ambivalent rock star), his furious piano playing, and deranged stage shows have made him a pop icon.

LEFT **Little Richard, most frenzied of the original rock 'n' rollers: the modern-day shaman who fulfills some need in his society.**

Sexual ambiguity is a characteristic of traditional shamanism, possibly reflecting a transformative need to embody opposites within a single form, or perhaps bringing into the open a universal tension between male and female components of the psyche. Some shamans were commanded by spirits during their initiation to assume a feminine personality, often much against their will. In the 1960s and 1970s, with the arrival of glamrock, transvestism, and androgyny were to become staples of the rock star's spectacular repertoire. The cover of the Rolling Stones' single "Have You Seen Your Mother, Baby" featured the band members wearing dresses. The phenomenon of androgyny is also apparent in David Bowie's earlier performances, which also featured references to shamanic flight into the upper world with such numbers as "Space Oddity." The blurring of the gender divide is now an established part of popular music: Boy George, REM, and Placebo are just three current performance groups carrying on what is now a tradition.

THE TAMBOURINE MAN

In the later 1960s, material produced by leading rock artists such as Bob Dylan, John Lennon, Jimi Hendrix, and Jerry Garcia took on a visionary, surreal quality, often describing dreams, ecstatic experiences, or demonic worlds. Dylan's earlier protest songs had become anthems of the civil rights movement, but in the mid-1960s a near-death experience following a motorbike accident coincided with a complete change of direction, toward a much heavier rock style. Dylan's lyrics are often visionary, with an obscurity that yields subjective and personal meaning only in combination with the music to create a shared experience with the audience. "In my dreams," he told the journalist Bill Flanagan, "I don't

really live in the actual world. . . There's substance to the dream, there's something in front of you. It's happened, it's been said, I've heard it: I have proof of it. I'm a messenger. I get it. It comes to me so I give it back in my particular style."

HE WAS THE WALRUS

John Lennon's work was already showing shamanic tendencies with songs such as "Strawberry Fields Forever" and "I Am the Walrus" before he left the Beatles in 1970. The cover of the Sgt. Pepper album (1967) shows, behind the marijuana plants and the psychedelically transformed quartet of musicians, a ghostly gallery of the spirits that dominate our extended Western clan consciousness, from Marx to Marilyn Monroe. Strongly influenced by the Japanese artist and performer Yoko Ono (he changed his middle name from Winston to Ono in 1969), Lennon used performance art as well as song to get across his utopian ideas before becoming yet another of the rock stars who suffered a violent and premature death.

RAVE ON

In the late 1980s, a form of ecstatic dance music quickly engulfed counter-cultural Western consciousness, acquiring a following of many millions—one of its names was "rave music." The music was based on a techno sound with a repetitive rhythmic pattern of about 130 beats per minute (nearly double the normal heartbeat), played at high volume, and incorporating otherworldly electronic effects. Using the designer drug MDMA, (methylenedioxymethamphetamine) known as Ecstasy, as well as more established psychotropic

drugs such as LSD (lysergic acid diethylamide), ravers say they experience a sense of well-being, generalized affection for those around them, increased energy, and sometimes hallucinations—and the ability to dance continuously for hours. Participants at raves often undergo a loss of ego sense and an absorption into a wider collective consciousness.

This merging of the individual into the collective is also seen at other mass gatherings, notably football games, but only at rave parties is it directed in a form of dance participation. The movement incurred the wrath of authoritarian and conservative forces in society, who seized on the destructive effects of the drugs to demonize the culture, but to little real effect. Parallels can be drawn between rave culture and various ecstatic cults that have developed throughout history, often among subjugated groups, notably the Dionysus cult of ancient Greece.

APOLLO AND DIONYSUS

Dionysus is the Greek god of madness and ecstasy, the god of two faces, the spirit of absence and presence. His emblem is the mask, the symbol of duality. This masked duality takes form in one of the earliest known depictions of a shaman, the figure carved into the ceiling of the cave of Trois-Frères in southern France, c. 12,000 BCE. Named "the Sorcerer" by the paleontologist Abbé Breuil (1877–1961), he wears the attributes of his spirit allies. He is dancing, and all around are murals of animals, among whom he presides as mediator between humans and their venerated animal kin. The tortuous passageways which lead to the chamber of the Sorcerer are reminiscent of the shaman's descent into the underworld where the animal spirits have their being. The shaman's mask shows his identity with them, but the mask is more than an invocation of the spirit. It contains the spirit itself.

THE POWER OF THE MASK

The mask is not just a disguise; it inspires awe and was traditionally kept in a sanctified place. Its supernatural essence can still be seen today at such occasions as Halloween or Mardi Gras

THE MYTH OF DIONYSUS

The myth of Dionysus describes a recognizably shamanic progress, but in a superhuman form more dangerous and wonderful than any human equivalent. Of both earthly and divine parentage (the god Zeus and the king's daughter Semele), he was rescued from fiery destruction while still a fetus, and reared by semidivine nurses, the Kouretes, from whom he was stolen by the Titans. These daimonic entities subjected him to a typically shamanic ordeal of boiling in a cauldron and dismemberment, but his heart survived and from this essence Persephone, queen of the underworld, reconstituted him in a new body. He returned to earth with a special power, like any shaman, except that the gift he brought was not healing but ecstatic madness, achieved through use of a psychotropic plant—the vine. He is a shaman god who enacts the mystery of creation affected by madness and overshadowed by death.

gatherings. In the early Greek world, Dionysus was the lord of the mask, of paradox, the god with two faces. Dionysus is the mad god whose cult gave rise to drama in the form of both tragedy and comedy. With the rise of Christianity he became a devil. "All the old gods are devils," wrote the Church father Tertullian. "Dionysus the old god is lord of the theater. Therefore, the theater belongs to a devil, the Devil."

Masked dancers performed the cult of Dionysus, embodying the invisible forces that worked through them. The

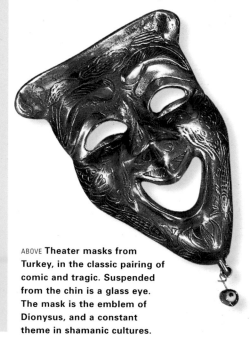

ABOVE **Theater masks from Turkey, in the classic pairing of comic and tragic. Suspended from the chin is a glass eye. The mask is the emblem of Dionysus, and a constant theme in shamanic cultures.**

mask is the unique characteristic and attribute of Dionysus, expressing the primal phenomenon of the god's duality, the incarnate presence of the invisible and transcendental. The aspect of his worship that expressed joy and mirth developed into comedy, while the aspect involving grief and mourning became tragedy. Thus from fertility rituals and sacred reenactments of the god's life emerged the subversive humor of Aristophanes and the uplifting, cathartic emotion of the great tragedians of fifth-century Athens.

As a shamanic god Dionysus is master of the dithyrhamb or double-door. Like many shamans, he is androgynous in appearance, yet capable of amazing feats

ABOVE **A seventeenth-century landscape with Apollo killing Python, painted by Gillis Neyts. Apollo and Dionysus were the prototypes for what became the two aesthetic poles: classical (objective, simple) and romantic (subjective, sensual).**

of strength. He is the raving god, accompanied by pandemonium and silence. He is associated with prophecy. He is the god of ecstasy and love, yet he is also the persecuted god, suffering and dying. His entourage includes satyrs, half-animal dancers recalling the masked figures of the Perigordian caves, and maenads, frenzied women entwined with serpents and clad in fawn skins (maenad is derived from the word for madness). Roaming the mountains, these descendants of the Kouretes suckle the young of wild animals, or tear them to pieces with their bare hands, recalling the dismemberment of the god child by the Titans. Those who resist the daimonic power of Dionysus are seized with destructive madness; those who embrace his worship enjoy divine rapture.

THE INDIAN CONNECTION

On earth, Dionysus voyaged far and wide, always accompanied by his band of ecstatic ravers, and wherever he went he brought madness and ecstasy. The women of the cities he visited welcomed him, becoming his devotees filled with ecstatic love reminiscent of the love which the Hindu god Krishna (the Dark One) inspired in his *gopi* followers. This personal realization of unity with the godhead through ecstatic love, a branch of yoga known as *Bhakti* (pure love) was rekindled in India by the sixteenth-century mystic Chaitanya, and can be seen today in the performances of the Hari Krishna sect in many Western cities. According to one tradition, Dionysus came originally from India, but he differs in a major respect from the god Krishna in the orgiastic nature of his cult. Krishna inspires divine madness with his flute, whereas Dionysus is himself 'the raving one'. He acts out his gift of ecstasy, participating in the madness with which he afflicts and graces his followers.

ENTER APOLLO

How did the cults of the raving god come to be transformed into masterpieces of formal art? Apollo was the god of the arts in ancient Greece, the most honoured of all the Olympians after Zeus himself. He was Phoebus, the shining one, lord of light, the antithesis of Dionysus the dark god. At Delphi, the navel of the world, Apollo's oracle became the fountainhead of prophecy, retaining its position into late classical times. But this oracle had once belonged to Gaia the earth goddess, whose sacred animal, the serpent Python, Apollo had slain with his arrows. Transfixing the earth force, the serpent energy, Apollo assumed its prophetic powers and transmuted them into civilized form. His priestess, the Pythia, uttered prophecies while in a state of trance, but these were delivered in a precise verse form – the hexameter. As the Italian classicist Robert Calasso writes, Apollo 'didn't want slovenly shamans, but girls still close to the nymphs, and speaking well-turned verse'. Apollo was the patron of the Muses, the wild women of Mount Helicon whom he trained in the gifts they were to confer on humankind: song, dance, music, poetry and epic.

Dionysus and Apollo were complementary as well as opposite. In the words of Calasso, 'both Apollo and Dionysus knew that possession is the highest kind of knowledge. For Dionysus, possession was the immediate unassailable reality; for Apollo, possession is a conquest to be articulated in meter. He wants to stamp the seal of form on the flow of enthusiasm at the very moment it occurs.'

> Apollo and Dionysus are both often to be found at the limit of what is acceptable. They provoke the back-and-forth in men, that desire to go beyond oneself which we seem to cling to even more than to our humanity, even more than to life itself.
>
> ROBERT CALASSO

RIGHT *The Drunkenness of Bacchus*, by Michelangelo (1496–7). Bacchus was the Roman equivalent of the Greek Dionysus, and Bacchanalia were orgiastic festivals in his honour; they were banned from Rome in 186 BCE, the perennial response to wild parties.

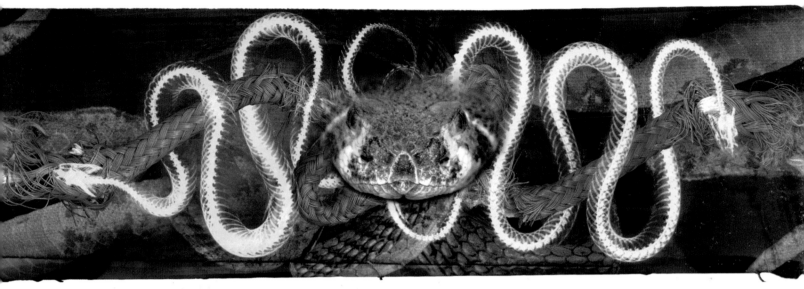

Apollo was lord of Delphi for nine months of the year. But for the three winter months Dionysus was in charge, presiding over the waking dead on the torch-lit slopes of Parnassus. His grave was located above the grave of Gaia's earth energy symbol, the Python, whose serpentine energy the death-and-resurrection god shares. In ancient Greece, spirit and matter were as inextricably linked as in any shamanistic society, at least until the emergence of analytic philosophy in the fourth century BCE.

'The universe is alive and filled with daimons,' proclaimed the pre-Socratic philosopher Thales (640–546 BCE). These 'daimons' included spirits of the dead, the ancestors, spirits of place and species, and even guardian spirits. Socrates (469–399 BCE) venerated his daimon as a guiding spirit that made itself known to him whenever he was about to make a mistaken decision. To this daimon he ascribed his success as a communicator of philosophical ideas. It was for teaching his students 'false *daimonia*' that Socrates' fellow Athenians condemned him to death. His successor Plato (428–347 BCE) considered that a 'divine daimon' resided in every human being, the irrefutable and inescapable witness who could intervene through a dream or a sign, or even appear personally to 'direct what is favourable towards us and to compensate what is evil'.

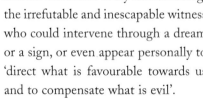

ABOVE **Python was the sacred animal of the earth Goddess Gaia. Its sinuous and rhythmic form is representative of the natural cycle of death and rebirth.**

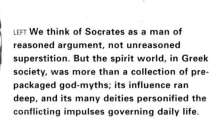

LEFT **We think of Socrates as a man of reasoned argument, not unreasoned superstition. But the spirit world, in Greek society, was more than a collection of pre-packaged god-myths; its influence ran deep, and its many deities personified the conflicting impulses governing daily life.**

GOOD AND BAD DEMONS

The psychologist Rollo May has defined the daimonic as any psychological function "which has the power to take over the whole person. . . the daimonic can be either creative or destructive, and is normally both. Demon possession is the traditional name through history for psychosis. It refers to a fundamental, archetypal function of human experience." Thus the separation between Apollo, god of reason, and Dionysus, daimonic god of passion, is far from clear-cut.

A degree of possession is implicit in the creative act, however "reasonable." At one level, the daimon is a guardian spirit who mysteriously protects the devotee. At another level it is totally destructive. To become creative, the human mind needs to be touched by a certain Otherness, which may form the most important part of the total creative process. The philosopher Plato believed that "God takes away the minds of poets and uses them as ministers, as it also uses diviners and holy prophets, in order that we who hear them may know that God himself is the speaker, and that through them is conversing with us." But inspiration requires interpretation. Successful interpretation of the inspiration leads to the creation of an artistic product imbued with that divine Otherness, which in turn affects all those who experience it. Thus, in a secular age, art has arrogated to itself the mysterious Otherness that gave religion its essential meaning in direct experience.

LEFT **Silenus is the Greek demigod who fostered Dionysus. Here, as painted by Rubens in c.1620, he enjoys the most widely experienced altered state of all, drunkenness, with the generous support of attendant satyrs.**

KIPLING'S DAEMON

The English writer Rudyard Kipling (1865–1936) believed unhesitatingly in the creative power of his daimon.

◎ **Let us now consider the Personal Daemon of Aristotle and others, of whom it has been truthfully written, though not published:**

> *This is the doom of the Makers—their Daemon lives in their pen.*
> *If he be absent or sleeping, they are even as other men.*
> *But if he be utterly present, and they swerve not from his behest,*
> *The word that he gives shall continue, whether in earnest or jest.*

Most men. . . keep him under an alias which varies with their literary or scientific attainments. Mine came to me early when I sat bewildered among other notions, and said: "Take this and no other." I obeyed, and was rewarded. It was a tale. . . called "The Phantom Rickshaw." Some of it was weak, much was bad and out of key; but it was my first serious attempt to think in another man's skin.

ABOVE **Mowgli, the boy brought up as a member of the wolf pack, is perhaps the most famous product of Kipling's "contract" with his daemon.**

. . . My Daemon was with me in the *Jungle Books, Kim,* and both Puck books, and good care I took to walk delicately, lest he should withdraw. I know that he did not, because when those books were finished they said so themselves with, **almost, the water-hammer click of a tap turned off. One of the clauses in our contract was that I should never follow up "a success," for by this sin fell Napoleon and a few others. Note here. When your Daemon is in charge, do not try to think consciously. Drift, wait, and obey.** ◎

FROM *SOMETHING OF MYSELF,* BY RUDYARD KIPLING (1937)

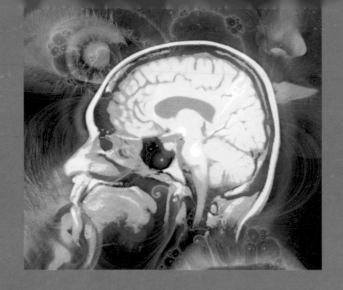

STRUCTURES
OF THE MIND

What a piece of work is a man! How noble in reason, how infinite in faculty . . .

WILLIAM SHAKESPEARE

WHAT IS CONSCIOUSNESS?

Consciousness is an adaptive system, continually altering in response to changes in the environment. What we consciously see and hear, feel, smell, and think is based on material that has only reached consciousness after passing through a whole series of filters and censors. From the infinite quantity of physical energies "out there" in the universe, the sensory outposts of the mind select only what is necessary for survival. A stringent elimination of nonessential information is the basis of our perception, controlled by a sensory apparatus unique to our species. This perceptual range provides the basis of so-called objective reality, and by the standards of many other organisms it is rather limited. It is created by the species-wide sensory range that unites our view of reality.

We create our own world: sounds from waves in the air, colors from electromagnetic radiation, taste from molecules that match areas in our tongues. We perceive what our senses tell us is there, both as individuals and as members of the same species. The world is a mass of individual illusions subsumed under a species-wide collective illusion. It is the anatomical equivalent of Castaneda's "Tonal" (see page 24), which "makes up the rules by which it apprehends the world." Like the Tonal, it "creates the world although it doesn't create a thing."

SMELL IT LIKE IT IS

Other species of course have very different sensory ranges. The sense of smell in dogs is so well developed that it can perceive "odor fingerprints," that is, the individual odor of living things at their unique genetic level. Salmon use the sense of smell to find their way across thousands of miles of ocean to the native streams where they were hatched. Eels do the same. All animals share the language of smell. The nerves from the nose are unique in that they reach the brain without any intermediate synapse. Smelling gives us our most direct experience of the world.

Analogous to odor are the chemical messengers called pheromones, hormones secreted from different parts of the body in different species. They are found throughout the

living world and are probably the oldest form of communication. Pheromonal messages underlie the amazing collaboration of animals living in communities, such as ants or termites, allowing them to act like a single organism. These pheromones apparently work in the same way as the chemical signals exchanged between cells within a single body. Mammals also use pheromones from specialized glands to mark their territories, as well as for recognizing mates and offspring. And pheromones have recently been discovered to play a major part in the lives of primates.

ABOVE **The "objective reality" of colors is a function of our sensory perceptions; if our eyes could access the infrared part of the light spectrum, the sky would be green and the trees red.**

The fact that human sweat takes on an odor only at puberty suggests that pheromones may have once been more important in human sexuality. The sexologist Alex Comfort writes, "Human beings have a complete set of organs which are traditionally described as nonfunctional, but which, seen in any other mammal, would be recognized at once as part of a pheromone system." These are the apocrine glands, located in areas of body hair, labia, and foreskin, and seem to be connected with sexual activity. "The assault on these recognizable pheromone-mediating structures (by shaving and deodorant) in many human societies implies an intuitive awareness that their sexual function goes beyond the decorative. A conspicuous and apparently unused antenna array presupposes an unsuspected communications system."

SECOND SIGHT

There are many other apparently "nonfunctional" perceptual areas within the human sensory range. Of the 70 octaves of electromagnetic radiation that exist, we perceive only one octave in the form of visible light, the spectrum between red and violet. But the skin of our hands emits infrared radiation, which in some circumstances allows us to, as it were, "see with the skin." Different colors absorb different amounts of infrared and reflect back the rest, which may be picked up by receptors in the skin. This can be tested by a simple experiment. Conceal a number of squares of differently colored paper beneath a covering, and then put your hands beneath the covering and see whether you can guess the color of the paper. "Guessing" here is a way of getting at the subliminal information that has failed to reach our consciousness, the "sixth sense" on which creative people rely.

RIGHT **Helen Keller in 1956, aged 75, holding a braille Bible. Her life became the subject of a play,** *The Miracle Worker,* **by William Gibson, subsequently turned into a movie.**

From the navigation methods of preliterate ocean-going peoples to the extraordinarily developed touch sense of congenitally blind people such as Helen Keller, there seems to exist a whole infrastructure of "nonfunctional" sense organs, which can be activated in certain circumstances. An altered state of consciousness is accompanied by, or develops, an altered state of perception, allowing "nonfunctional" senses to operate and so-called extrasensory perception to get through. The "hunch" of the gambler or the "flash" of the artist may be based on this kind of activity.

KNOCKING AT THE DOORS OF PERCEPTION

Thus it seems that the boundaries of the human perceptual range are not as fixed as they appear to be. "Nonfunctional" senses exist in latent form capable of operating beyond the conventional limits of ordinary consciousness. These limits consist not only of the species-wide biological constraints on what we perceive, but also a multitude of others, which have their origin as a result of psychological and social conditioning of the individual. Children from environments other than the rectangular urban world are not easily deceived by standard straight-edge optical illusions.

Moreover, we constantly adjust sensory information to fit in with what we expect to see. If seeing is believing, *not* seeing is often a form of *not* believing. The data-processing

centers, hard-wired in the brain, interpret sensory information to produce a representation of the world based on information necessary for survival. But this information is subjected to personal as well as collective selection before

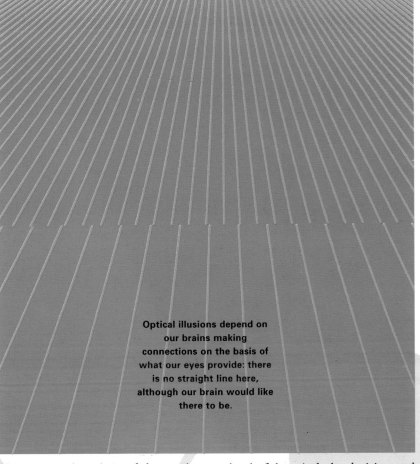

Optical illusions depend on our brains making connections on the basis of what our eyes provide: there is no straight line here, although our brain would like there to be.

being fed onto the next level of the mind, the decision and thought centers in the brain. The sensory function of eliminating all nonessential information and selecting only those items conducive to survival extends beyond the biological to the social and even the personal level.

THE BRAIN

The brain is the organ that allows humans to respond flexibly to events in the environment, enabling them to behave in different ways depending on present circumstances and previous experience. It regulates automatic functions, such as heartbeat, breathing, and blood pressure. It processes, interprets, and decides what to do with the information from the sensory organs. It controls the endocrine system, which mediates many physiological processes, including reproductive behavior and metabolic rate. It controls all complex functions such as attention, consciousness, sleep, memory, imagination, thought, and creative ability.

HOW MANY BRAINS?

It is a mistake to think that all this is done by a single processing system, like some vast computer. We have not one but at least three brains, if not four. The human brain evolved over millions of years, with the oldest part resembling the entire brain of many reptiles. Called the brainstem, this is the part that controls such basic functions as breathing and heart rate, as well as both REM (dreaming) and nondreaming sleep.

ABOVE **The limbic system is our "emotional brain," and the part chiefly susceptible to drugs. Hence perhaps the affinity between drug use and altered states of feeling and perception.**

Between the brainstem and the cortex is the limbic system, a structure found in all mammals. This controls emotions as well as primitive reactions. Thus our emotional apparatus is older than the uniquely human cerebral cortex, and to some extent independent of it. Emotional needs can dominate consciousness as strongly as more basic physiological needs. The limbic system, which coordinates many of the brain's operations, prioritizes the messages transmitted to the cortex. Its numerous connections with many parts of the "higher brain" provide the feeling that accompanies our thinking processes, the moods that color thoughts, and the emotions that interlink with creative activity and artistic appreciation. It lays the groundwork that makes complex consciousness possible. It is the seat of the emotions.

The limbic system "likes" drugs. Opiates, the most powerful known pain relievers and also the classic example of the addictive substance, find an abundance of receptors in the limbic system. This suggests an explanation for the emotional changes caused by opiates, especially for the rush of euphoria brought on by heroin injections. On a physiological level, drugs work with

and through the brain's neurotransmitters, the chemicals that facilitate or block neural activity. The study of opiate receptors has been one of the main ways into a scientific understanding of how drugs act on the brain, and has also furthered development of new pharmaceutical compounds, notably in analyzing the effects of antischizophrenic drugs on neural transmission. Psychotropic drugs also work by modifying neurotransmitters.

Above the limbic system is the "third brain," the uniquely human cerebral cortex where the world is organized, individual experiences are stored in memory, speech is produced and understood, paintings are seen, music is heard. It is divided into two hemispheres, connected by a bundle of fibers. All mammals' brains have a hemispheric division, but only in humans are the hemispheres specialized for different operations. The right hemisphere controls the left side of the body; the left hemisphere controls the right side of the body. Since the 1960s it has been established that, while both hemispheres are involved in higher cognitive thinking, each half of the brain is specialized in complementary fashion for different modes of cognition, although both hemispheres share a potential for many functions.

A TWO-WAY SYSTEM

Concepts of the duality of human nature and thought have been postulated by philosophers, teachers, and scientists from many different times and cultures. The key idea is that there are two parallel "ways of knowing," seen at its simplest in the age-old distinction between reason and emotion. The Taoist duality of Yang (positive, masculine, expressive) and Yin (negative, feminine, responsive) is one of the earliest and most concise summaries of this universal cognitive phenomenon. This duality of cognitive process was further developed by Freud in his proposal for a "primary process" of nonverbal

thinking, predominantly carried out through pictorial images, and a "secondary process" based on words. Since the 1960s, extensive research on the brain has established that this duality has an distinct anatomical basis, with left hemisphere activity identified as typically linear, sequential, rational, intellectual, cause-and-effect, analytical thinking, while right hemisphere functioning seems more concerned with pattern recognition, with wholes, with simultaneity rather than sequence.

In Western society rational thought is highly valued, and the function of language to give names to things has ensured the ascendancy of the rational, naming, faculty. In everyday speech, right is righteous, left is sinister. Likewise, at least until the arrival of Romanticism, reason was always preferred over the irrational. In the human body, paired structures occur everywhere and reveal a dominance of one over the other, from the dominant/recessive gene to the dominance of right over left in a range of human activities.

This pattern seems to be reflected in the brain hemispheres, but some researchers believe that linear thinking is greatly overvalued, especially among Western academics, causing us to exist for much of the time in an unbalanced, almost pathological state. Many altered-state experiences seem to involve an increased use of the right hemisphere mode of cognition. Subjects talk of seeing patterns in things, of simultaneously and instantaneously grasping relationships they cannot ordinarily grasp, of being unable to express these things verbally. The experience is usually reported as pleasant and rewarding and often is valued as a higher or truer form of cognition. Apparently left and right hemisphere functioning is more balanced or there may even be a shift to dominance of right hemisphere functioning. The experience does not lend itself to verbal description, but may be communicable in other ways, as through music or dance.

THE MULTITASKING MIND

However, although the left brain/right brain dichotomy seems to adequately describe the differences between the two brain halves, with rational processes dominant in the left hemisphere and intuitive, holistic processes on the right, more recent research reveals a more complicated picture. In the 1970s the neurologist Robert Ornstein developed electroencephalograph (EEG) procedures that identified numerous anatomical centers in the brain, mainly in the cortex but also in the limbic system, which "seemed to form coherent mental and behavioral units possessing a rich concentration of certain abilities." These range from the simplest to the most complex abilities, from movement and feeling to talking and knowing, and vary significantly from individual to individual.

ABOVE **We all have a "talent for moving," but if the relevant neural center is well-developed it can produce the unique brilliance of dancer Margot Fonteyn. . .**

Ornstein calls these neural colonies "talents," for they are innate abilities that are not only essential but also have creative potential. For example the "talent" of movement addresses a basic need, but in developed form produces a Margot Fonteyn, Martha Graham, or Muhammad Ali. Likewise, the ability to recognize place or face is a basic necessity for getting around, but when it is highly developed underpins success in the visual arts. The innate component of many talents may be traced to a well-developed neural center of this kind.

KNOWING YOUR SELF

Two specific centers have been identified in the brain, which are concerned with knowing: logical analysis in the left brain, and the ability to connect observations into a whole in the right. There is even a location for the governing talent of the "self," situated in the frontal lobes, which has the functions of organization, inference, interpretation, and control. Damage to this region may interfere with our knowledge of who we are. This "self" talent infers about the nature of the outside world and the person, and has the ability to command the different components of the mind. Independent of the rest of the mind, the "self" is nevertheless one of its many components. Nor does it have direct access to what is going on in the other minds—we often have to guess or infer what is happening. The emotional part of the brain may well know what it feels, but the rest of the mind usually must make separate inferences about it. However, the psychological phenomenon of cognitive dissonance (the ability to compare our thoughts within our own minds to achieve some kind of consistency) indicates that there is a mental entity capable of making these necessary compromises.

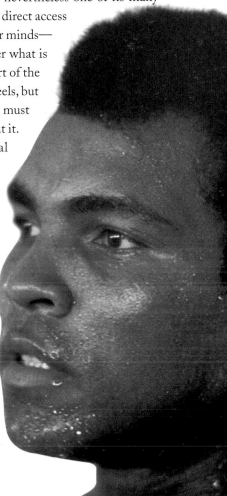

RIGHT **. . . or Muhammed Ali, the heavyweight boxer whose boast was "float like a butterfly, sting like a bee." What savage irony that his sporting career leached away the talent for movement that was its source.**

LEFT **Whether as a result of the challenge to identity of motherhood, or the cultural construction of woman as mother/lover/temptress, it is often suggested that women are more at ease with the idea of their multiple selves than are men.**

The centers of abilities or talents combine with mental operating systems, which are in essence self-contained minds of their own. These "small minds" are situation-specific and are changed according to the needs of the environment. We do not have access to all of these centers at once, consciousness being necessarily limited to a few items at a time. As Ornstein writes, "We wheel in and out of consciousness a certain number of these small minds to handle different situations." Different kinds of learning, knowledge, and memory coexist independently within the mind. Since consciousness splits to handle multiple needs, the governing self often has an insecure hold over these minds' functioning. Our mind is a coalition of competing entities, and we often do not know what we think or believe. On the other hand, we usually know what we feel. The basic talent of feeling connects with the components of arousal, amplifying experience and coloring thought.

Ornstein believes that high-level mental activities such as creative thought, judgement, and language take place in the same wheeling routines as do simple emotional reactions, with specific components of the mind "wheeled in and out of consciousness in a bewildering dance." We have a diverse collection of abilities, all of which make up our selves. And we show different sides of ourselves depending on the point of view of the situation and the onlooker. These different sides may really be the different small minds swinging into action. Everyone has a number of different personalities—at work, at home, in the family, in public—which respond to different environments. It seems quite probable that we construct our own idea of ourselves from the different kinds of information available.

THE DIVIDED SELF

The concept of the splitting functions of the mind, and their comparative autonomy within the general direction of a governing self, appears to find support in the dissociative condition known as Multipersonality Disorder (MPD). This is a mental condition in which two or more personalities apparently inhabit a single body, and take control of the person's behavior usually without his or her knowledge. Since 1970 it has been associated with severe and repetitive abuse during early childhood. Therapists who have treated MPD believe that the child, unable to bear the trauma, dissociates and creates an alternative personality or personalities, which may lead an independent existence unknown to the waking self. Periods of lost time, the sudden appearance of new possessions that they cannot recall having purchased, and bank withdrawals signed for in a strange handwriting are the common signs that lead victims to seek treatment, and successful therapy supposedly brings the other personalities into full consciousness, along with the memory of the original trauma.

ALL ABOUT SYBIL

MPD is believed to be an extreme form of a defense mechanism whereby the victim seeks to escape overwhelming fear and pain by imagining he or she is someone else. Instances of the phenomenon have increased exponentially since the publication in the 1970s of *Sybil*, the case history of a young woman who in the course of many years of therapy revealed no fewer than 16 different personalities or alters. These included one self-assured, intelligent, and compassionate character who seemed aware of the existence of all the others, and was described by the therapist as "the memory trace" of all Sybil's selves. Other personalities were characteristically violent and angry, or emotional and irrational, or possessed of artistic accomplishments unknown to the waking self. Two of the "alters" were male characters. As these subpersonalities were revealed to the therapist under hypnosis and encouraged to express themselves, the waking Sybil gradually became conscious of them and the original traumas that had led to their existence. Sybil was described by her therapist as a "depleted" person until her reintegration with her lost selves.

BELOW **How many people am I? We all have elements of a number of different personalities, but normally subordinated to an overall consciousness. Multipersonality Disorder mocks such efforts at unity.**

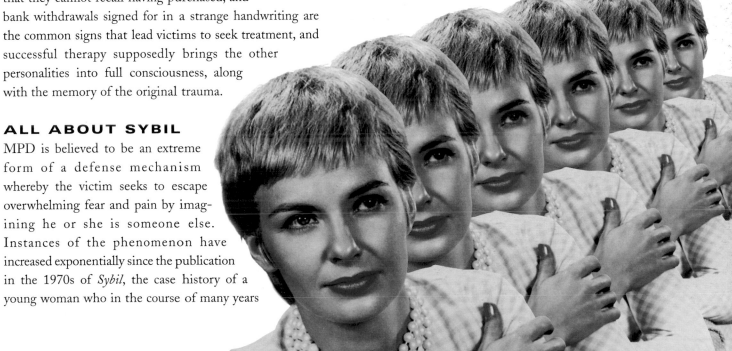

Historically, MPD has received little mention apart from a spate of occurrences in the later nineteenth century, when a number of cases of dual personality were studied by Freud and Charcot. It has echoes in the doppelganger or "wicked twin" myth, however, and was a theme used by several writers, notably James Hogg in *The Confessions of a Justified Sinner* (1824) and R. L. Stevenson in *The Case of Dr. Jekyll and Mr. Hyde* (1892). In its twentieth-century version, MPD usually includes more than one alter. It has been attacked in recent times on the grounds that the most extreme cases of child abuse, at Auschwitz for example, have not yielded a single known case of MPD, and the highly suggestible nature of most patients lends credence to the possibility of a therapy-led, iatrogenic origin. When the tapes of Sybil's case were released in 1998 it became clear that this too might have been a therapy-induced phenomenon. Skeptics also point out that recovered memory therapy is extremely unreliable and often creates images of abuse that are unrelated to real childhood events. Others have noted that MPD symptoms often appear only after therapy has begun, and tend to rapidly disappear when treatment is terminated.

BELOW **Anthony Perkins in *Dr. Jekyll and Mr. Hyde*, from the story by Robert Louis Stevenson, a classic early portrayal of dual personality.**

CREATIVE FRAGMENTATION

However, while it is clear that many cases of MPD are dubious, there are many cases where the existence of distinct, clearly defined personalities within the same body is hard to deny. These personalities may and usually do have different names, ages, likes and dislikes, different physical or mental abilities, differences in body language, speech and mannerisms, different histories, body movements, facial expressions, voice tone and pitch. In some cases they even have different brain patterns. One MPD victim has written, "Multiplicity is about hiding, pain, and survival. It is a desperate, completely creative, and wonderful survival mechanism. For the child who endures repeated and inescapable abuse, it may be their only escape. I consider myself to be blessed with MPD not cursed. It was a gift from God to me, to ensure my survival in a world that was full of insanity and reason not to survive." Alters typically include, in addition to the depressed, exhausted host: a strong, angry protector; a scared,

SYBIL

The multipersonalities of Sybil were so fascinating they became the subject of a movie starring Joanne Woodward.
◎ The selves, the doctor was now convinced, were not conflicting parts of the total self, struggling for identity, but rather defenses against the intolerable environment that had produced the childhood traumas. Sybil's mind and body were possessed by these others—not invading spirits, not dybbuks from without, but proliferating parts of the original child. Each self was younger than Sybil, with their ages shifting according to the time of the particular trauma that each had emerged to battle. . . integration would be

hurt child; a helper; and an internal persecutor who blames one or more of the alters for the abuse they have endured.

"Dissociation" is the term used for any condition in which a person becomes separated from objective reality. It covers functions such as daydreaming or absorption in an activity to the exclusion of all others; as well as pathological forms that signal avoidance of an unbearable memory. It is familiar to all creatives, for whom periods of reverie and obsessive concentration are characteristics, and many others also report "blank" times, the intervention of a guiding Other, and the production of work by unconscious or supernatural forces—all of which suggest an Ornsteinian "splitting" function.

There are other interpretations. Some have drawn analogies with the spirit possession of shamans; others believe that demonic possession of the kind described in the Bible may be a form of MPD. Plato's daimon, the guiding spirit who watches over and sometimes intervenes in the life of the waking person, seems to have a reference in Sybil's alter Vicky, the calm, sympathetic, and helpful "memory trace" of all the selves. Whatever the faults of MPD research and therapy, many creative people believe in and may have experienced the operation of unconscious selves within their own.

The Internet revolution puts a new light on multiple personality. It enables the self seated at the keyboard to assume any number of alternative identities, reaching different audiences projected across the Net in various E-mail and research situations. One "self" discusses intellectual subjects in an E-mail philosophy group; another may be sexual; a third may be into sports; a fourth may project a different gender, age, or whatever. Who is to know? Is this fragmentation or creativity? If the job of creativity is to bring disparates into a new unity, then Internet multiples seem to be its antithesis. But if fragmentation is necessary before a new entity can be conceived, then perhaps the Internet experience will be helpful in allowing users to confront different aspects of themselves and emerge with a new unity.

accomplished by getting the various selves to return to Sybil—the depleted waking self—the acquisitions and modes of behavior that they had stolen from the original Sybil. They had to return the knowledge, the experience, and the memories that had become theirs in the third of the total Sybil's life that *they* and not Sybil had lived. . .

. . . She could scarcely even endure just being awake. Waking, she knew one of the others might take over. Even when there wasn't an actual takeover, there was the everlasting internal pressure, the interference by the others. She felt alone, useless, futile. Convinced that she was never going to get better, Sybil was faced with self-recriminations and complaints. Certain that her life had stopped while she retraced a path that uncovered only anguish, Sybil felt that she had indeed come to the end of the line. She didn't want to live this way. She reached the Hudson River, brownish-green and deep. She envisioned herself in the water, sinking. Death would bring surcease.

Sybil walked closer to the river, but before she could actually reach it, her body turned, propelled by another's will. The body, controlled by Vicky, sought and found a phone booth in one of the apartment houses on Riverside Drive. After dialing, Vicky said in a firm, clear voice, "Dr. Wilbur, Sybil was going to throw herself in the Hudson River, but I didn't let her." ◎

FROM *SYBIL*, BY FLORA RHETA SCHREIBER (1973)

DREAMS AND THE UNCONSCIOUS

The madman is a walking dreamer.

IMMANUEL KANT

THE REDISCOVERY OF DREAMING

The development of "sleep laboratories" in the 1950s led to the discovery that dreaming is a universal phenomenon, using as much mental energy as the waking state. It was established that everyone dreams several times a night in the course of a recurrent nocturnal sleep cycle, the dreaming state being revealed by rapid eye movement (REM) in the sleeper. Dreaming periods occur three or four times during the night, gradually extending in length until the final stage of REM sleep. This last period may continue for as much as 45 minutes before waking, and dreams from this time are generally the ones recalled after the subject wakes up.

It was found that interruption of REM sleep had adverse effects on sleepers, who always showed an increased proportion of REM sleep to deep sleep when deprivation ceased. This "REM rebound" following dream deprivation indicated that we have a biological need to dream. Interestingly, psychotics showed a particular need

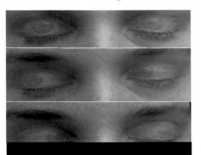

SLEEPING PERCHANCE

It is now recognized that we spend our lives in at least three completely different states of being: wakefulness, non-dreaming sleep, and REM (rapid eye movement) sleep. Each state is an active rather than quiescent process, with plentiful neural activity. Of these states, dreaming—REM sleep—has the closest affinity with creativity. In a sense, creativity is practical dreaming. NREM sleep also has its dreams, which may include somnabulism and certain kinds of nightmares and night terror.

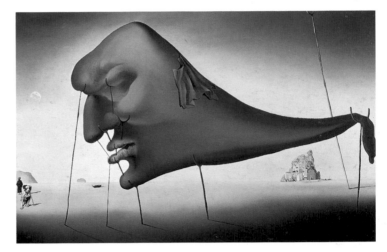

ABOVE *Sleep* by Salvador Dali, a famous painting by an obsessive whose work particularly focused on the strange visions experienced in dreamland.

for REM sleep when they were in remission from their illness. However, when they were ill, suffering from psychotic symptoms such as hallucinations or delusions, they showed no REM rebound after several nights of dream deprivation. The fact that psychotics appear not to need dreams to the same extent as normal people, as indicated by lack of REM rebound, suggests that the illness itself is a form of dreaming while being awake. Many dreams would be classed as psychotic activity if they took place in ordinary reality. In fact, by strict medical criteria each of us, when dreaming, is formally psychotic, delirious, or demented.

The bizarreness of dreams, the surreal shifts of person, place, and thought, include pathological elements such as: motor and visual hallucinations (including flying); spatial and temporal cognitive distortion (including flagrant violations of physical law); delusional acceptance of hallucinoid experience (acceptance of "impossible" events as experientially real); intensification of affect (strong emotion); and amnesia

LEFT *The Purity of a Dream* (1915) by Giorgio de Chirico. Even without the surreal juxtaposition of the distant frame, the looming tiers of empty arches capture the strangeness of dream-visions.

of dreams each night probably promotes mental health in ways we do not fully understand." However, the trivial and uninteresting nature of most dreams retrieved in laboratory situations has lessened the excitement generated by the original discovery. About 90 percent of REM dreams are judged to be "about as credible as descriptions of waking reality," claimed Dr. Frederick Snyder of the Association for the Psychophysiological Study of Sleep in California. "REM dream reports are generally clear, coherent, believable accounts of realistic situations in which the dreamer and other persons are involved in quite mundane activities and preoccupations…generally involving a familiar or commonplace setting."

Experiments have shown that dreams recalled at home rather than in the laboratory are generally more exciting, but the drab quality of so many dreams has led many people to believe that they are neither creative nor meaningful. The Nobel prize-winning zoologist Sir Peter Medawar has proposed that "many dreams may be assemblages of thought-elements that convey no information whatsoever."

Creative people have seldom seen dreams in this light. From Coleridge to Ginsberg, dreams have been a framework for creativity. Moreover, even a superficial review of one's own dreams reveals that they represent not one but many different states of mind. While most dreams are trivial, others may be particularly vivid and strongly colored, leaving an impression that lasts for hours or even days. Trivial dreams reflect the triviality of ordinary thought processes; unusual dreams deserve closer investigation. Images, ideas, and even entire works of art have been brought back from the dream state with great creative effect.

(tendency to forget the experience once it is completed). These conditions are what make dreams dreamlike, and they are also psychotic symptoms.

BRAIN-TIDYING OR CREATIVITY?

Not only do we all dream, but also we need to do so. As the psychologist Anthony Storr writes, "Entering the mad world

DREAM POWER

Dreaming is an altered state of consciousness that is universally shared and subjectively experienced (only in so-called lucid dreams are we aware that we are dreaming). The condition seems to extend wider than ordinary reality, ranging from banal events to out-of-the-body experiences, from meaningless happenings to episodes charged with intense, numinous feeling. Prophecy and poetry have always been associated with dreams. The bard is both dreamer and seer, according to a linkage that goes back to the earliest times and persists into our own period.

SHAMANIC DREAMING

Possibly the earliest representation of the professional dreamer is to be seen in a Lascaux cave mural, painted about 17,000 years ago, where a horned beast looms over a reclining figure (human forms are unusual in cave art) surrounded by weapons and a bird-topped staff. This emblematic staff, together with the prostrate figure's clearly emphasized erection (penile erection is an invariable feature of male REM sleep), suggests that he is a shaman in dream trance, while the animal looming over him is a psychic familiar or enemy.

From paleolithic times to the present, shamans have been professional dreamers who used their skill to assist the community through prediction and healing. Not accessible to ordinary consciousness, the dreamworld contains elements that endow the experiencer with extrasensory powers, such as telepathy and precognition. The skillful dreamer knows how to access these powers, and to interpret what they reveal.

ABOVE **Cave painting from Lascaux (near Montignac, southwestern France), probably showing (left) the outline figure of a dreaming shaman.**

A surprisingly large number of people believe in the precognitive and telepathic power of dreams. Some precognitions may arise as the result of subliminal signals stored by the mind but never accessed in consciousness. Signs of a defect in one's car, noted but instantly forgotten, may emerge in dream form as a car accident, which may then occur in reality. However, by no means all precognitive dreams can be explained in this way. Despite the best efforts of physicalist scientists, many people side with transpersonal psychologists in the belief that such paranormal functions are latent in the human organism, and manifest themselves most readily when the ordinary consciousness is asleep.

The practical value of dream skills was well understood in the ancient world. The Israelites seem to have been valued as interpreters, with Joseph prominent in Egypt and Daniel at Nebuchadnezzar's court in Babylon. The Greeks believed that "false" dreams came from the demonic world, entering through gates of horn, while "true" dreams come from the gods through gates of ivory. Dreams were used for diagnosis and treatment of sickness as well as for prophecy. The Greeks established shrines to Hypnos (the god of sleep) where sick people would sleep, hoping to be cured through dreams.

BELOW **Hypnos, represented in a fourth-century bronze sculpture. The son of Nyx (Night) and brother of Thanatos (Death), he fanned the weary to sleep with his wings.**

DREAMS AND THE ROMANTICS

With the birth of science in the seventeenth century the rational side of humanity took the ascendancy in the West, and the art of dreaming ceased to be valued by all except creatives, such as Henry Vaughan the Silurist (1622–1695), who dreamt he "saw Eternity the other night." But in the eighteenth century Jean-Jacques Rousseau (1712–1778) and Johann von Goethe (1749–1832) began a Romantic affair with the irrational dreamworld that challenged the sunny certainties of the Enlightenment. Dreams took on a new prominence. In the 1770s a new concern with the irrational power of emotion emerged with the German *Sturm und Drang* (Storm and Stress) movement, and from then on the law laid down by reason was no longer enforceable. The fantastic dungeons of the engraver Giambattista Piranesi (1720–1778) and the Gothic novels of Matthew "Monk" Lewis (1775–1818) or William Beckford (1759–1844) were early Romantic glamorizations of the dark side of human nature.

Now the eye of imagination was opened, and a different world came into view, whether the vision was William Blake's *Soul of a Flea* or Mary Shelley's *Frankenstein*. Different senses operate in the dark, and different entities are perceived. Freud, the cartographer of the irrational, was later to describe dreams as "the royal road to the unconscious," but for the Romantics there was no road, just a number of risky tracks into the unknown led by strange spirit guides. The Romantics were the first explorers of the unconscious, trusting the visions that brought them into contact with the underworlds and upper worlds. Some visions were involuntary—Blake saw his spirits with his own eyes, and brilliantly portrayed their features. Others used drugs—laudanum, opium, and hashish—to take them where their rational minds could not go. Writers such as Samuel Coleridge, Edgar Allan Poe, and Charles Baudelaire, artists such as William Blake, Théodore Géricault, or Caspar David Friedrich, used the power of dreams to assist, inspire, or even create their own work. To Coleridge, the imagination was "the organ of the super-sensuous," and the human mind was like an "Aeolian harp" responding to the vibrations of the invisible natural world.

> The Romantics understood that the world of the unconscious can only be approached by our feelings, by sensations with that tinge of otherness, which is a riddle to our conscious minds, and draws them to further comprehension.
>
> PETER REDGROVE

BELOW **Piranesi's engravings of imaginary dungeons blended architectural realism and grandeur with a strong element of Romantic fantasy.**

RIGHT *Soul of a Flea* by **William Blake. The imaginative breadth and visionary nature of Blake's work has assured his modern status: "I do not notice that which I see with my mortal eyes."**

THE PERSON FROM PORLOCK

The poet Samuel Taylor Coleridge described the genesis and fate of his poem "Kubla Khan," written in 1797.

◎ In the summer of the year 1797, the Author. . . had retired to a lonely farmhouse between Porlock and Linton, on the Exmoor confines of Somerset and Devonshire. In consequence of a slight indisposition, an anodyne had been prescribed, from the effects of which he fell asleep in his chair at the moment he was reading the following sentence, or words of the same substance, in "Purchas's Pilgrimage": "Here the Kubla Khan commanded a palace to be built, and a stately garden thereunto. And thus ten miles of fertile ground were inclosed with a wall." The Author continued for about three hours in a profound sleep, at least of the external senses, during which time he has the most vivid confidence, that he could not have composed less than from two hundred to three hundred lines; if that indeed can be called composition in which all images rose up before him as things, with a parallel production of the correspondent expressions, without any sensation or consciousness of effort. On awaking he appeared to himself to have a distinct recollection of the whole, and . . . instantly and eagerly wrote down the lines that are here preserved. At this moment he was unfortunately called out by a person on business from Porlock, and detained by him above an hour, and on his return to his room, found . . . that though he still retained some vague and dim recollection of the general purport of the vision, yet, with the exception of some eight or ten scattered lines and images, all the rest had passed away like images on the surface of a stream into which a stone has been cast. ◎

FROM PREFATORY NOTE TO "KUBLA KHAN"
BY SAMUEL TAYLOR COLERIDGE (1797)

THE CARTOGRAPHY OF THE MIND

The Romantics were looking for something beyond the grasp of the unassisted mind, and their work is full of dreamlike imagery. But Sigmund Freud (1856–1939) brought an organizing power to bear on the irrational, mapping out the primary mindworld of the unconscious. Like Plato, he saw dreams as representatives of a lawless nature that emerged during sleep. In *The Interpretation of Dreams* (1900) he proposed that dreams represented unacceptable sexual and aggressive desires repressed in the unconscious and sanitized through a process of disguise and distortion. In a later formulation he named his new territory, proposing an id ("it") for the unconscious part of the mind representing the basic libidinal and aggressive drives demanding immediate satisfaction ("the pleasure principle"), embodied in infantile sexuality. The repressed child of the id employs irrational, instinctive, and illogical "primary process" thinking to express its desires. The "secondary process" of conscious thought is the tool of the ego, which blocks out the id's desires or molds them into respectability, functioning as an intermediary between the inner world of the id and external reality. The "reality principle" of the ego modifies and redirects the id's libidinal impulses toward a necessary adaptation of reality. Failure of such modification leads to mental illness, neurosis, and psychosis. The process of adaptation begins with the moment of birth, which is "the first experience of anxiety, and thus the source and prototype of the affect of anxiety."

Freud sought to reconcile the conflict between biological factors of human existence and the civilizing aspects of human behavior: aesthetics, intellectual capacity, and religion. The intention of psychoanalysis is to "strengthen the ego. . . to widen its field of perception and enlarge its organization so that it can appropriate fresh portions of the id." The creative impulse itself was an attempt to sublimate these forces, bringing them to consciousness in an acceptable form.

Freud's intellectual power, vast erudition, and creative insights have earned him a pre-eminent place in the history of twentieth- century thought, but his insistence on the dark, dangerous, uncivilized nature of the unconscious shows him to be a man of his times, committed to a psychological version of the imperialist *mission civilatrice*. "I am not a man of science," he announced, "not an observer, not an experimenter, not a thinker. I am by temperament nothing but a conquistador—an adventurer, if you want it translated—with all the curiosity, daring and tenacity characteristic of a man of this sort." It was as a conquistador that he carved out his "royal road to the unconscious" interpreting his patients' dreams in the name of the civilizing mission of the ego. "We must make a dogma of [infantile sexuality]," he is said to have

BELOW **Sigmund Freud, the founder of psychoanalysis. The systematic approach he developed seems, in many of its details, rather narrow and dated, yet he remains a hugely influential figure.**

mission civilatrice. "I am not a man of science," he announced, "not an observer, not an experimenter, not a thinker. I am by temperament nothing but a conquistador—an adventurer, if you want it translated—with all the curiosity, daring and tenacity characteristic of a man of this sort." It was as a conquistador that he carved out his "royal road to the unconscious" interpreting his patients' dreams in the name of the civilizing mission of the ego. "We must make a dogma of [infantile sexuality]," he is said to have told disciple Carl Jung, "an unshakeable bulwark against the black tide of mud—occultism."

Freud suggested that the bizarreness of dreams arises from a process of intrapsychic disguise and censorship. In sleep, the control of the ego is lessened over the repressed impulses that comprise the id in the unconscious. Forbidden wishes intruding upon the conscious mind would disrupt the sleep state, therefore the "censor" disguises the unwelcome impulses through defensive transformations. Freud concluded that the bizarre manifest content of dreams must be dissected and interpreted to uncover the latent content that is the motive force of the dream process. However, his psychological theory is now believed to be overdependent on an outdated neurobiological conception of how the brain works, with nerve cells acting as energy transmitters.

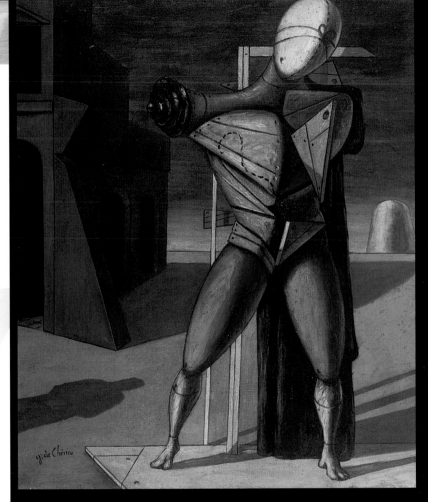

SURREALIST DREAMERS

Freud's insights opened a new territory for creative discovery, inspiring the Surrealists, who produced work that shared many of the dissociative features of dreams. However, as the artist and writer Susan Hiller points out, a distinction should be made between "dream" and "dreamlike." The proto-Surrealist Giorgio de Chirico (1888–1978) maintained that art should represent rather than explore dreams. "Without any sign of common sense or logic. . . [a work of art] will draw nearer to dream." René Magritte (1898–1967) wrote that his work was "a question of self-willed dreams, in which nothing is as vague as those feelings one has while escaping in dreams." The paintings of Salvador Dalí (1904–1989) are careful illustrations of Freud's theories rather than actual dream experiences.

ABOVE *Il Trovatore* by **Giorgio de Chirico. His dreamlike pictures from around 1910 had a considerable influence on the Surrealists.**

RIGHT **Dali's *Hallucinogenic Toreador* (1969–1970), with its nudes melting into faces melting into bullfighters, has a dreamlike quality, but also the distinct sense of a controlling hand.**

THE SCIENCE OF DREAMING

Neuroscientists have established that neurons located in the primitive brainstem, the "reptilian brain" at the base of the cerebral hemispheres, play a central role in sleep–wake alternation. The brainstem contains a "REM-on" population of cells uniquely active in REM sleep periods, while another group of nerve cells falls silent. The Harvard neuroscientist Allan Hobson has proposed that REM sleep and dreaming are the outcome of a change in the operating system of the brain, mediated by these two reciprocally interacting populations of brainstem neurons. The "REM-on" cells drive the eyes into motion, send excitatory pulses to visual and motor centers in the cortex, and inhibit access of input from the external world. At the same time, the muscles are prevented from receiving the relevant impulses from the brain, thus ensuring that we do not act on sensory stimuli produced in the dream.

Autoactivated, disconnected, autostimulated, the dreaming brain struggles to make sense of its internally generated stimuli, integrating them into a dream plot, which it synthesizes in the light of an individual's past experiences, ongoing concerns, settled character, and cognitive style. The form of dreams is related to the form of brain activity in sleep. The sensory-motor hallucinosis of dream experience arises from specific activation of sensory-motor neural centers, and it is because the visual and motor circuits are preferentially stimulated that in our dreams we see, move, even fly, more often than we taste, smell, or touch. Our subjective consciousness accepts improbable dream scenarios as experiential reality because the brain is deprived of external clues with which to construct an orientational framework. The unconstrained nature of the internal stimulus source, incompletely endowed with representational coherence and thematic unity, leads to distortions of time, place, and person. The intense feelings of the dreamer reflect a direct activation of the brain's emotional systems. The amnesia results from a corresponding failure to activate long-term memory circuits.

THE LUST FOR MEANING

Hobson believes that this system of information-processing is capable not only of reproduction and distortion of stored information but also of the elaboration of novel information. His theory of "activation synthesis" sees the brain as so inexorably bent upon the quest for meaning that it attributes and even creates meaning when there is little or none to be found in the data it is asked to process. The theory thus includes creativity among its assumptions. In this sense, the study of the dreaming brain is the study of the brain-mind as an auto-creative mechanism. The creativity of the dreaming brain shares a deep kinship with that of the artist: "Since dreaming is universal, it stands as testimony to the universality of the artistic experience. In our dreams, we all become writers, painters, and filmmakers, combining extraordinary sets of characters, actions, and locations into strangely coherent experiences." Hobson's activation-synthesis theory convincingly explains the biological processes of dream production, apparently precluding the need for Freudian dream interpretation. However, it begs the question of the psychological selection process, the experiential nature of dreaming. What is it that weighs some dreams with special meaning, and imparts an intense emotionality to others? Why do dreams often reenact familiar traumas in thinly disguised form? Why and how do they bring solutions and warnings, insights and inspirations, feelings of content and wonder?

THE JUNGIAN ANGLE

The Swiss psychologist Carl Jung (1875–1961) rejected Freud's emphasis on the sexual-aggressive nature of dream content and identified as "grand" dreams those that emerged from a deeper, nonsexual level of meaning. His discovery of parallels between psychotic delusions and ancient myths led him to explain human motivation in terms of a larger creative energy. Below the personal unconscious, where repressed feelings and thoughts developed during an individual's life, lay the collective unconscious, "the vast historical storehouse" of feelings, thoughts, and memories inherited and shared by all humanity.

ABOVE **The Wise Old Man, the upholder of authority, is one of the archetypal figures that, according to Jung, populate humanity's collective unconscious.**

COLLECTIVELY UNCONSCIOUS

Jung proposed that this collective unconscious had more or less the same structure among all peoples—hence the close similarities between mythological themes in unconnected cultures throughout the world. He felt further that these unconscious processes shaped people's mental and spiritual growth. Certain dreams were gateways to this world of "archetypes" —the primordial images that constantly appear not only in religions, myths, and folklore, but also in the individual's most meaningful dreams. Such archetypes include the Wise Old Man, a quasidivine authority figure; the Trickster, an antihero combination of the animal and the divine; the Persona, the mask that we use for waking life; the Shadow, the primitive, instinctive side of

ourselves; the Anima and Animus, the male and female potential present in all humans; the Great Mother, the archetype of feminine mystery and power.

Jung also discerned "connections between individual dream symbolism and medieval alchemy," which he saw not as chemical but psychic symbols and transformations. Alchemists sought to unify opposites such as white and black, sun and moon, male and female, to create a single unifying principle, the Philosopher's Stone. Jungian therapy aims to reconcile similar dualities within the individual psyche, and to integrate the personal unconscious with the collective unconscious in order to achieve a state of individuation, or wholeness of self.

Many creatives owe a conscious debt to the theories of Jung, from Hermann Hesse (1877–1962) the Swiss-German novelist and poet who became a cult figure in the 1960s, to the British composer Sir Michael Tippett (1905–1998), and the Scottish poet Edwin Muir (1887–1959). But the importance of Jung's work lies more in the way it has opened many people to the possibility that the great mythical themes reflected in dreams are parables of a timeless philosophy.

BELOW **Carl Jung, photographed in 1953. He developed an alternative to Freud's view of personality and the subconscious, and a different approach to the interpretation of dreams.**

CREATIVE DREAMING

To the creative, dream theory is less important than dream practice. The discovery that dreams work for you leads to a desire to develop this interesting, often enthralling area of cognition. The set of beliefs a person holds about dreams affects the way he or she uses them, but anyone who has tried keeping a dream diary knows that this exercise invariably improves both the quality and quantity of the dreams themselves, suggesting that there is a faculty here that can easily be trained.

LUCID DREAMS

Lucid dreaming, the awareness that one is in a dream, is a first step toward creative manipulation of the dreaming state of consciousness. Lucid dreamers subjectively experience the reality of the dream environment, but remain in possession of their normal intellectual faculties. With practice, they develop to some extent the ability to control the events of the dream, deciding where to go and what to do. A standard way of preparing a lucid dream is to concentrate on some object before falling asleep, and find it again in the dream. Recognition of the object will trigger the awareness that one is in a dream.

ABOVE **An Eskimo figurine from Alaska, believed to show a shaman leaving his physical body in order to fly in spirit form.**

The shaman's use of dreams involves conscious, volitional activity in a dream body, including flight to specific locations in this and other worlds. This technique is also reported by adepts in yoga and other mystical disciplines. What is brought back from these travels may constitute works of art, such as new songs or dances designed to give the shaman's experiences a performative reality, but these creative products are not intentional works of art so much as ways of recreating the shaman's experience and transmitting the supernatural message to the community.

One of the earliest Western accounts of lucid dreaming was recorded by the Dutch physician Frederik van Eeden in 1913, who first became aware that he was dreaming when he observed the extraordinary perfection of the landscape through which he was traveling—it was too perfect. On other occasions, some defect in the environment or functioning betrays the dream state. The dreamworld, according to van Eeden, is "a fake-world, cleverly imitated, but with small failures." This implies that it is constructed from the dreamer's own perceptions, transformed to accommodate stimuli released by the "REM-on" neural colony in the brainstem, rather than any external reality. However, there are well-attested cases of dreamers identifying real people, places, and objects, mysteriously suggesting that the individual's perceptual range is not confined to his physical perceptual organs. The age-old belief that the physical body contains a nonmaterial counterpart, or "subtle body," is found in most religions and was developed in the West by the theosophists in the nineteenth century, notably Annie Besant and C. W. Leadbeater, who developed a system of astral and mental thought forms based on Hindu Tantra.

Van Eeden's experiences have interesting similarities to shamanic accounts, recorded from an entirely different cultural perspective. For example, he described how he was able to slip from his sleeping body into his dreaming body, and the "double recollection of the two bodies ... leads almost unavoidably to the conception of a dream body." He noted that flying often indicated the onset of a lucid dream—another point of similarity with the shamanic experience.

OUT OF BODY OR OUT OF MIND?

Lucid dreams have affinities with another remarkable altered state of consciousness, known as the out-of-body experience (OBE). OBEs have been extensively reported, and usually occur during the hypnagogic state between sleeping and waking. In the late 1960s Charles Tart began the first laboratory tests with subjects who could have OBEs voluntarily. One of his subjects was able to repeat accurately a five-digit number from a card placed on a shelf about five-and-a-half feet above the bed where she lay sleeping. Tart calculated that the probability of her being right by chance was about one in 100,000.

However, the accuracy of OBE accounts has proved very variable. The psychologist Stephen LaBerge has proposed that OBEs occur when people lose input from their sense organs, as happens at the onset of sleep, while retaining consciousness. This combination of events is especially likely when a person passes directly from waking into REM sleep. In both states the mind is alert and active, but in waking it is processing sensory input from the outside world, while in dreaming it is creating a mental model independent of sensory input. When dreaming, we generally experience ourselves in a body much like the "real" one, because that is what we are used to. However, our internal senses reside in the physical body, which when we are awake inform us about our position in space and about the movement of our limbs. This information is cut off in REM sleep. Therefore we can dream of doing all kinds of things with our dream bodies—flying, dancing, running from monsters, being dismembered—all while the physical body lies safely in bed. This explains many OBE experiences, but does not account for the accuracy of a significant number of OBE reports.

LEFT *The Nightmare* (1790–91) by Johann Füssli, a vividly Romantic image. Füssli was a friend and contemporary of William Blake, and a great admirer of Michelangelo.

LUCID DREAMS

The Dutch physician Frederik van Eeden kept a record of his dreams from 1896 till 1913, when he submitted his "Study of Dreams" to the Society for Psychical research. In addition to classifying them into nine experientially distinct types, he described in detail the altered state of consciousness known as the lucid dream.

◎ I obtained my first glimpse of this lucidity [when] I dreamt that I was floating through a landscape of bare trees, knowing that it was April, and I remarked that the perspective of the ^ branches and trees changed quite naturally. Then I made the reflection, during sleep, that my fancy would never be able to invent or to make an image as intricate as the perspective movement of little twigs seen floating by. . .

Lucid dreams are also symbolic—yet I never remarked anything sexual or erotic in them. Their symbolism takes the form of beautiful landscapes—different luminous phenomena, sunlight, clouds, and especially a deep blue sky. In a perfect instance of this lucid dream I float through immensely wide landscapes, with clear blue, sunny sky, and a feeling of bliss and gratitude. . . Sometimes I conceive of what appears as a symbol, warning, consoling, approving. A cloud gathers or the light brightens. Only once could I see the disc of the sun. ◎

FROM *ALTERED STATES OF CONSCIOUSNESS*, EDITED BY CHARLES T. TART (1969)

ABOVE **A graphically literal depiction of an "out-of-body experience" (OBE). OBEs, "lucid dreams" (in which the dreamer is aware that "this is a dream") and "near-death experiences" (NDEs) are closely allied phenomena.**

BRIEF ENCOUNTERS WITH THE REAPER

A more extreme form of the OBE is the near-death experience (NDE). Victims of car crashes and cardiac arrests most commonly report NDEs. Their typical symptoms come in five stages, starting with a sensation of serenity and painlessness. Then comes a feeling of passing through a tunnel toward a point of bright light, and the arrival at a "place of light." Here they are greeted by figures from their past, some of them dead, and sometimes there follow religious visions. Before these events, many patients claim to have floated from their bodies to observe events in other rooms. One observed a glove lying on a window ledge outside the building, and this was discovered to be accurate. Another observed friends and relatives waiting in another room. Tests are at present being carried out at a well-known hospital in England to investigate the reality of NDEs over an extended period.

It seems that, just as the physical body creates its own reality through its sensory system, so the nonphysical body creates a reality through internally generated stimuli, and under certain circumstances these two realities interpenetrate.

THE CREATIVE PROCESS

The subconscious is ceaselessly
murmuring, and it is by listening to these
murmurs that one hears the truth.

GASTON BACHELARD

THE GERMINATION OF IDEAS

The creative process introduces change and development in the organization of subjective life; and this occurs on both a collective and an individual level. Creativity is the means by which new ideas enter the collective consciousness. The creative process is the course of action that enables this to happen. It emerges through individual producers, who not only share in a larger system of cultural conditions, social networks, and cognitive fields, but also add their own sets of mental operating systems to the equation. Thus the creative process cannot be disentangled from the creative person and the creative product. The process has affinities with procreation, including stages of germination, gestation, birth, and, finally, integration into the world. However, this process is not the concern only of those who follow a creative vocation in the arts, sciences, or philosophy—as a property of subjectivity it is as wide as life itself.

At a mundane level, most people achieve creative solutions to everyday challenges on a regular basis: circumstances demand new solutions to new problems. At another level, the creative process has its fullest expression in self-creation, the integration of disparate parts of one's personality into a unified whole. In meditation and mystical states of consciousness, this objective transcends the individual's personal consciousness, and the unity to be achieved is with an absolute reality. Within the individual, the process of integration, the development of the structure of a psychic life, is a process of continuous adaptation. For the creative artist, on the other hand, this integration is achieved through the work itself.

An artist's works are the outward form of ongoing development of personality, which is a never-ending process. In Jung's picture of the inner development of the personality, the work itself becomes the poet's destiny and determines his psychic development. "It is not Goethe who creates Faust," Jung wrote, "but Faust who creates Goethe." The creative person both defines and realizes the self in terms of the work produced. From its mysterious origin in the unconscious, to its realization in a completed object or idea that can communicate its meaning to others, the creative process interpenetrates ordinary reality while being separate from it. It exists in the individual, but is also part of a larger system. Many creative people have described this experience and, although there is often a self-mythologizing aspect to these accounts, there remains in even the most prosaic a sense of wonder. All agree that the end is never fully in sight in the beginning and comes into view only when the process of creation is completed.

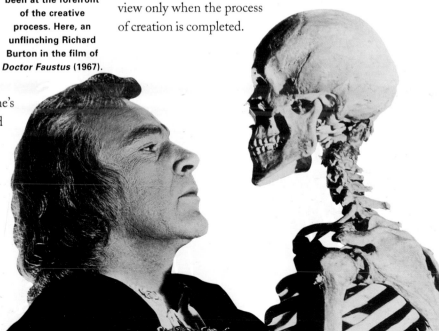

BELOW **Confrontation— with life, with death, and with self—has been at the forefront of the creative process**. Here, an **unflinching Richard Burton in the film of *Doctor Faustus* (1967)**.

THE ROLE OF THE UNCONSCIOUS

The creative process makes use of both unconscious and conscious processes, but the role of the unconscious is often seen as the key to creativity. "The unconscious is the ocean of the unsayable," wrote the Italian novelist Italo Calvino (1923–1985), "expelled from the land of language, removed as a result of ancient prohibitions." Externalizing the unsayable inner conflicts and giving them conscious form is the artist's work. It may be that the intensity of the conflict, the struggle with the daimonic element, is what gives force to the finished work of art. Factors underlying the creative processes in the unconscious include not only sexual, aggressive, and other feelings influencing conscious behavior" but also tender and loving emotions that may be just as inhibited in their expression. From the unconscious, too, come the promptings we vaguely call intuition and hunches.

ABOVE *Recalling the Faust Fantasy* (1866) by Mariano Fortuny. The first telling of *The History of Dr. Faustus* was published in Germany in 1587, and the story of Faust's deal with the Devil has since inspired numerous writers, artists, and composers.

According to Freud, the unconscious consists of elements derived from the individual's past that are kept out of consciousness because they are personally or socially unacceptable, but continue to exert an effect on conscious thought and behavior. A basic function of the ego's controlling mechanism is to alter and distort the unconscious material that wells up in dreams so that it cannot be recognized in consciousness. This view has been challenged by the recent work of neuroscientists, but the "primary process" thinking of the Freudian unconscious, which apparently uses a preverbal, visual language to express itself, is an experiential reality that has a resemblance to many features of the creative process. The unconscious uses right-brain images, and these are by definition less "analytic" than rational left-brain processes, which play little part in the germinative period of the creative process. Freud and his disciples believed that creative artists control the eruption of unconscious processes into consciousness, sublimating them into a form that is new and satisfying.

But some psychologists point out that although art may use the language of dreams, it seeks to communicate the vision, not to suppress it. Equally, if Jung's themes of the collective unconscious (Wise Old Man, Universal Mother, Hero, Shadow, etc.) are perceived as "germinative influences" appearing in dream or reverie, they nevertheless need to be transformed or changed to have creative effect. The value of art lies not only in the depth of its perceptions but also in the power with which it communicates them to others. The product of a creative mind, though formed in the unconscious, carries the shapes, patterns, styles, and compositional form characteristic of art. Even such "unconscious" artists as Coleridge and Blake were conscious and strongly motivated poets before any visions or poetic lines appeared in their dreams.

LEFT **Coleridge's reputation as literary critic and lecturer survived the decay of his early poetic career which was ruined—despite the visions—by opium addiction.**

Whereas dreams reflect the secret and forbidden desires of the dreamer in disguised form, the creative process seeks to resolve unconscious processes to produce revelation rather than concealment, lucidity rather than obscurity.

ALBERT ROTHENBURG

INSPIRATION

The German philosopher Friedrich Nietzsche, one of the most important and provocative thinkers of the nineteenth century, described how he was inspired to write his masterpiece *Also Sprach Zarathustra* (Thus Spake Zarathustra).

◎ **Provided one has the slightest remnant of superstition left, one can hardly reject completely the idea that one is the mere incarnation, or mouthpiece, or medium of some almighty power. . . One hears—one does not seek; one takes—one does not ask who gives: a thought flashes out like lightning, inevitably without hesitation—I have never had any choice about it. There is an ecstasy whose terrific tension is sometimes released by a flood of tears, during which one's progress varies from involuntary impetuosity to involuntary slowness. There is a feeling that one is utterly out of hand, with the most distinct consciousness of an infinitude of shuddering thrills that pass through one from head to foot. . . There is an instinct for rhythmic relations which embraces an entire world of forms. . . Everything occurs quite without volition, as if in an eruption of freedom, independence, power, and divinity. The spontaneity of the images and similes is most remarkable; one loses all perception of what is imagery and simile. . . This is my experience of inspiration. I have no doubt that I should have to go back millenniums to find another who could say to me: "This is mine also!"** ◎

FROM *ECCE HOMO*,
BY FRIEDRICH NIETZSCHE (1888)

ABOVE **Nietzsche, pictured on his sickbed at the Villa Silberblick, 1899: an oil sketch by Hans Olde. Nietzsche's heroic concept of creativity was an apotheosis of nineteenth-century thought.**

PLATO'S DIVINE MADNESS

Mental operations beyond the reach of thought take place both at the germination and during the elaboration of creative activity, but it is the original impulse, or inspiration, that seems most removed from ordinary reality. Plato defines inspiration as a form of possession, an altered state. This inspiration is a "breathing into" consciousness of the psychic pheromone that leads ultimately to a finished work of art, in turn capable of inspiring others. For creativity is an important, perhaps the most important, form of communication.

In ancient Greece, this inspiration was mediated through the Muses, daughters of Zeus and Mnemosyne (Memory), who each presided over an area of creative activity, and had been trained by the god Apollo, lord of music, light, and clarity. If Apollo suggests the divine, numinous quality of the creative process, Mnemosyne emphasizes the thorough knowledge and mastery of the field that all artists need to possess.

> The poet has no invention in him, until he has been inspired and is out of his senses and the mind is no longer in him. . . [Poets] are simply inspired to utter that to which the Muse impels them.
>
> PLATO

THE AHA! FACTOR

The phenomenon of inspiration, which may occur during the development of the creative process as well as at its point of origin, is typically experienced as a physical sensation expressed through an "Aha!" response, an alteration in breathing pattern. Some psychologists have noticed that inspiration is often accompanied by tension or anxiety, suggesting that it may embody unconscious conflicts, containing the seeds that eventually spur the poet or artist to insight. The "Aha!" is the bursting of the bubble containing the seed of the idea. The force required to break it is generated by disturbance or conflict in the unconscious. To these researchers, the creative process is an adaptive function working to resolve inner conflicts and externalize them in an acceptable form.

According to the psychologist Rollo May, "the daimonic is apt to come out when we are struggling with an inner problem, it is the conflict which brings the unconscious dimensions closer to the surface where they can be tapped. Conflict presupposes some need for a shift. . . within the person; he struggles for a new life, as it were. This opens up the channels to creativity." Thus the daimonic, the Dionysian element, the recessive gene of creativity, is there from the beginning.

The moment of inspiration, the germinative impulse that sets off the creative process, is characterized by unaccountable emotion, indicating the antirational component of creativity. The successful work of art is not only conceived in nonordinary consciousness, but also has the capacity to

> Art bids us touch and taste and see and hear the world, and shrinks from all that is of the brain only, from all that is not a fountain jetting from the entire hopes, memories, and sensations of the body.
>
> WILLIAM BUTLER YEATS

communicate something of its mystery, working not through reason but emotion. The ability of art to transmit emotion is one of the qualities that we value most.

The Romantic poets and artists used narcotics to puncture the membrane that held them in the rational, conventional world, and to gain access to their dark and chaotic inner reality. They believed in a mythic truth, which could be reached through the extremes of emotion, by means of a "disordering of the senses," as proposed by the French poet Arthur Rimbaud (1854–1891), and this caused them to respond more passionately and more dangerously to the initiatory promptings of the creative process. They were the inheritors of Plato's doctrine of divine inspiration.

CATCHING THE ELUSIVE MUSE

For others, the first awareness is often something more banal, though still mysterious, a mere glimpse serving as a clue to be developed. Creation begins typically with a vague, confused excitement. The English writer Martin Amis describes it as "a throb or a glimmer, an act of recognition on the writer's part. . . It may be that nothing about the idea appeals to you other than the fact that it's your destiny, that it's your next book. You may even be secretly appalled or awed or turned off by the idea, but it goes beyond that."

The American novelist Henry James (1843–1916) refers to "the stray suggestion, the wandering word, the vague echo, at touch of which the novelist's imagination winces at the prick of some sharp point, the fineness of which communicates the virus of suggestion." His germinative idea for *The*

Spoils of Poynton (1897) arose from a chance exchange with his neighbor at dinner in which "there had been but ten words, yet I had recognized in them, as in a flash, all the possibilities of the little drama of my 'spoils,' which glimmered then and there into life." The Russian poet Osip Mandelstam (1891–1938) was haunted by a rhythmic, wordless sequence that led him to create his work. Gustave Flaubert's (1821–1880) impulse was often visual: "It flits before your eyes, and that is when you must grasp it, avidly."

LEFT **"A throb or a glimmer, an act of recognition. . . your destiny, your next book"**: the germ of creation described by the novelist **Martin Amis.**

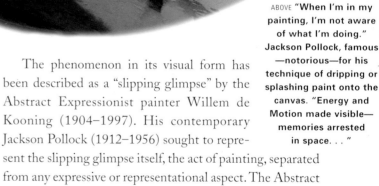

The significance of the apparently trivial material offered in the original impulse lies in the disproportionate excitement these half-visions evoke in the creative, and in their power to open the mind inward. They carry a strange emotional charge, sometimes leaving the subject feeling unwell. Many writers have commented on a sensation of physical unease at the onset of creative activity, a change in the inner weather leading to—or caused by—a subtle shift in the sensory apparatus. The poet A. E. Housman (1859–1936), for example, claimed that he had "seldom written poetry unless I was rather out of health, and the experience, though pleasurable, was generally agitating and exhausting."

ABOVE "When I'm in my painting, I'm not aware of what I'm doing." Jackson Pollock, famous —notorious—for his technique of dripping or splashing paint onto the canvas. "Energy and Motion made visible— memories arrested in space. . . "

BELOW *Devon* by Willem de Kooning. Whether in figurative or abstract mode, there is an element of free association in his work, a characteristic feature of Action Painting.

The phenomenon in its visual form has been described as a "slipping glimpse" by the Abstract Expressionist painter Willem de Kooning (1904–1997). His contemporary Jackson Pollock (1912–1956) sought to represent the slipping glimpse itself, the act of painting, separated from any expressive or representational aspect. The Abstract Expressionists' attempts to depict the irrational well-springs of creativity derive from the Surrealists' work, but differ in that it is the unconscious creative impulse that is portrayed, not its material in the form of imagery. For the Surrealists, apart from some work by Max Ernst (1891–1976) and Joan Miró (1893–1983), the imagery and logic of dreams are retrieved and recreated, but not portrayed. The violence of much Action Painting is a result of its closeness to the irrational surge that it seeks to capture.

RIGHT *Mythologization of Landscape* (1924–1925) by Joan Miró, a work which links with the cave painting of the dreaming shaman at Lascaux (see page 49), as well as with the dream pictures of the Surrealists.

INCUBATING THE IDEA

The psychologist Graham Wallas proposed a model of the creative process in terms of four stages: preparation, incubation, illumination and verification. In preparation, the individual formulates an idea and equips himself or herself for the project with constant input. During incubation, input becomes difficult because all is satiated to the point of compression. The transpersonal psychologist Carlisle Bergquist describes incubation as "the mysterious 'black box' stage in which the creation forms but remains inseparable, unknown, and unable to survive independently. It is symbiotic." The aggregate gestates, concluding with sudden illumination, and the accumulated resources thrust into a new, independent state of being that takes on a life of its own. Illumination is glamorous, appearing easy, as if the creative product springs forth effortlessly. The final stage, verification, reviews, refines, and adjusts the product of illumination to the realities of reason: it must actually work in its applied field. This stage separates fantasy from creation.

Wallas's model of the creative process understates the emotional intensity inherent in many of its functions. "Preparation" presumably includes the emotion-charged throbs, slipping glimpses, and other mysterious imperatives that set the whole thing off, as well as contemplation, self-instruction, and methodical research—which can be rare among many creatives. However, all share to some degree the reordering process of incubation that takes place in the brain when the germinative idea or inspiration is unconsciously scanned, compared with other mental contents, organized, or elaborated. The time taken for incubation can vary from a few minutes to months or even years.

ORDERING CREATIVE CHAOS

Both in creation and in preparation for it the mind nearly always requires some management. It has to discover the clue that suggests the required development, perceive the creative end to be reached, and assure certain and economical movement toward that end.

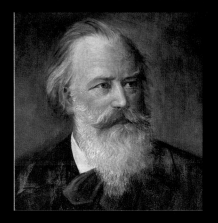

RIGHT **Brahms, painted around 1890 by Olga Miller zu Aichenholz. He was the "classical romantic," writing in a soberly disciplined style; yet some of his late, contemplative piano pieces are deeply imaginative and spiritual, contrary to his reputation.**

GESTATION FOR GENIUS

The composer Johannes Brahms (1833–1897) would deliberately turn to something else when a new idea came to him, and perhaps think no more of the new idea for several months. When he took it up again he would find that the idea had unconsciously assumed a different form, at which he would begin working. The period of gestation for Friedrich Nietzsche's *Also Sprach Zarathustra* (1883–1885) was "exactly eighteen months [which] might suggest, at least to Buddhists, that I am in reality a female elephant."

LEFT **Jean Cocteau face-to-profile with Maria Calvi. Poet, actor, playwright, artist, and film director: who better than Cocteau to tell us about the creative process?**

Though the nonlogical, instinctive, subconscious part of the mind must play its part in his work, the artist also has a conscious mind which is not inactive. The artist works with the concentration of his whole personality, and the conscious part of it resolves conflicts, organizes memories, and prevents him from trying to walk in two directions at the same time.

HENRY MOORE

To write, to conquer ink and paper, accumulate paragraphs, divide them with periods and commas, is a different matter from carrying around the dream of a play or of a book. . . The poet's role is humble; he must clean house and await its due visitation.

JEAN COCTEAU

ABOVE **Henry Moore found inspiration in primitive African and Mexican art, to which he brought a radical and vigorous aesthetic of his own. "Sculpture in stone should look honestly like stone."**

The will, which belongs to conscious life only, cannot make the creative move in directions not yet discovered, but when work must be done on something already defined, the will is useful in many matters assisting the creative process, helping the worker to stick to his or her discipline, stay at the desk, or deal firmly with distractions. It acts as a positive guiding organization and integration of self, which utilizes creatively, as well as inhibiting and controlling, the instinctive drives.

Louis Pasteur (1822–1895) wrote that "chance favors the prepared mind," and creative artists usually have a wide knowledge and expertise in their chosen fields. After the one percent of inspiration comes the 99 percent of perspiration. The psychologist Mihaly Csikszentmihalyi has proposed that no one can be "Creative with a capital C," unless they master all that went before them in the field or, like Freud or the flight-obsessed Wright brothers, create their own field. Csikszentmihalyi explains the creative process in his concept of "flow," that period when the task at hand is challenging enough to engage us totally, rescuing us from boredom, but not so challenging that we fail, allowing frustration to set in. Between the two extremes of boredom (too easy) and frustration (too hard) we find the flow channel—blissful execution, seemingly effortless progress, and an overall feeling of happiness. "Flow" is at work when a musician gets lost in his or her music, or when a painter becomes one with the process of painting.

The creative is attracted by the unrealized and drawn toward its realization. By its nature, the unrealized has an unconscious origin. However, the opposition between the conscious and unconscious activities in creation is only initial. The new order with which creation is concerned always has an affinity for consciousness. The artist works toward clarification, toward consciousness. He or she prepares the ground in which the germinative impulse from the unconscious can sprout, flourish, and give fruit.

ABOVE Louis Pasteur in his laboratory, 1885, as painted by Albert Edelfelt. As befits an inspirational scientist, Pasteur considered that the germination of a productive idea, as of a useful organism, required preparation and hard graft.

My ideas flow best and most abundantly when I am as it were completely myself. Whence and how they come, I know not; nor can I force them. Those ideas that please me I retain in my memory, and... provided I am not disturbed, my subject enlarges itself... Nor do I hear in my imagination the parts successively, but I hear them, as it were, all at once. What a delight this is I cannot tell!

WOLFGANG AMADEUS MOZART

[The poet] has acquired a greater readiness and power in expressing what he thinks and feels... All good poetry is the spontaneous overflow of powerful feelings: it takes its origin from emotion recollected in tranquillity: the emotion is contemplated till, by a species of reaction, the tranquillity gradually disappears, and an emotion kindred to that which was before the subject of contemplation is gradually produced, and does itself actually exist in the mind.

WILLIAM WORDSWORTH

AUTOMATIC CREATION

Perhaps it is the intensity of the inner conflict that imposes a certain automatism on creatives, many of whom have described at least some part of their invention as entirely spontaneous and involuntary. Coleridge's use of opium to stimulate automotive work is well known, but a degree of automatism is reported by most creatives, and no creative process has been demonstrated to be wholly free from it. At the least, something beyond the fully observable conscious construction takes place, and it is to the advantage of consciousness to be able to make use of it.

Full automatism is found in Blake, who asserted that an entire poem came to him word for word in a dream. A. E. Housman wrote that "there would flow into my mind, with sudden and unaccountable emotion, sometimes a line or two of verse, sometimes a whole stanza at once." He would write it down, "leaving gaps, and hoping that further inspiration might be forthcoming another day." If it was not, "the poem had to be taken in hand and completed by the brain, which was apt to be a matter of trouble and anxiety, involving trial and disappointment, and sometimes ending in failure."

ABOVE **The English poet A. E. Housman compared the pleasure of automatic creation with the grind of the mental effort required to complete a poem, "a matter of trouble and anxiety."**

NABOKOV'S PRIVATE MIST

This is the Russian novelist Vladimir Nabokov's description of how he wrote his first poem in a semiautomatic state:

When I was irrevocably committed to finish my poem or die, there came the most trancelike state of all. . . I found myself, of all places, on a leathern couch in the cold, musty, little-used room that had been my grandfather's study. On that couch I lay prone, in a kind of reptilian freeze, one arm dangling. . . When next I came out of that trance, my arm was still dangling, but now I was prostrate on the edge of a rickety wharf . . . I relapsed into my private mist, and when I emerged again, the support of my extended body had become a low bench in the park. . . Various sounds reached me in my various situations. I could hear the family phonograph through my verse. . . A tambourine, still throbbing, seemed to lie on the darkening moss. For a spell, the last notes of the husky contralto pursued me through the dusk. When silence returned, my first poem was ready.

FROM *SPEAK, MEMORY,* BY VLADIMIR NABOKOV (1967)

BLURRING THE SENSES

Another unusual aspect of the creative process mentioned by some artists is synesthesia, the interconnection of one sensual modality with another. Arthur Rimbaud and other Symbolists mentioned the "color" of individual sounds. Ludwig van Beethoven (1770–1827) could "see the image [of a musical work] in front of me from every angle, as if it had been cast." Robert Schumann (1810–1856) wrote that "certain outlines amid all the sounds and tones . . . form and condense into clear shapes." Wolfgang Amadeus Mozart (1756–1791) claimed that he could survey one of his compositions at a glance, "complete and finished, like a fine picture or beautiful statue."

BELOW **Beethoven: in music, he marked the transition from Classical to Romantic, projecting a new level of artistic self-awareness.**

The phenomenon of synesthesia is familiar to users of hallucinogenic drugs, who frequently claim to "see" sounds or "hear" colors. Some neurobiologists believe that synesthesia may be related to stimulation of the locus ceruleus, the funneling mechanism in the midbrain that integrates all sensory input. If the locus ceruleus acts to bring together all types of sensory messages into a general excitation system in the brain, stimulation of this area by psychedelics will cause the user to feel that sensations are crossing the boundaries between different modalities.

AUTOMATIC ART

The German-born surrealist painter Max Ernst always experimented with new ways to perceive and became interested in detaching the conscious mind from the creative process. Ernst described how, in 1925, he developed a process of automatic painting by dropping pieces of paper on the floorboards of his room and then rubbing the paper with blacklead. He called these works *frottages* (rubbings).

◎ The *frottage* process simply depends on intensifying the mind's capacity for nervous excitement, using the appropriate technical means, excluding all conscious directing of the mind (toward reason, taste, or morals) and reducing to a minimum the part played by him formerly known as the "author" of the work. . . . The author is present as a spectator, indifferent or impassioned, at the birth of his own work, and observes the phases of his own development. Just as the poet's place, since

the celebrated *Letter of a Clairvoyant*, consists in writing at the dictation of something that makes itself articulate within him, so the artist's role is to gather together and then give out that which makes itself *visible* within him. . . In trying all the time to reduce still more my own active participation in the making of a picture, so as to widen the active field of the mind's capacity for hallucination, I succeeded in being present *as a spectator* at the birth of all my works after August 10, 1925, the memorable day of the discovery of *frottage*. Being a man of "ordinary constitution" (to use Rimbaud's terms) I have done my best to *make my soul monstrous*. A blind swimmer, I have made myself clairvoyant. I have *seen*. I have become the amazed lover of what I have seen, wanting to identify myself with it. ◎

FROM "INSPIRATION TO ORDER" BY MAX ERNST, IN *THE PAINTER'S OBJECT*, EDITED BY MYFANWY EVANS (1937)

IMAGINATION AND FANTASY

Imagination, according to the American poet Wallace Stevens (1879–1955), is man's power over nature. The ability to imagine something that is not there allows one to deal with it when it arrives, and therefore there are good evolutionary reasons for the existence of such a mental operating system. The imagination has two sides: a passive, reproductive, aspect that creates mental images perceived by the senses; and an active, constructive or creative aspect that connects with many areas of the mind, emotional and irrational, to produce images connected to reality only loosely or not at all. The French philosopher Simone Weil (1909–1943) wrote that imagination and fiction make up more than three-quarters of our real life. In everyday waking consciousness, imagination works ceaselessly to make sense of the environment, fashioning understandable images from the material selected by the senses, and responding to what is going on. In dreaming, or hallucinations, imagination takes over the functions of perception completely, creating the world in a different, private reality not accessible to others—a subjective reality.

DAYDREAMS AND FANTASIES

Fantasies are the stuff of daydream or reverie, the state which Wordsworth described as being "both asleep and awake." This description calls to mind the strange phenomena of lucid dreaming and OBEs associated with the hypnagogic state mentioned in the previous chapter (see page 57), but the term "daydream" is more often associated with escapism and wish fulfillment. Essentially, it involves turning away from the external world and tuning in to the inner world, and occurs when there is an absence of pressing outside events demanding conscious attention. It can also be used as a means of escape from unpleasant reality. Escapism is often a neurotic symptom, brilliantly exemplified by American writer James Thurber (1894–1961) in his character Walter Mitty—an ineffectual and disempowered individual who indulges in fantastic daydreams of personal triumphs. Fantastic scenarios conceived during the daydream state are enacted in the imaginations of almost everyone to a greater or lesser degree.

However, reverie has a special significance in creative activity, generating images that may move consciousness from a dissociative, "in-between" state to a state of genuine trance, as described by numerous creatives. Freud identified the motive forces of fantasies as unsatisfied wishes, claiming that "every single fantasy is the fulfilment of a wish, a correction of an unsatisfying reality." Most fantasies are clearly wish fulfillments, and when they part company from the external world, the fantasy becomes a delusion. However, artistic imagination works with fantasy not merely to produce escapist material, but also to invent stories and characters that illuminate reality for the rest of humanity.

LEFT **Danny Kaye, who portrayed an unheroic hero in _The Secret Life of Walter Mitty_. But we all daydream, and probably need to.**

Thus artists use fantasy not merely as a form of escapism, a turning away from reality, but also as a preliminary to altering reality in the desired direction. Anthony Storr believes that an inner world of fantasy is part of human biological endowment, and the discrepancy between this inner world and the outer world compels people to become inventive and imaginative. We should use fantasy to build bridges between the inner world of the imagination and the external world. The artist's ability to synthesize elements of inner consciousness with external consciousness, and then to transmit this new kind of truth in a form valued by others, is their special task. Public recognition of the end product is the climax of the original, private recognition of the significant "something" that leaks through the membrane of the unconscious with disturbing effect.

This bridge-building function is primarily for the benefit of the creator, but has value to others—therein lies its creativity. The psychologist Otto Rank (1884–1939) wrote that the neurotic is the "artist manqué," the creative who cannot transmute his or her conflicts into art. Many elements, including mental disorder, go into the making of a work of art. The American novelist Herman Melville (1819–1891) even suggested that "all mortal greatness is but a disease."

There is no doubt that the creative process has a therapeutic function. Pollock's alcoholism was kept in check by his work. Vincent Van Gogh's (1853–1890) creativity did not overcome his emotional problems, but his letters attest to a steady increase in self-esteem as he gained confidence in the value of his work. The therapeutic function of the creative process is to sublimate the destructive daimonic element within.

LEFT *Pine Tree and Figure in Front of the Hospital Saint Paul* by Van Gogh, showing the hospital at Saint-Rémy where this most famous of mentally unstable artists was briefly treated. "Perhaps death is not the hardest thing in a painter's life."

A daydream is a meal at which images are eaten. Some of us are gourmets, some gourmands, and a good many take their images precooked out of a can and swallow them down whole, absent-mindedly, and with little relish.

W. H. AUDEN

An artist originally turns away from reality but finds his way back by making use of special gifts to mold his fantasies into truths of a new kind which are valued by men as precious reflections of reality. Thus in a certain fashion he actually becomes the hero, king, creator he desired to be without having to make alterations in the external world. But he can only achieve this because others feel the same dissatisfaction as he does with the renunciation demanded by reality.

ANTHONY STORR

THE PSYCHOTIC ELEMENT

Some psychologists claim that creative thought processes are used by the creator when he is in a perfectly rational and conscious frame of mind, not undergoing an altered or transformed state. The key aspects of creative thinking may have superficial similarities and connections with psychotic modes of thinking, but the processes that "mold and structure" themes are healthy, not pathological. Many artists, however, have chosen to explore the psychotic regions of the irrational in an attempt to bring back something new and wonderful. In 1922 the Prinzhorn collection of hospital-based psychotic art reached the public, and artists such as Max Ernst and Paul Klee (1879–1940) were strongly influenced by these "schizophrenic masters." Many features from the psychotic repertory have passed into the mainstream of contemporary art, from the Surrealists to Damien Hirst. However, it seems clear that creatives and psychotics, though both clearly dealing with the daimonic world, follow different policies. The permeable and flexible nature of the creative mind is able to dramatize the preverbal messages of trauma from the unconscious, and relate them to the human condition. Psychotics, it is said, merely address their own condition, without reference to others; their work is self-related and there is no attempt to communicate. However, if there is no attempt to communicate, why externalize the trauma at all? Is there a point at which the therapeutic value of art for many psychotics shades into the value of art in creating a new and valuable reality using psychotic elements?

LEFT *Mädchenklasse im Freien* by Paul Klee: a
visionary painter who could put real objects through
magical transformations. "I cannot be grasped in this
world. For I am as much at home with the dead as
with those beings who are not yet born."

THE CREATIVE PERSONALITY

6

Man's main task in life is to become what
he potentially is. The most important product
of his effort is his own personality.

ERICH FROMM

TALENTS AND INTELLIGENCES

The potential identified by the psychoanalyst Erich Fromm (1900–1980) will only develop positively, from talent to creative productivity, if conditions are favorable. Personality emerges from the interaction of heredity and environment, nature and nurture. Ornstein's "talent patches," the areas of the brain identified as governing different patterns of activity, reveal themselves in the earliest behavior of infants—some are more attentive, others more active, and so on. How a child

ABOVE **Albert Einstein, physicist, caricatured by Walter Trier. In Howard Gardner's list of intelligence-types, Einstein exemplified the logical-mathematical strand.**

copes with a difficult endowment will dictate the psychopathology reflected in his or her personality. Adaptation to unusual endowments may impose pressures on the emerging personality that will lead to pathology in human relationships.

SEVEN TYPES OF INTELLIGENCE

The psychologist Howard Gardner has drawn up a list of seven "intelligences" that resemble the Ornsteinian talents but are linked with personality. These "multiple intelligences" include: **linguistic intelligence**, the intelligence of words and the aptitude to master literacy; **logical-mathematical intelligence**, the intelligence of logic and numbers; **musical intelligence**, the capacity to perceive, appreciate, and produce rhythms and melodies; **spatial intelligence**, the ability to perceive and recreate images and pictures that are originated in the mind; **bodily-kinesthetic intelligence**, involving physical coordination and dexterity; **interpersonal intelligence**, the ability to understand and be responsive to others' desires, temperaments, and moods; **intrapersonal intelligence**, the ability to develop intuitively, to look inside oneself and discriminate feelings and emotions.

To this list of innate intelligences Gardner has recently added the **naturalist intelligence**, or the human ability to recognize plants, animals, and other parts of the natural environment. Classroom application of Gardner's theory would lead teachers to pay attention to the differences among pupils and try to use that knowledge to personalize instruction and assessment, to discover what is special about each child. Teachers could plan educational programs enabling children to realize desired end states (for example, the musician, the scientist, the civic-minded person).

INTELLIGENCE PERSONIFIED

While this is probably a desirable educational objective, Gardner's attempt to identify common characteristics in the personalities of leading exponents in each of these fields of intelligence is less persuasive. He lists T. S. Eliot (linguistic intelligence), Albert Einstein (logical-mathematical intelligence), Igor Stravinsky (musical intelligence), Pablo Picasso (spatial intelligence), Martha Graham (bodily-kinesthetic intelligence), Mahatma Gandhi (interpersonal intelligence), and Sigmund Freud (intrapersonal intelligence). Gardner has identified in all these people

LEFT **Mahatma Gandhi, lawyer and Indian nationalist leader, leading the "March to the Sea" in 1930 in protest against the government monopoly on salt production.**

such characteristics as strong-mindedness, early ability, rapid mastery of the chosen field or domain, the presence of childlike characteristics such as self-centeredness, intolerance, and exploitation of others, the making of "Faustian bargains" that often lead to disastrous personal lives, and so on. However, it would be possible to make a list of creatives who show different characteristics, because personality evolves within the individual's culture, and cultural pressures are not uniform.

> A poet has to adapt himself, more or less consciously, to the demands of his vocation, and hence the peculiarities of poets and the condition of inspiration which many people have said is near to madness. . . The problem of creative iting is essentially one of concentration . . . a focusing of the attention in a special way.
>
> STEPHEN SPENDER

But Gardner's profile does reflect the creative's need to balance an unusual range of endowments with outer reality. In some cases there is an overlap of talents, as in the case of music and poetry. Song lives in both domains, as creatives from the medieval troubadours to Bob Dylan have shown. But if the environment is hostile to the child's endowment, the future creative may be seen as backward (as the young Einstein was characterized), stupid (Picasso), or even feeble-minded (Flaubert). The ability to overcome environmental disadvantages is what will shape the creative artist's personality.

LEFT **Martha Graham, choreographer and dancer, the leading exponent of contemporary expressionist dance.**

OBSERVING CREATION

Pablo Picasso (1881–1973) enjoyed a long and productive career and did his best to describe the process of creation and his feelings as the need to create swept over him.

⊚ At the beginning of each picture there is someone who works with me. Toward the end I have the impression of having worked without a collaborator. . . One always has to begin with something. One can then remove all appearance of reality; one runs no risk, for the idea of the object has left an ineffaceable imprint. It is the thing that aroused the artist, stimulated his ideas, stirred his emotions. Ideas and emotions will ultimately be prisoners of his work; whatever they do, they can't escape from the picture; they form an integral part of it, even when their presence is no longer discernible. Whether he likes it or not, man is the instrument of nature; it imposes its character, its appearance upon him. . .

The painter passes through states of fullness and emptying. That is the whole secret of art. I take a walk in the forest of Fontainebleau. There I get an indigestion of greenness. I must empty this sensation into a picture. Green dominates it. . . It is not what the artist does that counts, but what he is. Cézanne would never have interested me if he had lived and thought like Jacques-Emile Blanche, even if the apple he had painted had been ten times

as beautiful. What interests us is the uneasiness of Cézanne, the real teaching of Cézanne, the torments of van Gogh, that is to say, the drama of the man. . . How would you have a spectator live my picture as I have lived it? A picture comes to me from afar off, who knows how far, I divined it, I saw it, I made it, and yet next day I myself don't see what I have done. How can one penetrate my dreams, my instincts, my desires, my thoughts, which have taken a long time to elaborate themselves and bring themselves to the light, above all seize in them what I brought about, perhaps, against my will? ⊚

FROM "CONVERSATION WITH PICASSO,"
BY CHRISTIAN ZERVOS (1935)

RIGHT **Picasso in his studio in 1929.
"The painter paints as if in
urgent need to discharge himself
of his sensations and visions."**

NATURE AND NURTURE

Natural endowments may form a basis or even a template for a creative personality, but will obviously not of themselves lead to creative production without a favorable nurturing environment. If talent is the creative capital, personality is its executive instrument, and will vary according to external conditions. For certain cultures, as well as many families, music has been almost a second language, a form of communication and shared experience that is part of their socialization. Mozart picked up a violin and began to play it as soon as he was physically able to hold one. J. S. Bach's (1685–1750) incredible productivity may partly have been due to an environment where music was in the air he breathed. And yet even here the connection between talent and creativity is not straightforward. For example, musical ability is obviously innate, at least to a large extent, but recent research indicates that opportunity, motivation, and hard work play key roles. Successful applicants to the prestigious Chethams Music School in Manchester, England, were found to have accumulated twice as much practice as those who failed. Dedication as much as talent underlies creative performance.

In this regard, the desire to please the parent may be a major factor in the artist's motivation, for many creatives have come from families where a parent was in the same profession. In addition, most surveys of leading creatives have shown that there is often one parent who has in some way been interested in a particular creative field. Thus, Mozart's father was a musician though not a composer, Eugene O'Neill's (1888–1953) father was an actor, Picasso's father was an art teacher. The creative person, in other words, may strive to fulfill a parent's implicit, unrealized yearnings. On the other hand probably many more parents have strenuously opposed their children's creative aspirations. Creativity seems to be more a way of life, a way of balancing the inner and outer worlds, than a particular personality type.

ABOVE **Mozart: almost a synonym for heaven-sent talent, but what were the effects, for better or worse, of his father's fanatical ambition on his behalf?**

THE MAD SCIENTIST SYNDROME

Passion for their work enables many creatives to function very well, despite dysfunctions that would probably put others into an institution. The Hungarian-born mathematician Paul Erdös (1913–1996), the most prolific and respected mathematician of the twentieth century, had no home of his own. His worldly belongings were contained in two battered suitcases. Erdös devoted his life to the discovery of mathematical proofs that were logically tight and aesthetically beautiful. In pursuit of these, he would turn up, often unannounced, at the home of a colleague whom he felt could help inspire a solution to a problem. His initially welcoming host would soon be exhausted by the intense work schedule, and Erdös would eventually go on his way—his motto was "Another roof, another proof." Within the mathematical community Erdös was a giant, coauthoring an

LEFT **Gauguin: a self-portrait from 1893. Early in his life he was a successful stockbroker who painted as a hobby, but he broke away from bourgeois existence to travel, paint, and generally immerse himself in the exotic.**

50 papers a year. Ideally, he believed, a mathematical result should not be cast in prose, but expressed in poetry.

"Mad scientists" like Erdös are the stuff of legend. Nevertheless, his personality expresses the common characteristic in virtually all creative people, a devotion to the chosen subject. W. B. Yeats (1865–1939) expressed this as a choice between "perfection of the life and perfection of the work." The painter Paul Gauguin (1848–1903) is only one of innumerable examples of this devotion at its most ruthless. Gauguin's art has all the appearance of a flight from civilization, of a search for new ways of life, more primitive, real, and sincere. His break with a solid middle-class world, the abandonment of family, children, and job, and his refusal to accept easy glory and easy gain are the best-known aspects of Gauguin's personality.

Psychologists speculate that this dedication to a creative ideal probably arises from early involvement with some aspect of the external world so strongly felt that it instills a feeling of admiration or awe in the subject. Some observers suggest that this involvement insulates the subject from psychological damage during nurture that would incapacitate others, making him or her relatively less vulnerable to the vicissitudes of upbringing. The novelist Anthony Trollope (1815–1882) passed his first 26 years in "suffering, disgrace, and inward remorse," leaving him disorganized, friendless, terrorized, and "an incorrigible dunce." He was able to reconstruct himself in his life and his work, until he became part of the establishment world he idealized in his books. Toward the end of his life he wrote, "As to that leisure evening of life, I must say that I do not want it. I can conceive of no contentment of which toil is not to be the immediate parent."

extraordinary number of papers, and confronting the most profound issues in the subject. Outside it he was a helpless child, unable to cook, drive, or organize his financial affairs. He once said, "Basically I have a psychological abnormality. I cannot stand sexual pleasure. It's peculiar." Right up to his death at 83 he continued to work 19-hour days and publish

ENDLESS LOVE

The artist's emotional involvement with the art is often intense enough to merit the title "love affair." Talking about his relationship to his art, Picasso describes an altered state of consciousness familiar to most people: being in love. Alarming—but for the most part highly pleasurable—being in love displays many of the altered state conditions listed by Charles Tart, but is also characterized by a passionate absorption in the object of desire, to the exclusion of much else in the world, a combination of arousal, love, and total focus.

Being in love with what one is doing underwrites almost all the other personality characteristics that have been observed of the creative person. It is because he or she is in love with his or her imagination that a creative artist can call on the necessary resources: courage, independence of thought and judgement, absorption, perseverance, commitment, high motivation, curiosity, wide knowledge of the subject, unconventional behavior, emotional force, etc. The creative artist is in a sense in love with his or her other self. Henry Miller (1891–1980) has described how after years of futile struggle "I heard my own voice. . . The fact that it was a separate, distinct, and unique voice sustained me. . . I had found a voice. I was whole again."

Being in love implies a relationship with another human being, however idealized. The other may be only a figment of the lover's imagination, but has a real existence somewhere, while the creative's love affair is with the imagination itself. For creatively gifted people, personal relationships are very often less important than the particular field of endeavor. The meaning of life is defined less by personal relationships than by the work. The conflict that this entails, both with the outside world and within the personality itself, is the challenge that the artist must take on, if his or her creativity is to be realized.

This need not be a cause for unhappiness. Many creatives have possessed equable temperaments that enabled them to lead a neurosis-free existence. Before the Romantic Age, the personalities of creative artists tended to reflect the temper of the time, unobtrusively adjusted to accommodate their gift. Thus the chronicler of the Roman Empire, Edward Gibbon (1737–1794), seems to have been conspicuously well balanced. "Happiness is the word that immediately rises to the mind at the thought of Edward Gibbon; and happiness in its widest context," wrote the biographer Lytton Strachey (1880–1932). Yet in at least one respect even Gibbon would appear to have been unfulfilled. As a young man he was forced to renounce his attachment for Suzanne Curchod, and sexual activity seems to have played little part in his life thereafter.

SEX ISN'T EVERYTHING

The modern belief that true happiness can only be found in intimate attachments, and particularly in sexual fulfillment,

> I could not live without devoting all my hours to art. I love it as the whole end of my life. Everything I do in connection with art gives me a tremendous joy.
>
> PABLO PICASSO

BELOW **Henry Miller, content to have found his voice. This photograph was taken at a press conference held in 1969 to launch his book *Sexus*.**

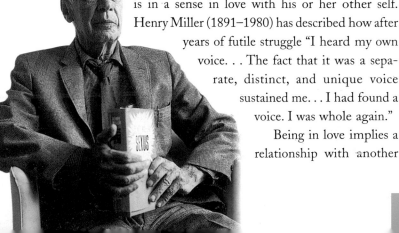

needs qualification in the case of many creative people who fail to make "mature" personal relationships. Some artists are extremely isolated, but the satisfaction of exercising their gifts, of hearing their own voice, and of reaching others through their work, outweighs the promise of alternative pleasures. This preference is most likely to occur in people who are also unusually attracted to novelty—or who have a great tolerance for change. Independence is a prerequisite.

I equally dislike the favor of the public with the love of a woman—they are both a cloying treacle to the wings of independence.

JOHN KEATS

The poet makes himself a seer, by a long, prodigious, and rational disordering of all the senses. Every form of love, of suffering, of madness; he searches himself, he consumes all the poisons in him, and keeps only their quintessences.

ARTHUR RIMBAUD

FALLING OUT OF LOVE

Love affairs can turn sour, but few creatives have altogether given up their love affair with their art. The great exception was the French poet Arthur Rimbaud, the founder of the Symbolist movement. Rimbaud's commitment to his art was ferocious, but at the age of 20 he ceased to write, becoming a trader in the Middle East. It is not clear that this turning away from creative life was not another form of self-creation. "By being too sensitive I have wasted my life," he wrote, and there are premonitions in his work of his future existence as a nomadic outsider. However, most creatives, especially in the visual arts, have continued until physically unable to go on. Even then they try to find a way: toward the end of his life Pierre Auguste Renoir (1841–1919) had his paintbrushes strapped to his crippled, arthritic hands, so that he could carry on his beloved painting.

LEFT **Renoir photographed in his studio in 1912, aged 72. Renoir's relationship with painting was no brief affair but a marriage which continued to the end of his life, by which time he had produced more than 6,000 canvases.**

CREATIVITY AS THERAPY

Involvement in creative activity may resemble dependency or addiction rather than love. It is generally recognized that creative work has often helped to prevent the disintegration of a precariously balanced personality. It is sometimes the only way to keep the inner demons at bay—demons inherent in the conflict underlying the artist's own creativity. The "driven" quality of many creatives has often been remarked on. This suggests that the creative may be inspired less by love of the subject than by need and anxiety.

However, creativity by itself is often not sufficient, although it may help the healing process. Vincent van Gogh is often regarded as a man who managed for a time to heal himself through his art. He was certainly a complete failure till he began to create, and gradually gained in self-esteem as his confidence in the value of his work increased. Yet his suicide at the age of 37 came when he was beginning to be recognized. It now seems clear that van Gogh's action was caused by his despair on hearing that his brother Theo, the "secret sharer" in his life and work, would soon die of an incurable disease. As the psychologist John Gedo writes, "The increment of self-esteem resulting from his creative activities did not save van Gogh from suicidal depression; rather, it was his brother's willingness to affirm that they needed each other equally that postponed the catastrophe." Van Gogh became an artist for his brother's sake. Theo's fatal illness brought the compact to an end.

TREADING THE THIN LINE

Since the Romantic period, creative activity has tended to concentrate on the inner world, where art is used to explore the irrational, unprocessed material that communicates in images rather than symbols. This is the language of the imagination, where nothing is impossible. But irrational messages lose content when translated into words, and often become unacceptable. As long as a message is primarily encoded in images, as are dreams, hallucinations, and "slipping glimpses," the irrational is not challenged. Once it is processed through the analytical system of language, it is limited by consensual reality and must either take form or be dismissed as a delusion. Hence the prevalence of the visual in psychotic art. Artists seeking to explore psychological traumas within themselves may need to enter temporarily the sphere in which psychotic people live their lives. The subject matter is the same for both, and the fact that so many artists have suffered psychotic collapse shows how permeable is the barrier. There may well be a psychotic narcissism implicit in creativity, for the creative is in love with the self-created world of imagination. The composer Richard Wagner (1813–1883) is often cited as an example of a pathological megalomania in the service of creativity.

THE SELF AS CREATION

There can be little doubt that creatives, like shamans, enter altered states to explore the other worlds of the unconscious. And, like shamans, they need to perform in order to communicate their message. In some cases the medium becomes the message, as with George Gordon, Lord Byron (1788–1824) or Oscar Wilde (1854–1900), who declared, "I put all my genius into my life; I put only my talent into my works." Since the days of Andy Warhol

BELOW **Oscar Wilde, writer and celebrated wit, died in 1900, but lived his life as a self-created persona in a way that gained much favor in the twentieth century.**

(1926–1987) the image of the "art star" has gained force, with Brit Art supremo Damien Hirst representing a good example of this postmodern blend of talent and self-advertisement.

Nearly all creatives are also "creative" when discussing their own lives and working methods. Such accounts are notoriously unreliable. This is partly because there is something sacred, or at least mysterious, about the creative process, not something to blab out to everyone. Such obfuscation is part of a necessary concealment of their true selves. A tendency to self-mythologizing combines with a certain caution. The painter Francis Bacon (1909–1992), who once announced that "I hope I shall go on painting—in between drinking and gambling—until I drop dead, and I hope I shall drop dead working," always insisted that he worked straight onto the canvas, in a sort of frenzy. But this claim seemed problematic after his close companion came forward after his death with material that could only have been studies for later paintings. Bacon had allegedly asked for the material to be destroyed, but in a rather equivocal fashion. Art critics have responded with great nervousness to the discovery, which is either a forgery or a collection of masterpieces by one of the great painters of the twentieth century.

The self-mythologizing tendency is present in the brilliant, innovative works of the English playwright Dennis Potter (1935–1994), notably *Blue Remembered Hills* and *The Singing Detective*. Potter was a confessional writer whose own experiences of abuse as a child led to a preoccupation with guilty sex. He used this experience to explore the self-deceptions, confusions, and occasional insights that arose out of that trauma, extending his investigation beyond the raw experience itself to the way he interpreted it and the fantasy world he constructed to make it bearable. Potter's life and work were inextricably tangled in a world of the artist's imagination. The imagination makes little distinction between fact and fiction, as can be seen in the autobiographies of most writers. The creative personality is as elusive as the creative process which it embodies. Creativity, as currently defined, runs as a continuum from the imaginative problem-solving practiced by almost everyone to the "intuitive genius" end of the spectrum, where the individual lives on the edge of psychosis. Personality characteristics will reflect inner pressures, but it is the creative artists' areas of activity, dictated by their particular endowments, their destiny in a sense, which will dictate whether, and in what form, they will mold a personality that is able to accommodate and express them.

MAKING POETRY

The British poet Stephen Spender (1909–1995) wrote eloquently about the requirement of artists to adapt their personality to the demands of their chosen vocation. The need to create may often lead to an unbalancing of the artist's personality in the service of a higher, artistic, equilibrium.

The concentrated effort of writing makes one completely forget for the time being that one has a body. It is a disturbance of the balance of body and mind and for this reason one needs a kind of anchor of sensation with the physical world. Hence the craving for a scent or a taste or even, sometimes, for sexual activity. Poets speak of the necessity of writing rather than of a liking for doing it. It is spiritual compulsion, a straining of the mind to attain heights surrounded by abysses and it cannot be entirely happy, for the only reward worth having is absolutely denied. . . At the moment when art attains its highest attainment it reaches beyond its medium of words or paints or music, and the artist finds himself realizing that these instruments are inadequate to the spirit of what he is trying to say. . .

Some poets write immediately works which, when they are written, scarcely need revision. Others write their poems by stages, feeling their way from rough draft to rough draft, until finally, after many revisions, they have produced a result which seems to have very little connection with their early sketches. . . Mozart thought out symphonies, etc. entirely in his head. . . and then transcribed them, in completeness, onto paper. Beethoven wrote fragments of themes in notebooks, working on and developing them over years. Often his first ideas were of a clumsiness that makes scholars marvel how he could in the end have developed from them such miraculous results. . . [but] genius unlike virtuosity is judged by the greatness of its results, not by brilliance of performance. The Mozartian type of genius is able to plumb the greatest depths of his own experience by the tremendous effort of a moment; the Beethovenian must dig deeper and deeper into his consciousness, layer by layer. . .

FROM "THE MAKING OF A POEM" BY STEPHEN SPENDER, IN *PARTISAN REVIEW* (SUMMER 1946)

ABOVE **Stephen Spender in 1940, drawn by Lucian Freud. He was part of the left-leaning literary landscape of Thirties Britain with Auden and MacNeice.**

RIGHT **Jung posited the notion of the artist as one peculiarly attuned to the symbolic realm and able to give these symbols a concrete form.**

THE ARTIST AS INSTRUMENT

The psychologist Carl Jung began his career as a disciple of Freud but eventually went his own way, and developed fascinating ideas on the nature of creativity, the impact of shared experience, and the significance of the collective unconscious.

Every creative person is a duality or a synthesis of contradictory aptitudes. On the one hand he is a human being with a personal life, while on the other he is an impersonal, creative process. Since as a human being he may be sound or morbid, we must look at his psychic makeup to find the determinants of his personality. But we can only understand him in his capacity of artist by looking at his creative achievement. . .

Being essentially the instrument for his work, he is subordinate to it, and we have no reason for expecting him to interpret it for us. He has done the best that in him lies in giving it form, and he must leave the interpretation to others and to the future. . . To grasp its meaning, we must allow it to shape us as it once shaped him. Then we understand the nature of his experience. We see that he has drawn upon the healing and redeeming forces of the collective psyche that underlies consciousness with its isolation and its painful errors; that he has penetrated to that matrix of life in which all men are embedded, which imparts a common rhythm to all human existence, and allows the individual to communicate his feeling and his striving to mankind as a whole.

FROM *MODERN MAN IN SEARCH OF A SOUL*, BY CARL GUSTAV JUNG (1933)

THE ROLE OF SOCIETY

7

Poets are the unacknowledged legislators of the world.

PERCY BYSSHE SHELLEY

THE CREATIVE PRODUCT

Creative products are the evidence of our evolution. Incessant innovation is the response to incessant change in the environment. From the domestication of the dog to the formation of the Internet, human creativity has introduced innumerable cultural modifications that have changed our world in every aspect. Creative products include ideas as well as objects: a novel solution to a mathematical problem; the discovery of a new process in science; the writing of a poem; the formation of a new philosophical or religious system; an innovation in law; a fresh way of thinking about social problems; a change in manners. All these are creative products, placed in external reality. Many believe that a product has achieved its "creative" aim if it communicates its maker's intention to someone else; it has been recognized. Nevertheless, in its role as a social construct, the creative product's value will depend on the judgement of the audience, which will reflect the values of the society at a certain time and place.

An oft-repeated definition of the creative product is something consensually determined to have both newness and positive value. However, this definition omits the important part that imaginative feeling plays in the process, the ability to inspire others with potentially transforming emotion. A creative product is new and valuable, of course, but it is also the gift of a mind seeking to communicate something hitherto unknown. This can be seen in a child's

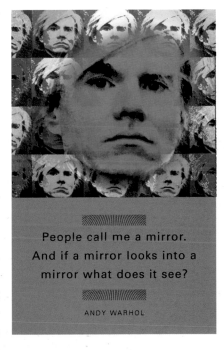

People call me a mirror. And if a mirror looks into a mirror what does it see?

ANDY WARHOL

drawing as much as in a groundbreaking scientific discovery. Part of the function of the creative product—its most important part, perhaps—is to convey its vision. There are basically two ways of passing on such a thing: by feeling (magic, illumination), or by explanation (representation, information).

ART AS RELIGION

Religious objects—icons, idols, symbols—are society's most powerful emotion-communicating entities, and their power is in proportion to the intensity with which the spectator shares their ideal. Where a society has few or disguised ideals, as in the modern Western world, such objects lose their symbolic strength but take on new references conferred by the onlookers. The objects become things of beauty rather than awe, conveying a general rather than a specific emotion. A shamanistic mask or a Byzantine icon is aestheticized by the onlooker into something of beauty and half-guessed spiritual power, but drained of its direct meaning. Thus, although empathic communication is the domain of religion and mysticism, many devotional objects are also works of art. Hence the large number of creatives who share Picasso's belief that art is magic. Perhaps it is also a kind of worship, the religion of a materialist age, reflected in pilgrimages to galleries, veneration before iconic paintings, and enormous expenditure. Or perhaps, in the postmodern context, it is a mirror reflecting nothing but itself.

THE SOCIAL BACKGROUND

The creative personality faces two ways, inward and outward. Those characteristics which are required for the development of the creative process itself refer inward toward the creative's own world of the imagination. And this personality, as we have seen, is characterized by a passionate involvement with the artform, driving the psyche to assemble a set of personality traits best fitted to achieve its realization. As a result, creative personality types may range from the unremarkable to the severely dysfunctional. The creative may verge on the psychotic, but is differentiated from one merely dreaming or deluded by the need to communicate. He or she has something to offer— the product of the quest. The perceived value of the product is what confers creativity, and this is a social effect.

Thus the created object stands apart from both process and person. It means one thing to the maker and another to the spectator. To the maker it represents the crystallization of a dream. This is what he or she seeks to communicate, but it may be different from what the spectator perceives. The finished picture is changed according to the condition of the one who looks at it, and it is through that person that the picture lives. The artist rages against the fact that the public has, in Picasso's words, "imposed on the pictures in the museums all their stupidities, errors, the pretences of our spirit. . . We cling to myths instead of sensing the inner life of the men who painted them."

> What I want, is that my picture should evoke nothing but emotion.
>
> PABLO PICASSO

RIGHT **Think of modern art, think of Picasso, prolifically creative, riding storms of criticism, but also finding a successful role in society. This is *Figures on the Seashore* (1931).**

UNSEEN ROSES

Can creativity exist without recognition? The psychologist Teresa Amabile has provided a strong statistical basis for the view that most creatives find that the interest, enjoyment, satisfaction, and challenge of the work itself provide sufficient motivation. Many researchers have found that the experience of performing a task for monetary reward significantly decreases the subjects' intrinsic motivation for that activity. It may well be that the strong link between creativity and intrinsic motivation is actually weakened when other types of reward are brought into the equation. On the other hand, both common sense and Sigmund Freud would approve of John Milton's claim that "fame is the spur" that drives the creative person to "scorn delights, and live laborious days."

> Whatever I do is done out of sheer joy, I drop my fruits like a ripe tree. What the general reader or critic makes of it is not my concern.
>
> HENRY MILLER

It would seem evident that, to be complete, a creative act needs to be brought into the public domain. It has to exist as a separate entity, and to be counted as creative requires the social honorific of certification as "new," "valuable," "useful," and "appropriate," conferred by members of society deemed qualified to judge its worth. Once its novelty has been accepted, and its value made apparent, it becomes part of society's continual adaptation to the environment, a contribution to the existing sum of human experience. Thus "social validation" is built in to most definitions of "creativity," the accolade that is conferred by the relevant authorities and ultimately by the public. To be complete, the creative act needs the approval of others. Creativity is achieved when possibilities, problems, skills, personalities, and the social milieu come together.

ECHOES AND DUPLICATIONS

The creative process of each individual is unique, being an emergent property of the creative's history, interaction with the chosen field, and social world. Therefore every product thus produced is also unique. Multiple creations of the same product, such as the simultaneous discovery of natural selection by Charles Darwin (1809–1882) and Alfred Russel Wallace (1823–1913), or of calculus by Gottfried Leibniz (1646–1716) and Sir Isaac Newton (1642–1727), may occur because research into a given domain has reached the stage where such a discovery is available. But, seen as part of the creative process, every product is unique because it emerges from a particular stage of development attained by a particular individual. He or she achieves a solution to the problem that began as a slipping glimpse from the unconscious. If there are two people there are two processes, even though the answer is the same. And the right answer is approved by society. In

LEFT **The ideas of Charles Darwin stirred and excited the nineteenth-century mind, perhaps not so differently from the musical ideas of Beethoven, leading to a new view of humanity.**

science and technology there is often a clear problem to be solved: scientists are often racing each other to be the first to make the discovery, as in the case of the structure of DNA in 1952 by Francis Crick and James Watson. The scientists use their own modes of creative and analytic cognition to arrive at their own product, which happens to be the solution society is waiting to reward.

GOOD AND USEFUL

However, social validation of a product is erratic. "Usefulness" is applicable only in the field in which something is used. Society is hostile to change, and revolutions are normally unwelcome. The basic conflict between the creative and society is that the one seeks out change, the other resists it. Conservatism, the spirit of "If it ain't broke don't fix it," is a biological imperative laid down by evolution. Institutions, too, are notoriously averse to development outside a previously defined area, as students of transpersonal psychology have often pointed out. How is the artist able to present his or her product so that it will be accepted? This depends on the nature of the society into which he or she is born. The accolade may be posthumously conferred, or it may be conferred and then withdrawn. The work's creativity fluctuates with its perceived value. Nobody considers Newton's work on alchemy with the veneration bestowed on his work on optics and gravity, yet the great scientist devoted at least as much time and creative energy to the former.

CREATIVE LEADERSHIP

The idea of valuable creativity becomes problematic when considering the creativity of leadership. Many, perhaps most, creatives have had a strong element of leadership in their personalities. It is a necessary trait for getting others to share one's vision, and in the case of those endowed with Gardner's "interpersonal intelligence" (Mahatma Gandhi is his example of such a creative, see page 78) it may have a significant effect on society. Highly endowed and fully operational, such figures have founded new religions, created new world orders, changed the face of history.

Few people have affected their times and later history more forcefully than Alexander the Great (356–323 BCE). A military genius, inspirational leader, and political giant,

Alexander infused the Greek idea so deeply into Western consciousness that it is with us to this day. Yet he was also a violent, vindictive, destructive, and seemingly psychopathic individual who was responsible for the deaths of many thousands of people in the name of his own military glory.

If history is the propaganda of the winning side, then the credibility of all "great leaders" such as Alexander is highly relative. And the same goes for creativity in general.

The mystery of creativity is this gap between the medium and the message. If the medium counts for as much as the message, if the process is as important as the product, then the idea that social value defines creativity must be modified. But it can't be, because the importance of the message is what confers the honorific of "creativity."

BELOW **Alexander the Great, King of Macedonia, pursuing his conquest of Persia. Great leader, genocidal general, or both?**

THE ARTIST AS SOCIAL PHENOMENON

In preagricultural societies where the function of artists, musicians, or storytellers was to serve the community by giving expression to traditional wisdom, their skills were valued but their individuality was not. The artist enters upon the stage of history when artistic creation becomes differentiated from other social functions and attains its own value, becoming an independent and legitimate pursuit rather than serving purposes of ritual. Biographies of artists began in ancient Greece c. 300 BCE, reappearing in Italy during the Renaissance; during the Middle Ages, when creativity was God's preserve, great art was anonymous.

The creative artist's ability to transmute imagination into reality is what distinguishes him or her from other people. Safe enough at the basic, problem-solving end of the creative spectrum, this imaginative power becomes potentially disturbing when it touches the imaginations of others and changes their reality too.

USURPING THE GODS

The Hebraic myth of Adam and the Greek myth of Prometheus both illustrate the view, held until post-medieval times, that creativity is a problematic activity, because making something from nothing is the role of the Creator, not the mortal human. By stealing fire from the gods and bestowing it on man, Prometheus, the benefactor of the human race, was also responsible for instilling in it the desire to substitute its own imaginative creations for the original act of divine creation. According to Plato, Prometheus' gift of the imagination is both a liberation and a curse—it makes possible a world where humans, having taken the place of gods and demigods, think their own imaginations divine. The imagination, with its elements of changeability and confusion, is to be regarded with suspicion.

RIGHT **Prometheus stealing fire from the gods for mankind's use, as seen by the seventeenth-century artist Jan Cossiers. Zeus countered Prometheus's act by releasing to mankind Pandora with her box of evils.**

LEFT **The workshop of
Phidias, as imagined by Pierre
Loommans. The tension
between art and craft is
expressed by the mantra "10%
inspiration, 90% perspiration."**

THE CONCEPT OF GENIUS

Where a special social position was conferred on creative artists, according to the Freudian Ernst Kris, this derived either from admiration at their skill, or awe at their inspiration. The artist was seen either as a master of his or her craft or as a divinely inspired genius. In the Western world, painters, sculptors, and architects reached the status of "genius" later than poets and musicians, and only since the sixteenth century has the differentiation gradually disappeared. Musicians have held a socially uneasy place in many societies, excluded as itinerant ne'er-do-wells at one level and accorded near-divine status at another. Performing artists have often been marginalized figures, traveling people making up their own nomadic societies on the edge of conventional morality, and owing allegiance perhaps to a much older tradition going back to preagricultural times.

ARTIST OR ARTISAN?

In the classical world there was a social division between different fields of creativity. Poets such as Homer or Aeschylus might be seen as inspired creators, divinely gifted, while sculptors, even Phidias, the genius of the Parthenon, were basically artisans. Admiration for painters was based on the accuracy of their representation of the subject—it was wonderingly reported that the grapes painted by Apelles were so "real" that sparrows had been deceived into pecking at them—while the odes of Pindar or the epics of Homer were the product of divine inspiration.

This division between magic and representation runs through Western art from its very inception, and is reflected in the way the artist is regarded by society. In medieval times the noble calling of poetry was sustained in the activities of the troubadours and trouvères, lyric poet-musicians of high social rank who composed and performed their songs as a manifestation of the ideal of chivalry.

Painting and sculpture, in contrast, continued to serve communal rather than individual interests. The medieval artist was often recruited from the lower ranks of society. It was only from about the thirteenth century that the names of individual painters began to be recorded. Artists were craftsmen whose chief task was to keep worshipers mindful of the truths of the Christian religion. The creativity of the artist lay in his faithfulness to the nature of his task, which was to glorify Almighty God. Originality, today seen as a defining component of creativity, was to be avoided in the service of a greater glory. The anonymous creators of Byzantine and Russian icons sought to express the sacramental nature of the divinity, avoiding any intrusion of human expression or personality. As means of instilling emotion in the onlooker, icons are intensely creative, but their makers strove *not* to be original.

In the fifteenth century, art and science combined to shift the creative aspect away from God and toward humanity. The new sciences brought anatomical realism and perspective into the domain of the arts, creating an idealized humanism that replaced the god-centered view of the world. The artist's work was presented from the onlooker's point of view. It was imbued with the artist's personal style, and bore the stamp of its maker. Vasari's *Lives of the Artists* (1568) conferred international celebrity on the great masters, from Giotto (1267–1337) to Michelangelo (1475–1564). Artists became personalities, even stars. Michelangelo's emotional intensity, or *terribilità*, which was a recurrent feature both of his work and his personality, gave him the status of "il divino Michelangelo" ("the divine Michelangelo").

THE TORTURED ARTIST

It was only comparatively recently, with the rise of individualism, that the artist came to be seen as a romantic outsider. Nevertheless, the complications inherent in a creative personality, arising from the perilous need to bring something across the bridge from imagination into reality, would always be likely to cause social difficulties for creative people in any age, irrespective of their formal standing in society. Inner stresses lead to aberrant behavior, with inevitable social consequences. The English poet Geoffrey Chaucer's (1340–1400) secure social position (his patron was the king) can be contrasted with the violent lives of

France's outstanding lyric poet, Francois Villon (1431–1465), and Sir Thomas Malory (d. 1471), author of *Le Morte d'Arthur*, who were both charged with murder. Michelangelo himself probably suffered psychotic attacks at several periods during his life. The modern image of the artist as a driven creature who struggles to impose his imagination on reality has many antecedents, and it appears to be a psychological fact as well as a social construct.

ROMANTIC HEROES

The Romantic movement, which dominated European and North American thought, art, and politics from the late eighteenth century until the end of the nineteenth century and beyond, empowered the creative artist with a new image. Lord Byron (1788–1824) came to typify the idea of the Romantic hero, rejecting convention and tyranny, and striving for individual liberty. Despite his great power as a poet, Byron's life seems to feature larger than his work. According to Bertrand Russell he was a major force for change in the nineteenth century and "more important as a myth than as he really was. . . Abroad, his way of feeling and his outlook on life were transmitted and developed and transmuted until they became so widespread as to be factors in great events."

LEFT **A detail from one of Michelangelo's frescoes for the ceiling of the Sistine Chapel. While God as creator is the subject, the ideal grace of the male figures speaks of a new vision of man as the measure of all things.**

BYRON: THE RAKE'S PROGRESS

The son of a notorious rake, Byron was brought up by his temperamental mother and a Calvinist nurse, who, he claimed, initiated him sexually when he was nine years old. At Trinity College, Cambridge, he was notorious for loose living and radicalism, leaving without a degree in 1807. In 1812 he became famous with the publication of part of *Childe Harolde's Pilgrimage*, written while traveling across Europe to Greece, where he swam the Hellespont and engaged in a series of romantic adventures. Back in London, Byron had a series of scandalous love affairs, including one with Lady Caroline Lamb, who famously described him as "mad, bad, and dangerous to know." Under a cloud of scandal, including suspicions of a sexual relationship with his half-sister, Augusta, he left England forever in 1816. His *Don Juan*, the first two cantos of which were published anonymously in 1819, was denounced in the English press as "a filthy and impious poem," but much admired by Goethe. In 1820 Byron became embroiled in the Italian patriotic movement, and in 1823 in the Greek War of Independence against the Turks. In 1824, he joined the Greek insurgents at Missolonghi where he formed a "Byron's brigade" and poured out his energy and financial resources for the cause before dying from a fever.

ABOVE **One Romantic artist's tribute to another: John Martin's 1837 painting based on Byron's epic *Manfred*, first published in 1817. The lonely hero in a landscape of brooding mountains is a touchstone of the Romantic sensibility.**

LIFE AS ART

Oscar Wilde's claim that he had put all his genius into his life, and only his talent into his works could perhaps also have been said of Byron. "Genius" originally meant a household god, or spirit of a place, conferring psychic atmosphere or mood. Its modern meaning of "exceptional intellectual or creative individual" dilutes the power of the original sense, which nevertheless still has validity. For genius goes beyond the individual to stamp its image on a whole period or field of activity, giving it form and identity.

In the case of Wilde himself, life was an art which, as Auden wrote, "he performed from the beginning, and continued to do so even after fate had taken the plot out of his hands." The fact that society did not recognize what he was attempting to do, and hounded him to death, made no difference. His genius is recognized today as distinct from the brilliant talent of his plays and other works. He presented not only a theory of art but also an emphasis on the importance of a quality of life. "His work survived as he had claimed it would," writes Wilde's biographer Richard Ellmann. "We inherit his struggle to achieve supreme fictions in art, to associate art with social change, to save what is eccentric and singular from being sanitized and standardized, to replace a morality of severity by one of sympathy. He belongs to our world more than to Victoria's."

The notion of the artist as the *poète maudit*, established by Rimbaud, has been familiar for more than a century. It continues to be central to the social perception of the creative artist, with countless biopics of tragic artists, from Van Gogh to Francis Bacon, from Toulouse-Lautrec to Dylan Thomas. Today, however, this idea of the artist sacrificing everything in the task of bringing a unique self-expression into the public domain has come into question. Following Andy Warhol, many now believe that the idea of the work of art as an original creation has been replaced by the image as a mechanically reproducible commodity.

In Warhol's multiple portraits of Jackie Kennedy or Marilyn Monroe, the idea of a unique human imagination producing a unique aesthetic object collapses into a play of infinite repetition. Images no longer reflect some transcendent reality. Postmodern imagery reflects neither the outer world of nature nor the inner world of subjectivity, but only itself. The artist Damien Hirst, whose best-known works consist of parts of animals preserved in formaldehyde and displayed in glass cases like exhibits in a natural history museum, has said: "I sometimes feel I have nothing to say. Sometimes I want to communicate this."

RIGHT **Commodification redoubled: Marilyn was already an invention of Hollywood before Andy Warhol took things a step further, offering a Marilyn production line, the apotheosis of mechanical aesthetics.**

CREATIVE SOCIETIES

Certain times and places have seen a remarkable upsurge in creative activity, from Athens in the fifth century BCE to New York in the postwar decades of this century, and the "Silicon Valley" of 1980s California. At a given time and place, a set of cultural rewards, practices, and values crystallizes uniquely to produce an abundance of unique ideas and products. Perhaps this is not in itself surprising. After all, creativity is a socio-cultural phenomenon and always reflects changes in the social environment, and if these are conducive to the production of art or science, then art and science will be produced. When patronage, status, and resources become available, the culture will grow according to the social nutrients provided. However, it is hard to believe that political, economic, and social factors alone explain the extraordinary efflorescence of art in, say, classical Athens, Renaissance Florence, or T'ang Dynasty China.

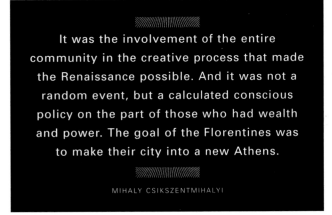

It was the involvement of the entire community in the creative process that made the Renaissance possible. And it was not a random event, but a calculated conscious policy on the part of those who had wealth and power. The goal of the Florentines was to make their city into a new Athens.

MIHALY CSIKSZENTMIHALYI

THE POWER OF PATRONAGE: RENAISSANCE FLORENCE

Civic pride clearly plays a major role in some instances, with wealth and new social priorities also important. Florence in the fifteenth century was a relatively small community that produced some of the world's greatest artists, including Donatello, Brunelleschi, Gentile da Fabriano, Masaccio, Botticelli, Leonardo da Vinci, and Michelangelo. The city had long been one of Europe's leading financial and manufacturing centers, and had just triumphed in a life-and-death struggle against Milan. Some writers believe that events at the beginning of the century, such as the discovery of long-buried Roman buildings and sculpture, and the influence of new ideas from the Middle East, helped to channel the consumption of wealthy Florentines into the patronage of works of art. The first 25 years of the century saw the installation of a number of key works, basic to the development of the Renaissance, the impetus coming either from rich individuals, or from one of the political or guild unions. To build the Duomo, the cathedral, a committee was set up to organize competitions, select the best entries, commission the winning artists, and pay for the finished product. A large proportion of the populace took part in the selection process.

The art historian Ludwig Heydenreich has written: "In this environment the patron begins to assume a very important role: in practice, artistic productions arise in large measure from his collaboration." Thus the starting point of production is not necessarily to be found in the creative urge, subjective self-expression, or spontaneous inspiration of the artist, but in the task set by the customer. Certainly, the artist has more chance of survival if a wealthy patron can be found. Few people, however, would believe that patronage told the whole story of the Renaissance flowering in Florence.

THE GOLDEN CENTURY: HOLLAND IN THE SEVENTEENTH CENTURY

In 1648 the Dutch, having finally won their independence from Spain, were fired with energy and nationalistic pride. Holland's cultural life achieved an international reputation in the seventeenth century with its scientists, cartographers, writers, and above all, its artists. By the mid-seventeenth century the Netherlands was the foremost commercial and maritime power of Europe, and Amsterdam was the financial center of Europe.

In the absence of a landowning nobility, and with a Protestant Church that discouraged adornment of religious buildings, Dutch merchants took the place of religious and noble patrons, commissioning portraits as a permanent memorial to their success. Frans Hals (1580–1666) painted only portraits, and portraiture played a significant role in the work of Rembrandt (1606–1669). Prices tended to be low, and paintings were bought by a far wider section of the population than elsewhere in Europe. Unlike the

art of Renaissance Italy, Dutch art was a record of "the men and the matter, the sentiments and habits, the deeds and gestures of the whole nation," according to Théophile Thoré.

THINGS FALL APART

But other observers have noted the Dutch preoccupation with *désagrégation*—a coming apart. Still lifes caught their subjects in the moment of perfect ripeness before decay. The animate and inanimate world of the Dutch was seen in a

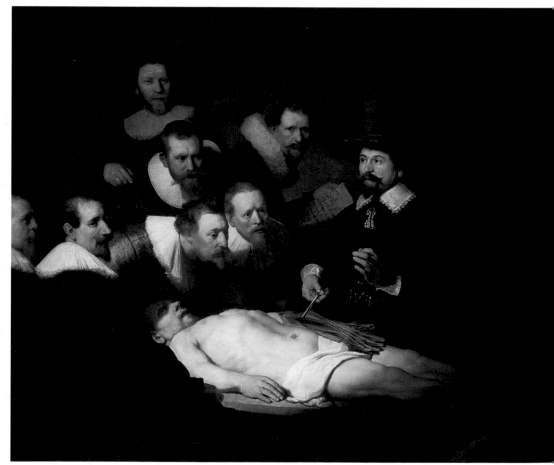

RIGHT *The Anatomy Lesson of Dr. Tulp* (1632) by Rembrandt reflects the Dutch interest in the "skull beneath the skin," a heroic Protestant refusal to idealize.

state of organic flux, a "secret elasticity," the essential kinetic quality for a country where the very elements of land and water seemed indeterminately separated. The Dutch interest in the underside, the transitoriness of the flesh, is seen in their preoccupation with anatomy and dissection, notably in Rembrandt's *The Anatomy Lesson of Dr. Tulp* (1632), the hypnotically precise scientific drawings of Anton van Leeuwenhoek (1632–1723), and the extraordinary work of the doctor and embalmer Ruysch (whose collection of bottled fetuses was acquired by Czar Peter the Great).

> The enterprise of Dutch art
> is like a liquefaction of reality
>
> PAUL CLAUDEL

Civic pride and mercantile patronage may have helped to elevate fifteenth-century Florence and seventeenth-century Holland, but elsewhere conditions have not been obviously favorable. In late nineteenth-century France, the era of Baudelaire, Rimbaud, Flaubert, Hugo, Rodin, Debussy, Courbet, and Cézanne, writers and painters were frequently at odds with the society that had brought them to birth. In Vienna at the end of the nineteenth century and the beginning of the twentieth —the Vienna of Freud, Mahler, Wittgenstein, Schoenberg, and Klimt—an anti-Semitic mood prevailed and Jewish artists were marginalized. Thus, even in spectacularly successful creative societies, the ingredients that form it transcend social boundaries to reach a wider expression of creativity.

LEFT **Gustav Klimt around 1912. From about 1900 onward his career was marked by controversy and conflict with the authorities, partly for stylistic reasons and partly because of the erotic element running through many of his paintings.**

PLAYFUL CREATIVITY

**Genius is simply childhood,
rediscovered by an act of will.**

CHARLES BAUDELAIRE

THE POTENCY OF PLAY

Play is the pure creative condition. In the book of Proverbs, Wisdom (in Greek translations, Sophia), God's companion at the beginning of Creation, describes herself as "playing in His presence continually, playing on the earth, when He had finished it, while my delight was in mankind." Perhaps it is the newborn child's imaginative faculty that is being hinted at here, the inborn ability of the mind to create its inner world in parallel with the world outside. Survival demands that the world inside our heads needs to approximate to the real world, the subjective to the objective. It is Sophia's role to make that approximation enjoyable.

The child psychologist Donald Winnicott has called this activity "creative apperception," the successful linking of subjective and objective, coloring the external world with the warm hues of the imagination. "It is creative apperception more than anything else," he wrote, "that makes the individual feel that life is worth living." When the subjective is so overemphasized that the inner world becomes entirely divorced from reality, we call those people mad. On the other hand, as Winnicott points out, when individuals suppress their inner world to such a degree that they allow external reality to be completely dominant, regarding the external world as something to which they just have to adapt, rather than as something in which their subjectivity can find fulfillment, their individuality disappears and life becomes meaningless or futile. Play is

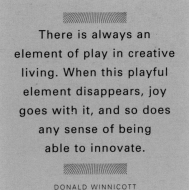

> There is always an element of play in creative living. When this playful element disappears, joy goes with it, and so does any sense of being able to innovate.
>
> DONALD WINNICOTT

RIGHT **The mind of the child is a fertile playground of associations and images without regard for logic and language. This playful element is essential to creativity.**

essential to creative development, and play requires a different mind-set from ordinary consciousness.

For every human being the world of sound and form predates that of name and language. Without language the infant (literally "the speechless one") creates its world in terms of sights and sounds. The need to identify objects in terms of shapes precedes the need to name them. This involves predominant activity by the eidetic (image-making) right-side brain rather than the analytic left hemisphere. Shapes and colors acquire multiple meanings before they are circumscribed in language. Pictures come before words, but perhaps sound comes before both. It is known that music affects humans even before birth, and this can be seen in the keen and pleasurable attention with which newborn children respond to music that has been played to them while they are still in the womb. According to Greek myth, it was the child god Hermes who transformed an empty shell into a musical instrument and thus first explored the possibilities of creative art. Musical intelligence may predate language in our species, and the call–response mode seems to be universal in all musical structures.

CHILDHOOD:
AN ALTERED STATE

Childhood is open to altered states of consciousness because it is a period when the boundary between imagination and reality is in the process of being defined. From daydream to trance, children travel easily between what might be and what is, slipping from reality to fantasy without difficulty, self-consciousness, or embarrassment. Consciousness is modified from babyhood to adolescence by the continual overlaying of preverbal perception with consensual name forms agreed by the prevailing culture and society.

Interest in, and admiration of, the otherness of children was a feature of the Romantic age, beginning with Rousseau and seen in England in the works of Wordsworth and William Blake, whose *Songs of Innocence* (1789) and *Songs of Experience* (1794) exalted the innocence of children and deplored their corruption by adult standards of belief and behavior. The Romantic movement's interest in children brought an enrichment of children's literature with myths, legends, and fairytales, notably the *Fairy Tales* (1812–1815) of the German Grimm brothers, which contained such stories as "Snow White and the Seven Dwarfs," "Hansel and Gretel," and "Rapunzel."

A classic attempt to show the world from a child's point of view was made by Lewis Carroll (Charles Lutwidge Dodgson, 1832–1898), a mathematics don at Oxford, in *Alice's Adventures in Wonderland* (1865) and *Through the Looking-Glass* (1872). Childish innocence and spontaneity escaped the constraints of civilization, but the world of childhood was subject to terrors as well as delights.

ABOVE **Blake's *Songs of Innocence* express an ardent belief in the power of childhood's unsullied imagination. It was a homemade book, printed by Blake and bound by his wife.**

CHILDREN'S MINDS

◎ The infant has to learn to construct the consensus reality of his culture. One of the main ways in which consciousness is shaped to fit consensus reality is through the medium of language. The word for an object focuses a child's perception onto a specific thing considered important by the culture. Social approval for this kind of behavior gives words great power. But the child's mind is autistic, a rich texture of free synthesis, hallucinatory and unlimited. His mind can skip over syllogisms with ease, in a nonlogical, dream-sequence kind of "knight's move" continuum. He nevertheless shows a strong desire to participate in a world of others. Eventually his willingness for self-modification, necessary to win rapport with his world, is stronger than his desire for autonomy. Were it not, civilization would not be possible. . . Maturity, or becoming reality-adjusted, restricts and diminishes that "knight's move" thinking, and tends to make pawns of us in the process. The kind of adult logic that results is dependent on the kinds of demands made on the young mind by parents and society. . . It is precisely this kind of childish strangeness that both frustrates us adults when we try to deal with children and excites our envy when we realize children have a certain freedom we do not have. ◎

FROM *ALTERED STATES OF CONSCIOUSNESS*, BY CHARLES TART (1969)

ART AS COMFORT BLANKET

Freud considered conflict to be a crucible for the formation of personality, with infantile sexuality and aggression as a kind of original sin to be socialized and civilized by processes of the ego. But Winnicott saw personality's origin in the early bonding of mother and child. Freud portrayed people as driven by the contradictions of desire into frustrating and ambivalent attachments, while Winnicott stressed that only in attachments can a human being find an authentic self. The child's first connection is with the mother's breast. The first interplay between imagination and reality is when the baby feels hungry and the mother offers her breast, "dipping" what is real into the baby's imagination so that the baby may feel it has created the world that nurtures it. Later, as the child begins to move out of the mother's physical sphere, he or she makes use of "transitional objects," a comfort blanket, or a piece of cloth, which are parts of the outside world but act as extensions of the child's inner world, substitutes either for the mother's breast, or for the mother herself as a secure attachment figure.

Winnicott considers that such objects help to mediate between the child's closely bonded relationship with the mother and its capacity to experience other people as autonomous beings. The transitional object exists as a separate entity from the child but at the same time it is heavily invested with subjective emotions that belong to its inner world. These objects are closely connected with the beginnings of independence and with the capacity to be alone. They encourage a process of mediation between inner and outer which might be described as the child's first creative act. A particular blanket, later on a doll or teddy bear, becomes a defense against anxiety, a comforter. Such objects may become at times even more important than the mother herself. The use of transitional objects suggests that the posi-

tive functions of imagination begin very early in life. Winnicott believes that art may play a similar role, mediating between the inner world and the external physical, social world.

ABOVE **There is darkness as well as light to be found in children's stories, not least in the stories by the Brothers Grimm.** *Rapunzel* **features kidnapping, imprisonment, and the blinding of the hero as well as a happy ending.**

A BEAR OF LITTLE BRAIN: WINNIE-THE-POOH

The most celebrated transitional object of the twentieth century is Winnie-the-Pooh, the teddy bear companion of Christopher Robin Milne (1920–1996). Pooh was the brainchild of Christopher's father A. A. Milne (1882–1956), a reasonably successful writer of light plays, novels, detective stories, and humorous essays. Milne created the character mainly, he wrote, to explore the genre of children's fiction; secondly to entertain his fey, elegant wife Daphne, of whom he was somewhat in awe; and only thirdly for "Christopher Robin" (who was never, in fact, known by that name), their only child, the nursery-domiciled, androgynous boy who was the actual owner of the toy.

The "Pooh Cycle" (1924–1928), which consists of two books of poems and two books of stories about nursery life, had spectacular success, especially the two Pooh books, *Winnie-the-Pooh* (1926) and *The House at Pooh Corner* (1928). This success continues to this day, notably in the familiar Walt Disney feature (which introduces a transatlantic chipmunk), but also in multiple spin-offs, such as cookbooks, expositions of Zen philosophy (*The Tao of Pooh* and *The Té of Piglet* by Benjamin Hoff), and management-type

books such as *Winnie-the-Pooh on Management*, *Winnie-the-Pooh on Problem Solving*, and *Winnie-the-Pooh on Success*. The Pooh books have been translated into most living languages and at least one dead (the Latin *Winnie-Ille-Pooh*). Despite the cloying sentimentality of many of the poems, there is something about the stories, together with E. H. Shepard's skillful and insightful illustrations, that has made the Pooh world part of our language and mythology. This is seriously playful creativity, with Pooh's use of right-brain logic providing the key to the kind of spin-offs mentioned above.

Milne never understood, and came to regret, the success of a creation that cast a shadow over all his other literary work. (The poems were savaged by the New York journalist

RIGHT **A. A. Milne with son Christopher, the Christopher Robin of the books. Whatever his actual qualities as a father, Milne's grasp of childish logic is unassailable.**

and wit Dorothy Parker, who suggested replacing the second line of the couplet, "Hush! Hush! Whisper who dares/Christopher Robin is saying his prayers," with "Christopher Robin is slaying his bears"). But the stories in which Milne described the adventures of the "bear of very little brain," together with Piglet, Eeyore, and other nursery animals living on the fringes of Ashdown Forest, have created a lasting resonance that transcends the somewhat dated whimsy of many passages.

POOH AND THE SHAMANIC TRADITION

Pooh's impact on the collective imagination may have to do with place rather than time. In 1924, when he embarked on Winnie-the-Pooh, the golf-playing, urbanite Milne had just acquired Cotchford Farm, a house in rural Sussex on the edge of one of England's untouched wildernesses. Even today Ashdown Forest, with its great stands of brooding beeches, its stretches of heathery, sandy heathland, and its blood-red, sunken, iron-laden streams, is an impressive place with a strong, strange atmosphere. In the 1920s, of course, it was considerably wilder.

Although not overtly apparent, Milne's synthesis of upper-middle-class nursery child with primeval forest yielded a mysteriously shamanistic character, a bear companion, in sanitized, suburbanized form; for Pooh shows signs of being a spirit ally as well as a Winnicottian transi-

ABOVE **E. H. Shepard's illustrations contributed greatly to the success of the Pooh stories. The children-only world of Pooh and Piglet stands against a familiar eternal background of thistle, pine, and beech.**

tional object for the four-year-old child. Pooh's ungainly form and weak reasoning faculty conceal characteristics, such as the ability to produce inspirations, poetry, songs, and paradoxical solutions, that mark his true nature as the bear companion. Forest and nursery interpenetrate. Rudyard Kipling was another author who tapped into the *genius loci* of Ashdown with his classic children's stories in *Puck of Pook's Hill* (1906). And indeed the name "Pooh" resonates with that of Puck, the trickster spirit friendly to man.

In his autobiography Christopher Milne wrote that Pooh was "only a year younger than I was, and my inseparable companion... In the last chapter of *The House at Pooh Corner* our ways part. I go on to become a schoolboy. A child and his bear remain playing in the enchanted spot at the top of the forest. The toys are left behind, no longer wanted, in the nursery... During the war they went to America, and there they have been ever since."

So the stories end with the beginning of the child's formal socialization. Christopher Robin is no longer allowed to "do Nothing, which was what he liked doing best." But Nothing is not nothing. According to Benjamin Hoff, enlightened Taoist sages are "Children Who Know. Their minds have been emptied of the countless minute somethings of small learning, and filled with the wisdom of the Great Nothing, the Way of the Universe."

ANIMALS AND NONSENSE

The ability of children to empathize with animals is another aspect of playful creativity that has its roots in right-brain, preverbal thinking. More than two-thirds of all children's dreams involve animals. It has even been suggested that children's affinity with and affection for small animals

ABOVE **Roald Dahl, hugely successful writer for children, whose books are often characterized by grotesquery.**

may have played a part in animal domestication itself. As we have seen, the earliest humans lived in close association with other animals, and drew spiritual strength from the animal life about them. Mystical feelings toward animals are reflected in myths and folktales, and anthropomorphic animal stories for children. From early fairy tales, such stories have featured largely in children's literature.

Rudyard Kipling's animal stories, including *The Jungle Books* (1894–1895) and *Just So Stories for Little Children* (1902), may have been originally stimulated by the tales of the American writer Joel Chandler Harris (1848–1908). His Uncle Remus books (from 1880), based on black legends and myths and written in black English, feature the trickster figure of Brer Rabbit and reflect West African and Native American notions of animal power.

A more domesticated approach is seen in the work of Beatrix Potter (1866–1943), the English writer and illustrator of children's books, who in 1893 wrote *The Tale of Peter Rabbit* for an invalid child. This story became a children's classic throughout the world. Potter is believed to have been not especially fond of children, and this characteristic has been suggested in other children's writers including Edith Nesbit (1858–1924) author of *The Railway Children* (1906), A. A. Milne, and Roald Dahl (1916–1990), the most successful of modern children's writers, whose best-known work is *Charlie and the Chocolate Factory* (1964).

INSPIRATIONAL ALICE

In contrast, Lewis Carroll, who famously observed that he was "very fond of children, except boys," delighted in the company of young girls to an extent that seems obsessive today. Alice Liddell, the nine-year-old daughter of the Dean of Christ Church for whom Carroll wrote his *Alice* books, was only one of hundreds of little girls befriended by the shy academic. Carroll was a talented photographer, and many of his camera portraits were of children in various costumes and poses, including nude studies. He abruptly abandoned photography in 1880, apparently because his posing of little girls was criticized. However, nude studies of children were not unusual in Victorian art and photography, and it seems unlikely that Carroll's feelings were overtly sexual. He once said that the greatest pleasure he could have was to converse freely with a child, and feel the depths of her mind. In telling stories he often took his cue from the child's remarks, making the story a personal possession for her.

BELOW **An illustration from *The Jungle Book*. Kipling's animals have a nobility and vivid power that resonates for the child-reader.**

Nevertheless, it has often been pointed out that Carroll's stories appeal more to adults than to children. The weirdness of Carroll's work is seen most powerfully in the great nonsense epic *The Hunting of the Snark* (1876), written for Gertrude Chataway, a clergyman's daughter whom he met at a seaside resort on the Isle of Wight in 1875. However, it is the *Alice* stories that have attracted most attention. Humpty Dumpty's statement that "When I use a word it means just what I choose it to mean" has challenged linguistic philosophers. The supposed psychotropic properties of the Caterpillar's mushroom have given Carroll an honorary status among modern dope enthusiasts. And the dreamy precision of Carroll's words and images—for example, the wood "where things have no names"—presents a convincing alternative reality that trembles on the brink of understanding, inducing an almost hallucinatory mood. It is not surprising that the names and sayings of characters such as the March Hare, the Mad Hatter, and the Red Queen have become part of everyday speech.

BELOW **Charlotte Henry in the 1933 film of** *Alice in Wonderland*, **directed by Norman Z. McLeod, one of several undistinguished Alice movies.**

LEWIS CARROLL

One of Lewis Carroll's "little girls" was Isa Bowman, a child actress who played Alice in the first stage version of *Alice in Wonderland*. In 1888 Carroll took Isa on an extended visit to Eastbourne (August 29 to October 3). Here is her account of their holiday.

⊚ When I got very tired we used to sit down upon the grass, and he used to show me the most wonderful things made out of his handkerchief, [which he] rolled up to look like a mouse and then made to jump about by a movement of the hand. . . By a sort of consent the handkerchief trick was kept especially for the walk to Beachy Head, where there was tea waiting in the coastguard's cottage. . .
It was in the coastguard's house or on the grass outside that I heard most of his stories. Sometimes he would make excursions into the realms of pure romance, where there were scaly dragons and strange beasts that sat up and talked.

In all these stories there was always an adventure in a forest, and the great scene of each tale always took place in a wood. The consummation of a story was heralded by the phrase, "The children now came to a deep dark wood." When I heard that sentence, which was always spoken very slowly and with a solemn dropping of the voice, I always knew that the really exciting part was coming. I used to nestle a little nearer to him, and he used to hold me a little closer as he told of the final adventure. ⊚

FROM *LEWIS CARROLL AS I KNEW HIM*,
BY ISA BOWMAN (1899)

THE PURPOSE OF LAUGHTER

Much creativity achieves its effect through humor. Laughter is an altered state, a massive response on the level of physiological reflexes, but serving no apparent biological purpose. Laughter is liberating in the sense of tension-relieving, but it prevents the satisfaction of biological drives such as sex and aggression, and deflates emotions such as anger, anxiety, or pride. Humor reflects the double-edged use of opposites that underlies most definitions of creativity. The writer Arthur Koestler (1905–1983) coined the term "bisociation" to make a distinction between the routine skills of thinking on a single plane, and the creative act, which always operates on more than one plane. The former may be called single-minded, the latter a double-minded, transitory state of unstable equilibrium, where the balance of emotion and thought is disturbed. The pun is perhaps the simplest example of such bisociation.

However, humor is much more. It is simultaneously subversive and sacred, as evidenced by the Fool kept at every medieval court, who performed the role of satirical commentator on the follies of the great and the wise. The purpose of folly may have been to inoculate the existing order with a vaccine of ridicule strong

ABOVE **Spike Milligan's influential radio scripts, books and TV programs have made him a major comic figure, but he has also experienced periods of despair and instability.**

LEFT **Charlie Chaplin in trademark outfit. Though his comic style may seem most suited to the silent era, he was an outstandingly creative individual.**

enough to release any resentment against the powers-that-be but not so strong as to threaten those powers. Jesters had to walk a difficult line between being too anodyne and too pungent, and modern comics have suffered the same fate. Everybody loves comics (in England lack of a sense of humor is perceived as an irremediable defect), but their lives and careers may be insecure and often tragic, as witness the fates of, say, Tony Hancock or Woody Allen. Humor lives in the irrational. Many comic geniuses, such as the English comedian Spike Milligan, have suffered, both from their own personalities (the need to balance subversion and sanity) and from society's disapproval. Milligan was the moving spirit of the groundbreaking radio show *The Goons* (1951–1960), the fount and origin of all subsequent alternative comedy. Milligan's inspired humor is often too uncomfortable, too clearly allied to pain and madness, to make his work easily transferrable to other cultures. However, his influence on British comedy is all-pervasive and deeply satisfying.

PRODIGIES AND INFANT PHENOMENA

The word "prodigy" has associations of genius, wonder, perhaps even a certain freakiness. Mozart's ability to compose minuets before he was four years old is so extraordinary that it seems to break the laws of nature. And indeed it does break the rules of development laid down by the Swiss psychologist Jean Piaget (1896–1980) and his followers. These propose a connection between behavior and age, and have assembled the evidence for human development in terms of interactions of biological determinants and environmental events. Piaget showed that young children reason differently from adults and are often incapable of understanding logical reasoning. His experiments suggest that cognitive development occurs in four stages: sensory-motor intelligence (birth–2 years), preoperational thought (2–7 years), concrete operational thought (7–11 years), and formal operational thought (12 years and older). Yet John Stuart Mill (1806–1873), the British philosopher-economist, began to study Greek at the age of three, and by the age of 17 had completed advanced and thorough courses in Greek literature and philosophy, chemistry, botany, psychology, and law. At an age when Christopher Robin was "doing Nothing," that is, inhabiting a rich imaginative world with his teddy bear transitional object, Mill was translating Homer and Virgil.

Despite the examples of Mill and others, musicians, mathematicians, and chess players seem to dominate the strange world of the prodigy. Mozart, Beethoven, Schubert, Mendelssohn, and Brahms had all achieved a mastery of their field before they had reached their teens. Chopin played a concerto in public before he was nine. Bobby Fischer at 13 was the youngest national junior US chess champion, becoming the youngest senior champion the next year. Ruth Lawrence took an Oxford first in mathematics when she was 13. Nevertheless, many child prodigies go on to become no more than competent adult performers. A prodigy is not always a "genius."

RIGHT **Bobby Fischer, genius, prodigy and chess champion, pictured at the 1966 US Championships. Now he is a myth, maverick and news-item.**

HOW PRODIGIES ARE MADE

According to the psychologist David Feldman, the prodigy represents an exceptional innate pretuning to an already existing body of knowledge, an intersection of person and field

> Between seven and eleven, life is full of dulling and forgetting. It is fabled that we slowly lose the gift of speech with animals, that birds no longer visit our windowsills to converse. As our eyes grow accustomed to sight they armor themselves against wonder.
>
> LEONARD COHEN

of activity so remarkable as to suggest the two had been made for each other. Feldman identifies a number of complementary sets of forces that have to be sustained in nearly perfect coordination for early remarkable development to occur. These include: the natural capabilities of the child; responsive and interested parents; a field or domain available early enough to engage the child's energy and enthusiasm; and a favorable cultural and social environment where a set of cultural rewards, practices, and values crystallizes uniquely in a given place and time.

Family traditions play a vital part in the process. Prodigies born in a family of musicians find that music is all around them from their earliest days, even before birth, and it is played, enjoyed, and lived as if it is the most important and central thing a person can do. We have seen how some preliterate peoples regard music as a form of socialization, not a skill, and in such an environment it is unnatural not to make music. This seems to be the situation in many musical families, and the same is true to a lesser extent in families of artists and writers.

ABOVE **Children's incapacity to distinguish between their imaginative world and the "real" world is the source of their enviable creative enthusiasm.**

In some cases, the prodigy seems to be the outcome of a conscious decision on the parents' part. The Hungarian psychologist Lazslo Polgar trained his daughters Zsuzsa, Judit, and Zsoti to become world chess champions, beginning at the age of four, and this was a preplanned course of action. It seems that the "creativity" here lies in the parenting. Preparing a prodigy requires vast adjustments in child-rearing, family life, and aspirations, as well as a willingness to devote virtually total attention to the prodigy's development. Developing a child's ability at a precocious age may be a way of improving the prospects of the whole family—Mozart's father, for example, milked his son's ability in a lucrative series of tours of European capitals.

In altered states of reality, such as dreams and reverie, all kinds of transformations are possible. Children have a far closer contact with their subjectivity than do adults, so that when the preconscious energy of the child's imagination is directed toward goals that have an existence in external reality, and this energy is supported by suitable innate endowment, the gap between real and imaginary, even the normal and the paranormal, may narrow sharply—the association of children with poltergeist and other extrasensory phenomena is well attested. As Picasso says, "What might be taken for a precocious genius is the genius of childhood. When the child grows up, it disappears without a trace. It may happen that this boy will become a real painter some day, or even a great painter. But then he will have to begin everything again, from zero."

MOZART

The musical prodigy Wolfgang Amadeus Mozart describes clearly how the creative work has all taken place in his head before he writes down a single note. He regards the ideas as God given; they just seem to come to him. Many prodigies experience the same sensation.

◎ When I am as it were completely myself, entirely alone, and of good cheer—say, traveling in a carriage, or walking after a good meal, or during the night when I cannot sleep; it is on such occasions that my ideas flow best and most abundantly. *Whence* and *how* they come, I know not; nor can I force them. Those ideas that please me I retain in my memory, and am accustomed, as I have been told, to hum them to myself . . .

All this fires my soul, and provided I am not disturbed, my subject enlarges itself, becomes methodized and defined, and the whole, though it be long, stands almost complete and finished in my mind, so that I can survey it, like a fine picture or a beautiful statue, at a glance. Nor do I hear in my imagination the parts *successively*, but I hear them, as it were, all at once. What a delight this is I cannot tell! All this inventing, this producing, takes place in a pleasing, lively dream. Still, the actual hearing of the *tout ensemble* is after all the best. What has been thus produced I do not easily forget, and this is perhaps the best gift I have my Divine Maker to thank for.

When I proceed to write down my ideas, I take out of the bag of my memory, if I may use that phrase, what has been previously collected into it in the way I have mentioned. For this reason the committing to paper is done quickly enough, for everything is, as I said before, already finished; and it rarely differs on paper from what it was in my imagination...But why my productions take from my hand that particular form and style that makes them *Mozartish* and different from the works of other composers, is probably owing to the same cause that renders my nose so large or so aquiline, or, in short, makes it Mozart's and different from other people. For I really do not study or aim at any originality. ◎

FROM *THE LIFE OF MOZART*, BY EDWARD HOLMES (1912)

LEFT **The ten-year-old Mozart in Paris in 1766. Mozart's account of his composing process may seem startling, but how else could he have achieved the sheer quantity of his output?**

CREATIVITY

AND DISEASE

Is getting well ever an art,
Or art a way to get well?

ROBERT LOWELL

THE ART OF SICKNESS

Creativity appears to encompass the concepts both of disease and of cure. By introducing a new thing into the cultural mainstream, a virus inhaled—inspired—through the lungs of the unconscious, it disrupts and destroys well-established forms of thought and behavior. On the other hand, by bringing something in from outside that counters the hardening of overused arteries and habits, it facilitates and improves the species' interaction with the environment. The creative, the carrier of this virus or antibiotic, is threatened both by the nature of the gift and by the response of society. For while creativity may be a natural condition, perhaps the most natural of all, according to Rousseau, Blake, and others, it is far from being a normal one, in the sense of "not deviating from the standard." Creatives rarely conform to a regular standard. They are "abnormal," not only in terms of their own personalities, but also in the way they are seen by society. This

may extend from eccentricity, tolerated but not necessarily condoned, to a condition requiring the sufferer to be locked away for his or her own and others' safety. For these, sickness is both a metaphor and a reality.

Physical illness may initiate, or at least accelerate, the creative's pursuit of his or her vocation. The artist Henri Matisse (1869–1954) was a lawyer's clerk at 20 when he became ill with appendicitis that developed complications, forcing him to refrain from work for a long period. During

RIGHT *Luxe, Calme et Volupté* (1904), an early essay in pointillism by Matisse. His more characteristic use of bold, pure color dated from his move to the brilliant light of the South of France.

> When I started to paint, I felt transported into a kind of paradise... In everyday life I was usually bored or vexed by the things people were always telling me I must do. Starting to paint I felt gloriously free, quiet, and alone.
>
> HENRI MATISSE

this time he obtained a paintbox. Matisse's decision to live in the south of France, which completely altered his painting style, also came about for health reasons. The wind at L'Estaque had brought on bronchitis so he went to Nice to cure it—and remained there for practically the rest his life. The English novelist George Eliot (1819–1880) believed that "some forms of debility, ill health, and anemia may produce an effect on poetry," while George Pickering has argued that the enigmatic French novelist Marcel Proust (1871–1922) took refuge in illness in order to procure the seclusion necessary to achieve his vast enterprise in the multivolume *À la recherche du temps perdu*. The German novelist Thomas Mann (1875–1955), believed that a close connection existed between disease and artistic creation.

Both physical illness and creativity involve altered states of consciousness, arising on the one hand from bodily changes and on the other from imaginative affects. Fever, delirium, lassitude, depression, and perceptual alterations in time and space are some of the effects of illness that resemble and also nourish aspects of creativity. The creativity born of using derangement of the senses as a means of exploring the inner world, dating from the Romantic age and before, has induced many creatives to simulate these conditions by means of drugs and physical austerities. Deliberate derangement of the senses takes the practitioner into yet another state of consciousness—fear.

> I have cultivated my hysteria with delight and terror, and today... I have received a singular warning, I have felt the wind of the wing of madness pass over me.
>
> CHARLES BAUDELAIRE

THROUGH THE PAIN GATE

Pain is a central fact of human existence, biologically attested by not one but two types of nerve fibers—one for acute and the other for nagging pain. Both types cut through other forms of consciousness. "To kindness, to knowledge, we make promise only; pain we obey," wrote Marcel Proust, whose own relationship with his ill health was complicated and exploitative. President Thomas Jefferson (1743–1826) spoke for all but the most masochistic when he said that "the art of life is the art of avoiding pain." Yet suffering can ennoble as well as degrade. At a biological level, pain warns the organism of damage, but it may also act as a stimulus to activity, even a goad to creativity, as Nietzsche believed.

Many creative artists have used their pain as the subject matter for their art. Frida Kahlo (1907–1954), the Mexican painter, taught herself to paint after sustaining terrible injuries in a road accident in 1925. She underwent many operations and was probably already suffering from a congenital spina bifida

condition. A number of her self-portraits endow her suffering with an almost spiritual element, using powerful imagery to convey her physical disintegration. In *The Shattered Column* (1944), for instance, her body, encased in a metal brace, is open to reveal a broken pillar in place of her spine. For Kahlo, physical and mental suffering was interwoven in her difficult relationship with her husband, the painter Diego Rivera (1886–1957).

English playwright Dennis Potter (1935–1994) was another creative who used his experience of physical and psychic pain to powerful effect in his work, notably *The Singing Detective* (1985). Mental suffering is even more pervasive in creative production. In fact, inner conflict is often seen as the cause of creativity itself. However, it is the ability to transcend conflict rather than merely to describe it that endows great art with its unique quality.

LEFT **A graphic representation of illness and pain:** *The Shattered Column* **(1944) by Frida Kahlo, who underwent both physical and mental ordeals in her short life.**

SENSORY DEPRIVATION

Blindness is obviously a calamity, especially for visual artists, but it has not been seen as an unmixed evil by all creatives. In antiquity, loss of sight was connected with prophecy and poetry: music and song exist independently of sight. The tradition of the blind poet bard, first found in Homer, is continued to the present in such figures as Stevie Wonder (b. 1950) and Ray Charles (b. 1930). Tiresias, the Theban seer who revealed that Oedipus had killed his father and married his mother, was blinded by the goddess Athena because he had seen her bathing, but was then recompensed with the gift of prophecy. Inner sight is superimposed on and replaces outer sight, as in the vision of St. Paul on the road to Damascus. The visionary must lose ordinary vision in order to "see"—the metaphor of Tiresias' blindness has been used by poets from Tennyson to T. S. Eliot. Loss of sight allows the inner eye to explore the heights and depths of the imagination. "One eye sees," wrote the painter Paul Klee, "the other feels." Physical blindness appears to facilitate the development of subliminal senses, as in the extraordinary story of Helen Keller. The failing eyesight of the English writer Aldous Huxley (1894–1963), was paralleled by his interest in inner visions, culminating in the experiences described in *The Doors of Perception* (1954).

On a more mundane level, John Milton (1608–1674) observed that "to be blind is not miserable; not to be able to bear blindness, that is miserable." Milton was isolated and embittered by his condition, but completed *Paradise Regained* (1671) when all sight was gone. James Joyce (1882–1941) thought that becoming blind was "the least important event in his life," while Jorge Luis Borges (1899–1986) wrote that "gradual blindness is not a tragedy. It's like a slow summer twilight … but then I think of letters and roses." Sight is by far the most important of our senses, and its loss irreparable, but its absence may allow other senses to develop in unusual ways.

> One eye sees, the other feels.
>
> PAUL KLEE

RIGHT **Pianist and singer Ray Charles in 1969. Blind from the age of six, he forged a successful career from the 1950s onward, principally in rhythm 'n' blues but branching into jazz.**

SOUNDS OF SILENCE

Deafness somehow seems a more wretched affliction than blindness. It imposes an unwelcome effort on both deaf people and their interlocutors, and may lead to feelings of paranoia in the deaf, a sense that people are talking about them behind their backs. Not all deaf people can share the equanimity of the novelist Henry Green (1905–1974), who wrote, "The very deaf, as I am, hear the most astounding things all around them, which have not, in fact, been said. This enlivens my replies until, through mishearing, a new level of communication is reached."

The social effect of deafness, the inability to decipher speech, is only one part of the condition of hearing loss. Musicians may experience it differently. Hearing is basically a specialized form of touch, the ear picking up vibrating air, which it converts to electrical signals to be interpreted by the brain. Thus sounds are both heard and felt. The profoundly deaf Scottish percussionist Evelyn Glennie (b. 1965) learned to distinguish roughly the pitch of notes by associating pitch with where on her body she felt the sound before losing her hearing. The low sounds are felt mainly in the legs and feet, while particular places on her face, neck, and chest indicate different high sounds. The sight of a drum or cymbal vibrating enables her subconsciously to create a corresponding sound.

ABOVE *Saturn Devouring One of his Children* by Goya, a horribly grotesque vision. Personal physical and mental afflictions contributed to Goya's pessimism.

BELOW **Beethoven's oncoming deafness caused him much anguish, but by a supreme effort of will he overcame the disability to write the profound music of his final years.**

The English composer Sir Michael Tippett (1905–1998) wrote that some music "comes by instinct, a reawakening inside the physical body, so that the stomach perhaps moves as the music moves." Beethoven's misery at his loss of hearing was due at least as much to its social as its creative disadvantage, since much of his greatest work was written when he was entirely deaf. Perhaps in his deaf world he was able, as his biographer Maynard Solomon suggests, "to experiment with new forms of experience, free from the intrusive sounds of the external environment . . . free, like the dreamer, to combine and recombine the stuff of reality, in accordance with his desires, into previously undreamed-of forms and structures."

Deafness struck the Spanish painter Goya (Francisco José de Goya y Lucientes, 1746–1828) when he was 47. This may have been the result of lead encephalopathy, a condition also characterized by depression and personality change, probably caused by poisoning from lead in his paint. Thereafter, a mood of pessimism entered Goya's work, from the print series *The Caprices*, to *The Disasters of War* (1810) and *Absurdities* (1820–1823). It seems likely that his isolation drove him to record his nightmare visions. However, his firsthand observation of the bloody years of the Napoleonic occupation of Spain would have been cause enough for the grim despair of these paintings.

IN THE SHADOW OF DEATH: TB, CANCER, AND AIDS

Some writers maintain that certain diseases, in particular tuberculosis, may exert a distinct effect on creative production. Dr. Philip Sandblom believed that "the slight fever livened the associations and filled the thoughts with fantastic, dreamlike pictures... A greater zest for life, which could not be satisfied in reality because of the lassitude produced by the disease, found an outlet instead in imagination, often with an erotic touch." The music of Chopin, the poetry of Keats, the novels of the Brontës, contain ingredients that lend credence to this view. Keats' death wish, "Now more than ever seems it rich to die,/ To cease upon the midnight with no pain," shares with Chopin's *Nocturnes* the same feeling of "sweet sadness." Robert Louis Stevenson (1850–1894) wrote how the patient was "tenderly weaned from the passion of life" as the disease progressed. However, TB was a wholesale killer for many generations (and is likely to become so again), so that any serious generalization is unlikely to be statistically useful. The work of the tubercular George Orwell (1903–1950), for example, or of Anton Chekhov (1860–1904), seems to fit uneasily in any dispositional theory of TB.

The idea that certain illnesses confer creativity has been reversed in recent times to suggest that creativity confers the illness. The comparatively recent discovery of the link between emotional states and the immune system, giving substance to the popular conception of, say, a "broken heart," provides this problematic proposal with scientific backing. The unhappiness caused by the inability to express oneself really does have a genuinely physical effect. Nor can it be denied that the boldness and interest in experimentation fundamental to the creative personality may often expose the creative to physical risk.

The ambivalent and potentially hypocritical attitude of society toward such people is seen particularly with reference to sexually transmitted diseases, from syphilis to AIDS.

AIDS, a destruction of the immune system resulting from infection with the human immunodeficiency virus (HIV), has struck more than 30 million people since its appearance in the early 1980s. Initially concentrated in the homosexual community in the United States, the AIDS epidemic continues to expand throughout the world, particularly in Africa, where more than 90 percent of HIV infection is thought to be due to heterosexual transmis-

LEFT **Charlotte Brontë. Writers of this period applied a special tenderness to death, Romantic sentiment brought to bear on the ever-present threat of tuberculosis.**

sion. Creatives and celebrities who have died from AIDS include the dancer Rudolf Nureyev, actor Rock Hudson, rock star Freddie Mercury, and film-maker and painter Derek Jarman. Diagnosed as HIV-positive in 1987, Jarman (1942–1994) became a powerful advocate for AIDS-related causes while continuing to paint and direct movies. During his final years he made several movies that dealt directly with his life with AIDS. Although Jarman's sight eventually deteriorated

With the modern diseases (once TB, now cancer), the romantic idea that the disease expresses the character is extended to assert that the character causes the disease—because it has not expressed itself. Passion moves inward, striking and blighting the deepest cellular recesses.

SUSAN SONTAG

to the point of blindness, his artistic vision remained strong. His final work, *Blue* (1993), consists of more than an hour of unaltering blue screen over which the audience hears music and voices, many of which describe Jarman's illness and its effect on his body.

ABOVE **Derek Jarman, artist, filmmaker and gay activist. Latterly he lived in a cottage on the bleak coastline near Dungeness nuclear power plant in southern England, and tended a garden in characteristic life-affirming defiance of both his surroundings and his illness.**

MIND SICKNESS

Eccentricity is the acceptable face of the creative. Most societies tolerate eccentrics, and even approve of them, in theory. "They just don't like them living next door," as the English eccentric Julian Clary observed. The philosopher John Stuart Mill believed that "the amount of eccentricity in a society has generally been proportional to the amount of genius, mental vigor, and moral courage which it contained." But one person's eccentric is another's lunatic. In a world where analytic, linear thinking has proved so successful, deviance from the step-by-step approach may sometimes yield results, but is more often seen to be disconcerting or disruptive.

The creative's tolerance of ambiguity, interest in the new, ability to accept conflicting ideas simultaneously, and form new syntheses, are all eccentric but acceptable characteristics. Thus eccentricity may often be no more than the label of "strangeness" conferred on anyone who doesn't fit in. This can be seen even in the simplest examples of creativity, where any surprising or unexpected solution to a problem is met with suspicion.

Such a reaction is familiar. But in the case of the many creative artists whose search for meaning takes them deep into the irrational, eccentricity may be only one symptom in a larger pattern of mental disturbance. Nor is this seen as a disadvantage—in some undertakings it

> One of the greatest pains to human nature is the pain of a new idea.
>
> WALTER BAGEHOT

> Men have called me mad, but the question is not yet settled, whether madness is or is not the loftiest intelligence—whether much that is glorious—whether all that is profound—does not spring from disease of thought—from moods of mind exalted at the expense of the general intellect.
>
> EDGAR ALLAN POE

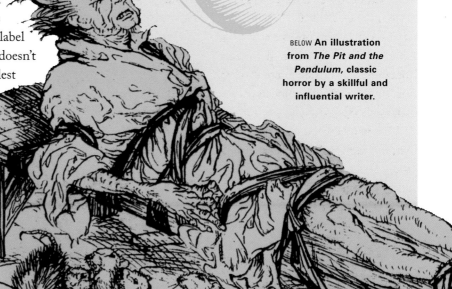

BELOW **An illustration from *The Pit and the Pendulum*, classic horror by a skillful and influential writer.**

may even be a prerequisite. Socrates believed that madness came from God because it was connected with the art of prophecy (thus recalling the age-old shamanic tradition), and this view has been shared by many creatives from the Romantic age to the present. Some poets, such as Rimbaud and the Symbolists, have seen it as part of their vocation actively to seek out madness.

The psychologist Albert Rothenberg has argued that, although pathological and creative thought processes share many features, such as the ability to think in opposites, and even to live in two worlds, the differences are fundamental. However, even Rothenberg concedes that the lines between the two are thin, and "the

crossover sometimes occurs." He instances the cases of the poet Sylvia Plath (1932–1963) and dramatist August Strindberg (1849–1912) as examples where "some crossing over between psychotic and creative thinking occurred at different periods of time, and only trained literary skills seemed to prevent florid disorganization in the work that was produced. Creative processes may turn to psychotic ones."

The thin line between creativity and psychosis is graphically illustrated by the lives of August Strindberg (left) and Sylvia Plath (above), both of whom crossed it at various times. Plath killed herself in 1963 after a period of depression, while Strindberg's aptly named autobiography *Inferno* described his spiritual crises and attacks of persecution mania.

PSYCHOTIC ART

One problem with the connection between creativity and pathology is that creativity is something generally recognized as positive, pleasurable, even joyful, despite its mysterious and therefore suspect nature. Illness, by contrast, is something to be cured, not something to be developed. How can the condition of creativity also be pathological? Perhaps the two conditions interface rather than overlap, with creativity acting as a means of coping with intolerable inner pressures. And perhaps madness is a spur to creativity. Many creatives have seen the condition as part of a Faustian bargain.

Madness is a painful, tragic, dangerous, and often life-threatening affliction. At the same time, it may be socially decreed and medically rubber-stamped. Social misfits can easily be seen as insane. "What is an authentic madman?" asked Antonin Artaud (1896–1948) in *Van Gogh: The Man Suicided by Society* (itself written while Artaud was confined in a mental institution, and published in 1947). "It is a man who preferred to become mad, in the socially accepted sense of the word, rather than forfeit a certain superior idea of human honor. . . A madman is also a man whom society did not want to hear and whom it wanted to prevent from uttering certain intolerable truths."

ABOVE **Richard Dadd's tenuous grip on mental health resulted in his incarceration, but also contributed to the phantasmagoric vision behind *The Fairy Feller's Master Stroke* (1855–1864).**

In *Madness and Civilization* (1971), the French philosopher Michel Foucault (1926–1984) showed how, in the Western world, madness—once thought to be divinely inspired—came to be thought of as mental illness. He believed that Western societies have traditionally repressed the creative force of madness. This idea was taken further by the psychiatrist R. D. Laing (1927–1989), who proposed that "madness need not be all breakdown. It may also be breakthrough. It is potential liberation and renewal as well as enslavement and existential death."

Many creative artists have suffered from various psychotic symptoms, and many psychotics have followed creative activities. There sometimes seems to be a fatal attraction between the two. The Romantic discernment of madness as a liberation from the fetters of reason has granted a privileged place to the altered states conferred by the condition, and therefore has always attracted the attention of those professionally interested in the unusual—in other words, creatives. The madness of the shamanistic Merlin, King Arthur's magician adviser, is recorded in the earliest of all Arthurian narratives, Geoffrey of Monmouth's *Historia Regum Britanniae* (c. 1136). Shakespeare explored insanity in *King Lear*. Many painters have gone to madhouses either as visitors (Goya, Hogarth, Géricault) or as patients (Richard Dadd, Van Gogh). The rollcall of creative artists who have also been mental patients is substantial.

DEGENERATE ART?

But psychotic art entered the mainstream, so to speak, with the collection of works assembled and published by the German psychiatrist Hans Prinzhorn in 1922. In terms both of subject matter and techniques, the art of these "schizophrenic masters" has had a profound effect on artists, from the Surrealists to the Art Brut movement of the 1960s. Many of these artists were later murdered as "incurables" by the Nazi authorities, themselves a product of homicidal mania. The Nazi exhibition of "Degenerate Art" in 1938 included work by Beckmann, Van Gogh, Kandinsky, and Picasso, alongside works by psychotic artists such as Franz Karl Bühler, Heinrich Mebes, and Else Blankenhorn. Meanwhile, practicing artists took from psychotic art whatever insights and methods would benefit their own work, while for the most part misunderstanding the very different motivation behind the two types of production. For the work of psychotic artists is essentially static, an endless confrontation with the shattered facts of their existence, while creative art seeks to transmute often painful experience into a new and communicable reality. According to Foucault, "Madness is the absolute break with the work of art; it forms the constitutive moment of abolition, which dissolves in time the truth of the work of art."

Many critics have pointed out the essential difference between psychotic and genuinely creative art, namely that the former relates to a sealed, private world while the latter seeks to communicate it. Nevertheless, the borderline between the two is both permeable and shifting. There are so many value judgements involved in definitions both of creativity and of madness. It has to be said that many paintings by hospitalized manic-depressives are coherent and well organized, obeying a tantalizingly elusive logic. Creative work offers a way of structuring painful experience, and channeling the frenzy of ideas, associations, and images produced in manic phases. The art historian Caroline Douglas suggests that this "instinctive self-defense" is the origin of the spontaneity of artistic production. The depression that follows performs a role as counterbalance to the preceding frenzy, by slowing down thought and feeling, allowing for reflection and focus. However, it is generally agreed that artistic production does not occur during acute phases of the illness, but only in the period of recovery.

MANIC DEPRESSION

The psychiatrist and academic Professor Kay R. Jamison has observed that manic depression, or hypomania, has many features that seem conducive to the original thinking found in creativity, at least during certain phases of the disease. In fact one of the standard diagnostic criteria for a phase of the disorder mentions "sharpened and unusually creative thinking and increased productivity." The extreme mood swings characteristic of manic depression have been recorded by numerous creatives, including William Blake, Lord Byron, and Alfred, Lord Tennyson. In modern times, mania or depression has enforced hospitalization on many creatives, including the poets and writers Antonin Artaud, William Faulkner, John Berryman, Robert Lowell, Sylvia Plath, Theodore Roethke, and Virginia Woolf. Many painters and composers have been similarly afflicted.

Hypomanic patients typically use rhyme and other sound associations, and form synonyms or other word associations much more rapidly than is considered normal. What causes this qualitative change in mental processing is not yet fully understood, but it represents an altered cognitive state that may well facilitate the formation of unique ideas and associations. As Jamison observes, "Such chaos in those able to transcend it or shape it to their will can provide a familiarity with transitions that is probably useful in artistic endeavors."

Hypomania and creative accomplishment also share certain other features, such as the ability to function well on little sleep, the concentration needed for intensive work, bold and restless attitudes, and an ability to experience a profound depth and variety of emotions. Biologically, the manic-depressive temperament is an alert, sensitive system that reacts strongly and swiftly, responding to the environment with a wide range of changes in terms of emotion, perception, intellect, behavior, and energy. Is it possible that the disease could itself confer certain creative advantages? It has been observed that most manic-depressives do not possess extraordinary imagination, and most accomplished artists do not suffer from recurring mood swings. Nevertheless, there does seem to be evidence that these diseases can sometimes enhance or otherwise contribute to creativity in some people.

Hypomania is a terrible affliction. Before the late 1970s, when the drug lithium first became widely available, one in five manic-depressives committed suicide. Lithium and anticonvulsant drugs have proved effective, but it is believed that these drugs may dampen a person's intellect and limit his or her emotional and perceptual range. For this reason, many manic-depressive patients stop using them.

LEFT **Caricature of the composer Hector Berlioz conducting a concert in 1846: it seems that Berlioz is in one of his hypomanic phases, and it's altogether too much for the audience.**

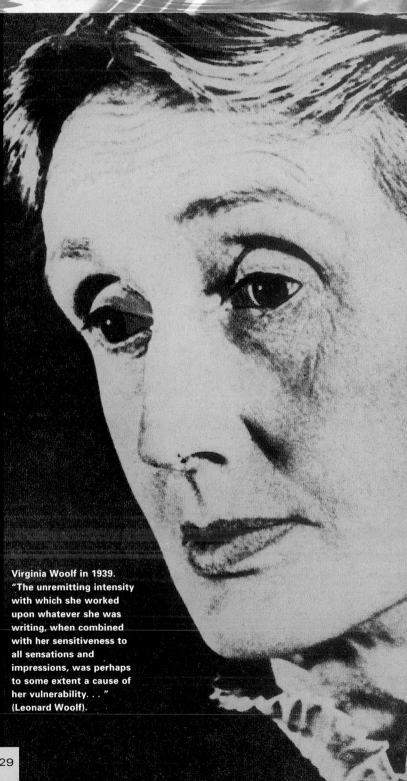

ANATOMY OF MELANCHOLY

This extract is from the diary of Virginia Woolf (1882–1941),
the English novelist, who had an innovative influence on
the twentieth-century novel. Her husband Leonard was ill in
hospital when she recorded this passage.

◎ **March 1, 1937**

I wish I could write out my sensations at this moment. They
are so peculiar and so unpleasant. . . A physical feeling as if
I were drumming slightly in the veins: very cold: impotent:
and terrified. As if I were exposed on a high ledge in full
light. Very lonely. . . Very useless. No atmosphere round me.
No words. Very apprehensive. As if something cold and
horrible—a roar of laughter at my expense were about to
happen. And I am powerless to ward it off: I have no
protection. And this anxiety and nothingness surround me
with a vacuum. It affects the thighs chiefly. And I want to
burst into tears, but have nothing to cry for. Then a great
restlessness seizes me. I think I could walk it off—walk and
walk until I am asleep. And I cannot unfurl my mind and
apply it calmly and unconsciously to a book. And my own
little scraps look dried up and derelict. And I know I must go
on doing this dance on hot bricks until I die. This is a little
superficial I admit. For I can burrow under and look at myself
displayed in this ridiculous way and feel complete submarine
calm: a kind of calm moreover which is strong enough to lift
the entire load: I can get that at moments; but the exposed
moments are terrifying. I looked at my eyes in the glass
once and saw them positively terrified. ◎

FROM *THE DIARY OF VIRGINIA WOOLF,*
VOLUME V (1936–41)

Virginia Woolf in 1939.
"The unremitting intensity
with which she worked
upon whatever she was
writing, when combined
with her sensitiveness to
all sensations and
impressions, was perhaps
to some extent a cause of
her vulnerability. . . "
(Leonard Woolf).

SCHIZOPHRENIA

The schizoid is characterized by a reluctance, even an inability, to make human contacts. Schizoid artists seek in their work a meaning and purpose for life which others find in human community. Success may cause them to feel that they have managed to restore the lines of communication to a lost world. The scientific disciplines require an objectivity and lack of emotionality which may appeal to pathologically withdrawn, emotionally "flattened" personalities of the kind associated with certain kinds of schizophrenic disorder. As

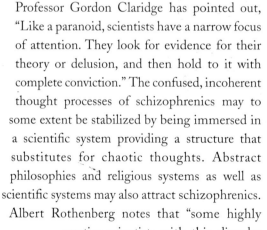

BELOW **Sir Isaac Newton (1642–1727):** a long and distinguished career, but might he have been a schizophrenic?

Professor Gordon Claridge has pointed out, "Like a paranoid, scientists have a narrow focus of attention. They look for evidence for their theory or delusion, and then hold to it with complete conviction." The confused, incoherent thought processes of schizophrenics may to some extent be stabilized by being immersed in a scientific system providing a structure that substitutes for chaotic thoughts. Abstract philosophies and religious systems as well as scientific systems may also attract schizophrenics. Albert Rothenberg notes that "some highly creative scientists with this disorder have succeeded immeasurably," and he lists Michael Faraday, Johannes Kepler, Tycho Brahe, and "very probably" Sir Isaac Newton.

Schizoids, according to Dr. Anthony Storr, suffer from an inability to make close relationships without feeling threatened. Their desperate need for love is thwarted by a desperate fear of close

ABOVE **Franz Kafka** reflected in his writings the mental difficulties and dislocations he felt himself, not only making them vividly clear as individual experiences but managing in the process to create a compelling portrait of institutional sickness.

involvement. Franz Kafka (1883–1924), the Austrian (Czech) Jewish writer, portrayed this dilemma and also used avoidance in real life so that he could employ his writing as a means of preventing "behavioral disorganization." It was his painful achievement to anticipate in his own pathology the oppression and despair of an entire age. Feelings of loneliness, guilt, and dread in the face of anonymous forces beyond the individual's control have become a cultural commonplace in the late twentieth century. Thus Kafka's themes reflect the individual's powerlessness, blending reality with fantasy and creating a nightmarish, claustrophobic mood.

THE BLACK DOG

Depression has been described as a condition in which the individual's aggression has been repressed to such an extent that it becomes directed inward in the form of self-reproach. It is characterized by feelings of worthlessness and despair, and is the commonest mental illness in the West today. Depressives complain of an empty feeling inside, a void which can never be filled. Alternatively, there is a feeling of being stifled, a "darkness visible" described by the novelist William Styron (b. 1925) as "the diabolical discomfort of being imprisoned in a fiercely overheated room. And because no breeze stirs this cauldron, because there's no escape from this smothering confinement, it is entirely natural that the victim begins to think ceaselessly of oblivion." Others have seen it in terms of a pitiless exposure. "O the mind, mind has mountains; cliffs of fall/Frightful, sheer, no-man-fathomed," wrote the Jesuit priest and poet Gerard Manley Hopkins (1844–1889).

Many depressives with creative ability have been writers, choosing to send out versions of themselves rather than to expose their own depreciated reality. The frailty of their condition is such that it may be adversely affected by success as well as by failure. The abstract expressionist painter Mark Rothko (1903–1970) was unable to cope with success after years of struggle. Displaying the self-depreciation typical of the depressive he feared that he was overrated and succumbed to suicidal melancholia.

ABOVE **Black on Maroon** by Mark Rothko (1958). Rothko explored the effects of pure color, creating large canvases containing only blocks or stripes, perceived as "atmospheric" or "peaceful."

Another famously depressed figure, the English writer Graham Greene, (1904–1991) declared that "writing is a form of therapy," but he extended its curative reach beyond the creative to include human experience in general. "Sometimes I wonder," he writes, "how all those who do not write, compose, or paint can manage to escape the madness, the melancholia, the panic fear, which is inherent in the human situation." Sandblom observes that the melancholy of the manic-depressive and the panic fear of the schizoid are essential symptoms of the two psychopathic temperaments which prevail in creative individuals; but Greene is surely right in suggesting that creativity has a power that goes beyond professional expertise. At one level it gives meaning to life—or relief from the disease of life. If avoidance of pain is "the art of life," then this is an art which everyone should develop.

> Sometimes I wonder how all those who do not write, compose, or paint can manage to escape the madness, the melancholia, the panic fear, which is inherent in the human situation.
>
> GRAHAM GREENE

EPILEPSY AND MIGRAINE

Physical changes in the brain reflect the altered perceptual states that characterize psychosis. In the cases of epilepsy and migraine, it is the physical disorder of neural function, seen in EEG patterns, that brings about the altered states. Sensory hallucinations precede many epileptic seizures, and are also found in migraines.

EPILEPSY

Epilepsy is a disturbance of the electrical activity of the brain, characterized by repeated convulsions or seizures. These include loss of consciousness, convulsive jerking of parts of the body, emotional explosions, or periods of mental confusion. Known as the "sacred disease," it was the subject of a treatise by Hippocrates (c.460–c.370) in the fourth century BCE, who ascribed its cause to blockages of the brain.

Despite its alarming appearance, epilepsy is rarely associated with severe mental disorder, but it has afflicted a number of creative artists, including Byron, Flaubert, Molière, Dostoyevsky, Swinburne, Pascal, and Petrarch. Its effect on individual behavior varies and may even be turned to advantage—Flaubert's epilepsy seems to have had the beneficent effect of preventing him from continuing with an unwanted career at law school, and freeing him to return home and develop his vocation.

In the case of Fyodor Dostoyevsky (1821–1881), the condition seems to have been of much greater importance. Most experts believe that he suffered from psychomotor epilepsy, caused by a lesion in the temporal lobe, but the preseizure aura of ecstasy that he experienced was unique. The effect of these auras was to give a mystical depth to the realistic psychology of his work. Dostoyevsky describes this condition in several of his novels, notably in *The Idiot* (1869). However, terrible depression, accompanied by feelings of guilt and shame, followed the attacks. These too were recorded in his work, as in his account of Smerdiakov in *The Brothers Karamazov* (1880).

ABOVE **Hippocrates, the Greek physician known as the father of medicine, investigated the causes of epilepsy.**

In certain moments, I experience a joy that is unthinkable in ordinary circumstances, and of which most people have no comprehension. Then I feel that I am in complete harmony with myself and the whole world, and this feeling is so bright and strong that you could give up ten years for a few seconds of that ecstasy— yes, even your whole life.

FYODOR DOSTOYEVSKY

LEFT **Dostoyevsky's epilepsy may have been an unusual variant. But then his whole life was hardly typical: as a young man he narrowly escaped execution as a revolutionary.**

EPILEPSY: A CASE STUDY

The Russian novelist Fyodor Dostoyevsky was an epileptic. In *The Idiot* he ascribed his sensations and experiences to the gentle hero, Prince Mishkin.

◎ He was thinking, incidentally, that there was a moment or two in his epileptic condition almost before the fit itself. . . when suddenly amid the sadness, spiritual darkness, and depression, his brain seemed to catch fire at brief moments, and with an extraordinary momentum his vital forces were strained to the utmost all at once. His sensation of being alive and his awareness increased tenfold at those moments which flashed by like lightning. His mind and heart were flooded by a dazzling light. All his agitation, all his doubts and worries, seemed composed in a twinkling, culminating in a great calm, full of serene and harmonious joy and hope, full of understanding and the knowledge of the final cause. But those moments, those flashes of intuition, were merely the presentiment of the last second (never more than a second) which preceded the actual fit. This second was, of course, unendurable.

Reflecting about it afterward, when he was well again, he often said to himself that all those gleams and flashes of the highest awareness and, hence, also of the "highest mode of existence," were nothing but a disease, a departure from the normal condition. . . "What if it is a disease?" he decided at last. "What does it matter that it is an abnormal tension, if the result, if the moment of sensation, remembered and analyzed in a state of health, turns out to be harmony and beauty brought to their highest point of perfection. . . " ◎

FROM *THE IDIOT*, BY FYODOR DOSTOYEVSKY (1869)

BELOW **Manuscript page from one of Dostoyevsky's notebooks for *The Devils*, featuring a startling self-portrait.**

MIGRAINE

A migraine is a severe headache that frequently occurs over one side of the head only, is caused by a constriction of blood vessels within the head, and may be brought on by hormone-level changes, endocrine imbalances, and stress. Like epilepsy it is often preceded by an aura, involving sensory hallucinations, dislocations of perception of time and space, and trancelike states. The hallucinations often take the form of phosphenes—brilliant sparks, stars, flashes, or geometric forms across a visual field. Some patients experience an overall brightening of vision, dreamlike sensations, and apparent alteration in the size of objects. The latter are graphically described by Lewis Carroll, a migraine sufferer, in his account of Alice's experiences in *Alice in Wonderland* as first she shrinks ("What a curious feeling! I must be shutting up like a telescope") and then expands "like the largest telescope there ever was. Goodbye, feet!"

LEFT **The migraine has been implicated and embodied in various artistic productions. The vivid manuscript illuminations (left) by the twelfth-century abbess Hildegard of Bingen show signs of migrainous symptoms, while the telescoping of Alice (below) reflects a common experience of migraine sufferers.**

According to the writer and psychiatrist Oliver Sacks, Hildegard of Bingen (1098–1179), the German mystic, abbess, composer, and writer, experienced visions that "were indisputably migrainous in nature." In two manuscript codices Hildegard left a magnificent visual and literary record of her visions, illustrating in great detail such physiological effects of a migraine as phosphenes, scintillations, and fields of light. "Hildegard's visions," writes Sacks, "provide a unique example of the manner in which a physiological event, banal, hateful, or meaningless to the vast majority of people, can become, in a privileged consciousness, the substrate of a supreme ecstatic inspiration."

ALCOHOLISM

Alcoholism is thought to arise from a combination of a wide range of physiological, psychological, social, and genetic factors. In the West, and probably worldwide, alcohol is the commonest substance for altering consciousness, and its general availability, its power to stimulate and to relax, as well as its ability to reduce anxiety, make it the drug of choice for many. Those who are exposed to anxiety-inducing situations are likely to use it more than others, and creatives form a group where anxiety is never far away. The process of unearthing unconscious material contains elements that are both threatening and uncomfortable, and exposure to the public also causes anxiety. Consequently, a considerable number of performing artists—actors and musicians in particular—have been dependent on alcohol. It has been prevalent among jazz musicians (Bix Beiderbecke is one example among many), and among actors and actresses. However, the condition of stage fright applies not only to the performing artist but also to the writer faced with a blank sheet of paper ("writer's block"). It is therefore not so surprising that individuals from both groups may rely on the disinhibiting power of alcohol to such an extent that dependence follows.

ABOVE **Ernest Hemingway, one of a raft of writers who have coexisted with alcohol. It didn't preclude a distinguished career, but he was prone to depression and shot himself in 1961.**

Famous authors who have also been alcoholics include Charles Baudelaire, Truman Capote, John Cheever, Stephen Crane, Theodore Dreiser, William Faulkner, Ernest Hemingway, Victor Hugo, Malcolm Lowry, Edgar Allan Poe, John Steinbeck, Dylan Thomas, and Tennessee Williams. Lowry's novel *Under the Volcano* (1947) is a classic description of alcoholism, tracing the physical and spiritual breakdown of the protagonist in grotesque and nightmarish detail. Most creative alcoholics, however, have not made their condition a major focus for their work. Creative activity has often been used to keep the condition under control, as in the case of the painter Jackson Pollock, and it seems that few writers have produced their best work while inebriated.

Ethnic factors may also be involved. Many successful twentieth-century writers have come from Irish backgrounds, where a high incidence of alcoholism is linked, according to some observers, with an association between drinking and masculinity. Two Irish writers of genius who were also alcoholics are Brendan Behan (1923–1964) and Flann O'Brien (1911–1966). In the US, this tradition has developed an impetus of its own. Alcoholic writers with Irish backgrounds include John O'Hara and Eugene O'Neill; but the pattern is also apparent in the lives and work of authors such as Ernest Hemingway (1899–1961) and Raymond Carver (1939–1988). In personal terms, alcohol may be seen as a secret ally, while it enables the writer to present a tough-guy image.

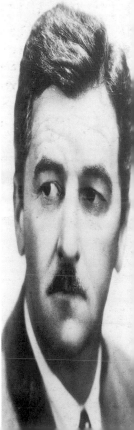

RIGHT **William Faulkner, a contemporary of Hemingway, came from a long line of drinkers. He won the Nobel Prize in 1949, but by then his undoubted talent had been lost to the bottle.**

SEX AND CREATIVITY

When woman's unmeasured bondage shall be broken, when she shall live through and for herself. . . she too will be a poet.

ARTHUR RIMBAUD

THE POWER OF THE WOMAN

Sexual and creative activity have something in common —at least, they are both altered states of reality. But more than that, both play with reality—there is a courtship and foreplay before the irreversible moment of penetration and insemination, a period when reality and imagination can be intermingled for both the lover and the creative. The invisible comes into being through a conjunction of opposites, a "bisociation" of genetic codes. During the period of gestation the zygote/idea undergoes systematic transformation within the womb of the creating mind/body according to pre-ordained processes and sequences. The new entity is further transformed at birth, which brings it (painfully for the bearer) into the light of the external world as a unique product/individual. Finally, there is the raising or rearing of the child/entity to become an acceptable and valuable addition to the totality of the species' experience, as perceived by others.

But procreation is dominated by the woman. The male acceptance of woman's unique power finds form in the most ancient human art works—the Palaeolithic "Venus" statuettes. From the Aurignacian period, 30,000 years ago, and throughout the New Stone Age, "female power" was acknowledged in innumerable works, from the tiny statuette from Willendorf, Austria, to the landform sculpture of Silbury Hill, England. Nor is this acknowledgement confined only to female creative power. The Great Mother is seen as the tomb as well as the womb of humanity. Life energy is female, as Shakti, the Supreme Energy of Hinduism, expresses. She contains within herself the three states of creation, preservation, and dissolution. At the time of dissolution she replaces the seeds in her pouch ready for the evolution from her womb of the next universe. Her male counterpart, Shiva, lies prostrate as she dances on his inert form. The *lingam* of Shiva combined with the Shakti's *yoni* in the primordial act of union forms the central shrine of all Shaiva temples.

ABOVE **The "Venus of Willendorf," a limestone statuette painted in red ochre, dating from around 20,000 BCE. Belly, breasts, and buttocks are emphasized, and it was probably a fertility or house goddess.**

GENDER AND CREATIVITY

The male contribution to the procreative process is a comparatively minor, though obviously essential, ingredient in the totality. The German-American psychiatrist Karen Horney (1885–1952) has suggested that "the tremendous strength in men of the impulse to creative work [is] due to their feeling of playing a relatively small part in the creation of living beings, which constantly impels them to an overcompensation in achievement."

An extension of this idea suggests that emphasis on the creative spark or flash may be an unconscious identification on the part of the male with masculine orgasm, a drama, or "doing," while the bringing into being, and the processes implicit in continuous nurturing existence, belong in the female sphere. The old idea that "man does, woman is" may be reflected in the male dominance of the fine arts, while women have until recently found—or been forced to find—creative fulfilment in, say, the decorative arts. Where they achieved entry in the male preserve, they had to assume masculine attributes and even sometimes, as in the case of the French novelist George Sand and artist Rosa Bonheur, a quasi-male appearance.

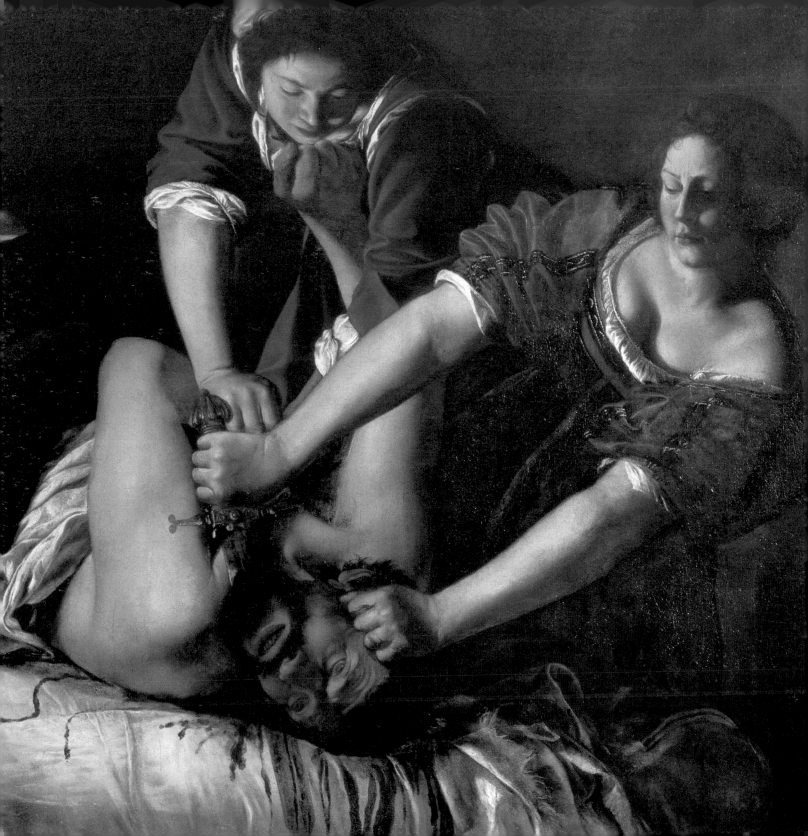

ABOVE *Diego and I* (1949), by the Mexican painter Frida Kahlo. Her tortuous relationship with the painter Diego Rivera was only one of many torments visited on her.

For many centuries "high" creativity has been largely a male preserve—but is this through nature or design? While it is true that there are no female equivalents of Michelangelo, Goethe, Beethoven, Joyce, or Matisse, remarks the cultural theorist Linda Nochlin, "the fault lies not with our stars, our hormones, our menstrual cycles, or our empty internal spaces, but in our institutions and education—education understood to include everything that happens to us from the moment we enter, head first, into this world of meaningful symbols, signs, and signals." The notion of a "feminine" form of creative activity finds no corroboration in the very different work of artists such as Artemisia Gentileschi, Georgia O'Keeffe, Angelica Kauffmann, and Louise Nevelson, or writers such as Murasaki Shikibu (regarded as one of the greatest Japanese novelists), Jane Austen, Emily Dickinson, George Sand, Virginia Woolf, Gertrude Stein, and Toni Morrison.

THE GENDERED BRAIN

It has been pointed out that biological differences between male and female include differences in the brain. Neurologists have observed that women have less specialization between their

LEFT *Judith and Holofernes*, a graphic seventeenth-century depiction of sexual antagonism and a favorite theme of the painter, Artemisia Gentileschi (c.1597–1651).

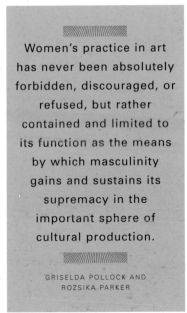

Women's practice in art has never been absolutely forbidden, discouraged, or refused, but rather contained and limited to its function as the means by which masculinity gains and sustains its supremacy in the important sphere of cultural production.

GRISELDA POLLOCK AND ROZSIKA PARKER

hemispheres than do men—damage to one side will affect a woman's brain functions, on average, less than it will those of a male. This suggests a less complete reliance on left-brain analytic thinking, and a corresponding strength in eidetic, intuitive, right-brain cognition. Furthermore, traditional female roles such as household management or childrearing typically require a holistic (right-brain) approach rather than an analytic one. There may well be, as feminists insist, a self-defining female energy, a female way of being and experiencing the world, even though, according to the Australian feminist writer Germaine Greer, "we are still not close to understanding what it might be." But Greer also believes that there is a fundamental, non-physical difference between male and female. "Every mother who has held a girl child in her arms has known that she was different from a boy child and that she would approach the reality around her in a different way."

However, the recent cultural and social convergence of male and female roles of activity in the Western world has not released new forms of creativity so much as brought about a parity within the old. Sexual partnerships between artists are often fraught with conflict, as seen in the interrelations of Georgia O'Keeffe and Alfred Stieglitz, Frida Kahlo and Diego Rivera, Elaine and Willem de Kooning, and Lee Krasner and Jackson Pollock.

SEXUALITY, ANTAGONISM, AND CREATIVE IMPULSE

Some authorities maintain that sex lies at the center, the power point that defines the "Other," and is also the center around which sexuality distributes its effects. Sex stands for the Other in its essential difference, and expresses itself through the activity of sexuality, interlacing function and instinct. But the French political philosopher Michel Foucault questions whether "sex" is in fact the anchorage point that supports the manifestations of sexuality, rather than an idea that takes form in the different strategies of power and the roles played therein. Sex is meaningless without sexuality.

Sexuality involves notions of power, mastery, and submission, whether or not it is an expression of something else. Sexuality rather than sex has the most direct bearing on artistic creativity, since the tension it generates has traditionally been seen as an energizer of the imagination, and a dangerous one at that. The persistent contradiction between the idealization of women and their exploitation in practice is an ancient conflict that may provide the energy for much creative activity.

Coitus is set so deeply within the larger context of human affairs that it serves as a charged microcosm of the variety of attitudes and values to which culture subscribes. Among other things, it may serve as a model of sexual politics on an individual or personal plane.

KATE MILLET

Tamed as it may be, sexuality remains one of the demonic forces in human consciousness... Even on the level of simple physical sensation and mood, making love surely resembles having an epileptic fit at least as much as, if not more than, it does eating a meal or conversing with someone.

SUSAN SONTAG

The violence and antagonism implicit in the sexual act both attract and repel. Since it involves opposite yet at the same time complementary activities, the act of heterosexual intercourse must have a different meaning for each participant, with overtones of compulsion and coercion for one partner, and submission and manipulation for the other.

But whence does this male violence arise? "Masculine identification processes," according to the American feminist sociologist Nancy Chodorow, "stress differentiation from others... Feminine identification processes are relational, whereas masculine identification processes tend to deny relationship. There is no need for a separation process to occur for the female child to develop her identity, since mother and daughter are of the same sex; whereas a male child must first identify himself with his mother, then separate himself from her in an attempt to find his own identity. Thus he is defined by and in opposition to her, a conflict that explains the combative, separatist approach linked with masculine modes of discourse."

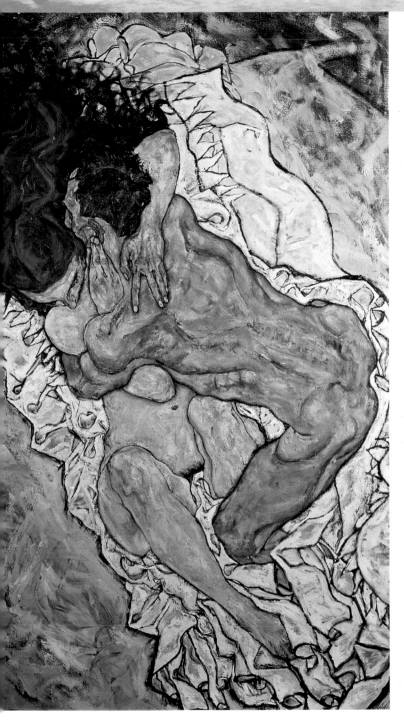

LEFT **Egon Schiele's painting *The Embrace* (1917) hints at the tension between tenderness and aggression in the sexual act with the awkward contorted posture of his couple.**

AGGRESSIVE POSSESSION

Sexuality in Western myth seems to be expressed very largely in the form of aggressive penetration, with rape and abduction the norm. The god possesses the object of his desire, and impregnates her with his divine seed. The impregnation is not necessarily sought or desired. Thus the idea of possession has both creative as well as sexual connotations. However, to be possessed is one thing, to be a possession another. Seen in social terms, the idealization of "woman" and the rape of women represent an awkward incongruity embarrassingly evident in the male psyche. But this is still accepted, or at least defended. The post-feminist writer Camille Paglia says, "You have to accept the fact that part of the sizzle of sex comes from the danger of sex. You can be overpowered." However, in the view of the American novelist John Updike, this major cause of conflict between the sexes may paradoxically provide the possibility of reconciliation.

In asking forgiveness of women for our mythologizing of their bodies, for being unreal about them, we can only appeal to their own sexuality, which is different but not basically different, perhaps, from our own. For women, too, there seems to be that tangle of supplication and possessiveness, that descent toward infantile undifferentiation, that omnipotent helplessness, that merger with the cosmic mother-warmth, that flushed pulse-quickened leap into overestimation, projection, general mix-up.

JOHN UPDIKE

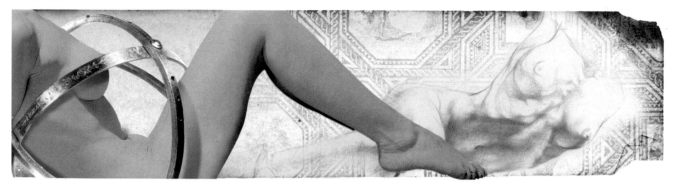

In the late twentieth century, images of sex and violence pervade the media, but their presence is noted and recorded assiduously because we are in the middle of a social and sexual revolution unprecedented in history; and with the steady empowerment of women it is no longer necessary to guess what they feel about such things. Contemporary women increasingly enjoy their own power, their own money, their own sexuality. They are unimpressed by promises of marriage or of men, or the easy seductions of motherhood. According to the English journalist Julie Burchill, the two roles traditionally assigned to women—mother and whore—can be seen as a kind of challenge. Those who choose the path of the whore, who "may only have one partner but will try anything," she finds preferable to the mother, who may have many partners for socioeconomic or other reasons, but is temperamentally timid and self-seeking. Whores, she argues, have chosen adventure over cowardly domesticity.

Freud believed that "sexual love is undoubtedly one of the chief things in life, and the union of mental and bodily satisfaction in the enjoyment of love is one of its culminating peaks." At the same time, he noted the possibility that "something in the nature of the sexual instinct itself is unfavorable to the realization of complete satisfaction." It was Marshall McLuhan (1911–1981), the Canadian communications theorist, who pointed out that for those for whom "the sex act has come to seem mechanical. . . there often remains a hunger which can be called metaphysical but which is not recognized as such, and which seeks satisfaction in physical danger, or sometimes in torture, suicide, or murder."

ABOVE **The objectification of the female body reflects the desire to depersonalize sex, to make it an aesthetic rather than a relational experience.**

WOUNDING BY CONSENT

Sadomasochism, according to Susan Sontag, "has always been the furthest reach of the sexual experience: when sex becomes most purely sexual, that is, severed from personhood, from relationships, from love. It should not be surprising that it has become attached to Nazi symbolism in recent years. Never before was the relation of masters and slaves so consciously aestheticized. Sade had to make up his theater of punishment and delight from scratch, improvising the decor and costumes and blasphemous rites. Now there is a master scenario available to everyone. The color is black, the material is leather, the seduction is beauty, the justification is honesty, the aim is ecstasy, the fantasy is death."

The characteristically masculine conflation of sex with violence may perhaps find its counterpart in those women who use sexuality to manipulate and disempower, as in the biblical examples of Delilah and Samson, or Judith and Holofernes. Both men and women use sexuality as a means to power rather than sensual pleasure. However, most if not all Delilah figures operate within the context of a male-dominated society; from Cleopatra to Jean Harlow they have been largely male constructs.

PICASSO AND THE WOMEN

Donjuanism (from Don Juan, the legendary Spanish libertine), involving compulsively promiscuous activity, has characterized the lifestyles of many creatives. Picasso, whose appetite for women is well attested, is described by the psychologist John Gedo as "for the most part venting his anger and contempt on women." However, the importance of women to Picasso is evidenced, according to his biographer John Richardson, by the fact that his work changed whenever the women in his life did. The centaur, the satyr, and most importantly the minotaur (man-bull), which appear in Picasso's etchings of the 1930s, represent the duality in men and in the artist himself. The critic Anthony Blunt describes

Picasso's use of the minotaur as at times "a symbol of violence and brutality, as in the scenes in which it is about to rape a sleeping girl. . . at other moments it is gentle and domesticated." Picasso's minotaurs, like man himself, yearn to be kinder, more human.

Henry Miller noted that Picasso's erotic paintings "have a playful quality which adulterate the sensuality one looks for in such work...his scenes are more amusing, delightful, and titillating than exciting." One clue to Picasso's complicated inner attitude to women, as opposed to the sometimes crude exterior, can be found in a drawing that he made toward the end of his life, in 1970, when he drew himself as an infantile old man, dwarfed by a huge circus equestrienne. According to Richardson, this figure almost certainly refers to the equestrienne Rosita, whom he sketched and made love to as a fifteen-year-old schoolboy. "Rosita appears again, resurrected in the phantasmagoric circus, brothel, bullring, and studio of Picasso's imagination nearly three-quarters of a century later."

LEFT *Minotaur and Dead Mare in Front of a Cave* (1936) by Picasso. The symbolism of power, possession, sexuality, and rape run through Picasso's paintings and etchings of this period.

MUSES, ICONS, AND SEX GODDESSES

The divine origin of women's sexual power was recognized in the ancient world in the practice of temple prostitution, the *hierodoule* of Greece and the Middle East, and the *devadasi* of Hinduism. Perhaps the idea of divine female sexuality came to be transmuted by the formative power of Apollo via the Muses into the idea of the female as inspirational force—Dante Alighieri (1265–1321), the Italian poet, was inspired by his meeting in 1274 with the nine-year-old Beatrice, whom he exalted as the symbol of divine grace, and for whom he composed *La Divina Commedia* (The Divine Comedy). One of the most

RIGHT **Robert Graves, novelist, classical and literary scholar, and probably the finest love poet of his generation.**

eminent literary figures of recent times, the English poet and writer Robert Graves (1895–1985), also revived the belief that poets derive their gifts from the Muse, a view which emerged during his long and turbulent relationship with the American poet Laura Riding (1901–1991). Riding, a destructive and domineering woman who brought chaos into many lives, lived with Graves for 13 years (1924–1937). In *The White Goddess* (1948) Graves identified the Muse in less personal terms as the primitive matriarchal moon goddess, the female principle, once dominant but now disastrously dispossessed by male values of reason and logic.

GOODBYE NORMA JEAN

There have been innumerable female icons through history, from Helen of Troy to Diana, Princess of Wales. But it has only been since the 1930s that the emergence of the mass media has given feminine iconization a global manifestation. Star quality, like creativity itself, is both innate and socially conferred. Perhaps the greatest Western icon of modern times is Marilyn Monroe (1926–1962), the American movie actress who died from an overdose of sleeping pills. "The consummate sexual doll," according to the feminist critic Andrea Dworkin, she "is empowered to act but afraid to act, perhaps because no amount of acting, however inspired, can convince the actor herself that her ideal female life is not a dreadful form of dying."

To the British writer Angela Carter (1940–1992), author of *The Sadeian Woman* (1979), the essence of her physicality "is a wholesome eroticism blurred a little round the edges by the fact she is not quite sure what eroticism is. This gives her her tentative luminosity and makes her, somehow, always more like her own image in the mirror than she is like herself."

The American dramatist Arthur Miller (b. 1915), whose short-lived marriage to Monroe appeared to unite idealized beauty and high creativity, could only say, "All my energy and attention were devoted to trying to help her solve her problems. Unfortunately I didn't have much success."

It has been pointed out that the most loved female figures of recent decades, the true icons, have tended to be largely silent, deeply suffering creatures such as Marilyn Monroe, Jackie Kennedy Onassis, and most recently, Diana, Princess of Wales. It seems that we like our female icons best when they are in distress. The feminist author Joan Smith writes of Diana that she is "a creature of pop modernity and solemn tradition, uniquely stylish and yet Ms. Everywoman, and in the last year or two, a woman both utterly broken and supremely powerful... Death was the logical, operatic end to Diana's story."

RIGHT **Norma Jean and "England's Rose." What they had in common was underlined when Elton John adapted "Candle in the Wind" for Diana's funeral.**

HOMOSEXUALITY AND ANDROGYNY

In *A Room of One's Own* (1929) Virginia Woolf, claimed that art required a mingling of both genders to obtain a universality. "The androgynous mind," she wrote, "is resonant and porous... naturally creative, incandescent, and undivided." It is an amalgam of the best of both genders, flowing through the nonsexed writer's prose. "In every human being a vacillation from one sex to the other takes place, and often it is only the clothes that keep the male or female likeness, while underneath the sex is the very opposite of what it is above." Woolf had a long affair with the writer Vita Sackville-West (1892–1962), from whom she drew the inspiration for the androgynous protagonist of her novel *Orlando* (1928). "It's all about you," she wrote, "and the lusts of your flesh and the lure of your mind."

THE GAY ARTIST

Many highly creative people have been homosexual, from Aeschylus to Leonardo da Vinci, from Walt Whitman to W. H. Auden, from Sappho to Gertrude Stein. However, homosexuality is not androgyny. The first implies an active, the second a passive or even unconscious sexuality. Although attitudes to homosexuality have varied widely through time and place, in the West homosexuality as a way of life is associated with the new urban cultures of the early modern period. Cities allowed groups of people who felt differently to come together in relative anonymity, and develop alternative

ABOVE **Virginia Woolf aged about 20. Her extraordinary novel *Orlando* is a comic tour-de-force combining historical fantasy with a witty critique of contemporary perceptions of gender and sexuality.**

lifestyles. At first, these subcultures were secretive and subject to strong persecution. During the twentieth century, however, they gave rise to ever more complex social networks, and to a strong sense of community among self-identified homosexuals. The gay liberation movement, originating in the New York Stonewall Riots in 1960, has powerfully asserted the equal validity of homosexuality with heterosexuality.

Questions of sexual identity, personal relationships, attitudes to authority, and the relation of the individual to society have always been of special concern to homosexuals. These issues become prominent in society as a whole during periods of cultural and social change, when individuality is emphasized over community. As a result, some writers have sought to link homosexual creative prominence with certain periods in history, such as Classical Greece and democracy, Renaissance Italy and humanism, the postwar period and Western individualism.

Homosexuals have traditionally been prominent in the performing arts, particularly dance, film, and theater. According to the psychologist Albert Rothenberg, this may partly be because homosexuals are "not at all intolerant of so-called feminine behavior, psychological tendencies toward exhibitionism, and the display of body in dance and voice in theater, while experience with shifting identity provides advantages for effecting shifting characterizations."

LEFT **Tennessee Williams, the American playwright, claimed that homosexuals developed greater artistic sensibility as a result of societal pressures**.

Homosexual persons may well have experiential access to aspects of the inner world of both sexes ... Ability to depict dual-gender experience in literature, music, and visual art may also be enhanced by homosexual life and orientation.

ALBERT ROTHENBERG

Sexuality is a part of our behavior. It's part of our world freedom ... It is our own creation, and much more than the discovery of a secret side of our desire. We have to understand that with our desires go new forms of relationships, new forms of love, new forms of creation. Sex is not a fatality; it's a possibility for creative life. It's not enough to affirm that we are gay but we must also create a gay life.

MICHEL FOUCAULT

Gay activists, on the other hand, argue that sexuality is a matter of choice, and that the divide between homosexuality and heterosexuality is a social and historical one, rather than one based in any fundamental, essential, or biological reality. What ultimately matters is whether homosexuals can live fulfilled lives. Sexual stereotyping, favorable or unfavorable, is just another form of constraint. There is no statistical justification for the claim that homosexuals are more successfully creative than heterosexuals.

WAYS TO
CREATIVITY

The way is to the destructive element
submit yourself, and with the exertions of
your hands and feet in the water make the
deep, deep sea keep you up.

JOSEPH CONRAD

THE BRAIN–MIND CONTINUUM

As we have seen, recent advances in neuroscience have put into question the psychoanalytic model of the mind, initiated by Freud, which essentially proposed a conflicting duality between conscious and unconscious processes. Conscious processes may, as Freud suggested, operate to transform unwanted and damaging impulses into acceptable activity; they may sublimate conflict into creative art. But the unconscious impulses do not necessarily emanate from a repository of suppressed desires. Consciousness is now seen more as the operation of certain areas of the brain in response to internal or external stimuli—danger, pain, sexual desire, etc.—which require the individual to make adjustments in subjectivity. The American neuroscientist Joseph Bogen believes he has identified the neural basis of "subjectivity" itself in a subsection of the thalamus called the intralaminar nuclei.

Creativity involves an adjustment of an individual's subjectivity. The numerous semi-independent mental operating systems, anatomically located mainly in the cortex but also in the limbic system of the brain (the so-called emotional brain), occupy consciousness for a particular purpose. And there is a "governing self" in addition to the others, located in the frontal lobe, which links the operation of the separate small minds to ensure a constant personality. Damage to this region causes a loss of identity (see page 42).

ABOVE **Few minds can have been more extensively investigated than Van Gogh's. This is his portrait of Dr. Paul Gachet, his doctor in Auvers.**

THE CREATIVE LOBE

Researchers in North America claim to have found in the temporal lobe, adjacent to the frontal lobe, a focus which when stimulated gives rise to thoughts of the divine, immortality, spirituality, and the infinite. Perhaps creativity too has a location in the brain. The onset of a form of brain deterioration known as frontotemporal dementia has recently been found to induce exceptional creativity, indicating that there are areas of the brain where musical and visual abilities develop—failure in one part of the brain could spark life in another. Bruce Miller of the University of California believes that Van Gogh may have suffered from this disease.

However, the identification of physical areas corresponding to specific mental activities does not begin to solve the mystery of creativity. The countless interrelations, resonances, and associations within the cerebral galaxy make our minds unique. The Colombian neuroscientist Rodolfo Llinás has compared the human brain to a "well-tuned musical instrument," containing an enormous number of "sympathetic" chords that make our internal resonances infinitely complex. "The association cortex, the indirect connections, are the features which really make us different from other animals." In particular, it is our capacity to imagine new things (our ideas or imaginations) out of pieces of things, or out of properties of the external world, that allows us to invent things that don't exist.

Neurological preparation for creative activity is part of the creative process. Some would-be creatives have evolved elaborate rituals to get themselves into a receptive frame of mind. The poet John Keats (1795–1821) described a state which he called "Negative Capability . . . when a man is capable of being in uncertainties, mysteries, doubts, without any irritable reaching after fact and reason." This technique of unfocused attention resembles the mental process known as meditation, which involves the individual's withdrawal from the active mode of normal consciousness in order to enter the complementary mode of receptivity. Psychologically, meditation produces an altered state of consciousness that combines alertness and relaxation. At one level, it is a way of relaxing the left-brain grip on consciousness, and allowing the right free expression; at another, it is a way of dissolving personal consciousness into superconscious reality. It is the way of the mystic.

DEVOTION AND THE AESTHETIC IMPERATIVE

Mental and physical disciplines, rituals, music and dance, psychotropic drugs—these are all time-tested ways of dramatically altering the ordinary state of consciousness to access a different reality. But do these altered states give access to "creativity," defined as the use of the imagination to bring something new and valuable into the external world? Many such states may be seen as ends in themselves, or as means to a personal rather than a social end. But for the creative person, the point of the exercise is not only the vision but also the often laborious transformation of the vision into external reality. For the vision-seeker, there is a different objective. Creativity is subsumed within the larger enterprise of going beyond oneself, not to create any particular thing but to experience a greater reality.

ABOVE **Top modelmakers: James Watson (left) and Francis Crick with their model showing the structure of the DNA molecule, a key to life and reproduction.**

The Romantic poet Percy Bysshe Shelley (1792–1822) wrote, "The mind in creation is as a fading coal which some invisible influence, like an inconstant wind, awakens to a transitory brightness." That invisible influence acts on the "fading coal" of the mind so as to produce something that is valuable to others. But the motivation of the creative affects the perception and even the nature of the product. Devotional art has a religious purpose, while modern Western artists attempt to express a personal vision that may or may not have universal significance. The creative impulse, the urge to give form to something beyond oneself, transcending the boundaries of consciousness in order to make something new and valuable, is as old as humanity itself; it is the application of this impulse that changes.

THE CREATIVE AESTHETIC

In one way or another, every creative product must have an aesthetically pleasing quality. Creative contributions in mathematics or science are perceived as aesthetically satisfying no less than in the arts, as in the case of Watson and Crick's exquisite model of the DNA double helix. Even the simplest creative solution earns the aesthetic accolade of "neat." But the aesthetic emotion differs importantly from direct, unmediated attraction or repulsion. There is something fastidious about it. Joyce suggests through Stephen Dedalus in *Portrait of the Artist as a Young Man* (1916) that "the aesthetic emotion is static. The mind is arrested and raised above desire and loathing." The emotion inspired by a beautiful painting should not induce desire for or dislike of the object represented. In other words, a successful work of art is not regarded as a reference to something else, inspiring emotion for that thing, but as a thing in itself. This is perhaps the aesthetic touchstone of creativity. It sets the creative apart from other investigators of altered states of consciousness.

The purpose of religious art is to guide the viewer's mind to thoughts of the divine, and this is at variance with the end-in-itself nature of ordinary creativity. This does not prevent artists from using religious power in the service of their own work—Picasso's fascination with West African votive masks is an example. Artists are attuned to resonances that chime in with their own, wherever they come from. Thus the American artist Barnett Newman (1905–1970) draws on Judaism to produce the cosmic minimalism of *Creation*. In contrast, Francis Bacon plays demonic games with the Christian ideal in his horrifying *Figures at the Base of a Crucifixion* (1945). Creatives must deal with the forces, spiritual or demonic, that come to them as best they can, from the moonstruck visions of Samuel Palmer (1805–1881) to the Tantric inspirations of Nicholas Roerich (1874–1947). The Russian painter Wassily Kandinsky (1866–1944), whose exploration of the possibilities of abstraction make him one of the most important innovators in modern art, believed that art's endurance does not lie in external reality but in the deep roots of mystical inner thought.

> The spiritual life to which art belongs and of which it is one of the mightiest agents, is a complex but definite movement above and beyond, which can be translated into simplicity.
>
> WASSILY KANDINSKY

LEFT **Much art was (and is) created to serve religion. There can also, however, be a more hostile relationship between the two: this is a detail from Francis Bacon's *Three Studies for Figures at the Base of a Crucifixion*.**

MYSTICS AND CREATIVITY

Many—perhaps all—mystics have been creative, but their creativity has been by default. The creative product is not the end product but part of a wider celebration of divinity. Thus the German religious mystic Hildegard of Bingen (1098–1179) experienced intense visions, notably recorded in her book, *Scivias*, but also expressed in numerous paintings, poems, and musical compositions. As we have seen, the neurologist Oliver Sacks believes that Hildegard's visions were derived from her migrainous condition, specifically the premigraine aura when a range of hallucinatory states are experienced (see page 134). But this is a woeful understatement of the sense of cosmic interdependence that pervades her work. Hildegard's "Word" is similar to the Hindu *prana* or the Taoist *ch'i*. "The Word is living, being, spirit, all verdant greening, all creativity," she writes. "The entire world has been embraced by the Creator's kiss." Hildegard may very well have suffered from migraines, but her achievements as mystic, poet, painter, composer, and adviser to leading statesmen of the time go far beyond neurological rationalizations.

THE GNOSTIC VISION

During the revival of Gnostic beliefs in Western Europe in the early modern period, the English hermetic philosopher Robert Fludd (1574–1637) attempted to synthesize Christianity and Gnosticism in mesmeric images of creation in his treatise *Utriusque cosmi. . . historia* (1617). The idea of a conflict between the light and the dark, so prevalent in the work of the greatest creatives, was proposed by the Gnostics, who flourished in the early

RIGHT **Man's place in the universe as seen by philosopher Robert Fludd. His highly ordered view attempted to make a unity of physical and spiritual truth.**

centuries after Christ and presented a challenge to the orthodox version of Christianity. Gnostics believed that a deformed, evil god, or demiurge (craftsman), created the universe. The divine sparks that dwell in humanity fell into this universe or else were sent there by the supreme God in order to redeem humanity. The Gnostics identified the evil god with the God of the Old Testament, which they interpreted as an account of this god's efforts to keep humanity immersed in ignorance and the material world and to punish its attempts to acquire knowledge.

William Blake implicitly shared many of these views. In his *Prophetic Books* he describes a conflict between the light and the dark—the heavy tyranny of Urizen, false god of reason, and the light of the imagination. In his dual nature of visionary and creative artist, Blake exemplifies his own view of the interreality of physical and spiritual.

LEFT **Blake's worldview held the imagination to be the spark of the divine in humanity.**

Man has no Body distinct from his Soul; for that call'd Body is a portion of Soul discern'd by the five senses . . . If the doors of perception were cleansed every thing would appear to man as it is, infinite. For man has closed himself up, till he sees all things thro' narrow chinks of his cavern.

WILLIAM BLAKE

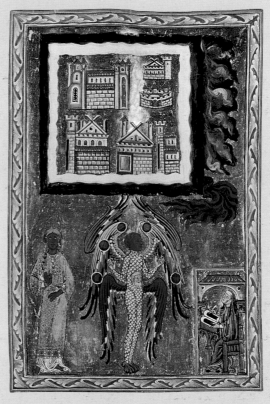

DEVOTION

And so the Spirit sweeps through the universe with resounding, inspiring, and igniting power, evoking the response of renewed vitality until the last day. This is the purpose and action of God, who has no beginning and no end. He created humanity as the wonderful work of his hand, by equipping people with an impulse and inclination to higher things by enabling them to make their own responses. God did this because he loved people. After all, he is Love itself.

FROM *LIBER VITAE MERITORUM,*
BY HILDEGARD OF BINGEN

ICONS AND MANDALAS

Mystics offer accounts, guides, and maps of the other worlds, which may incidentally be valued creative products in this one. But the intention of the mystic is to efface personal expression, not to express or project it. From the seventh century onward, painted icons of Christ, the Virgin, and various saints became the primary religious images of the Byzantine, Greek, and Russian Orthodox churches. The icon was believed to be sacred in itself as well as an aid in contacting the divinity it represented. To avoid any association with objects of idolatry, the icons were endowed with a formalized, deliberately stylized aspect that emphasized otherworldliness rather than any human feeling or sentimentality.

The work of the icon painters often combines spiritual grace and technical excellence to a marvellous degree, yet their personal input is almost invisible. The painters usually remained anonymous, but two, Andrei Rublev and Theophanes the Greek, are known by name. The work of these artists, active in the late fourteenth and early fifteenth centuries in Russia, represents the supreme achievement in icon painting, and yet

ABOVE **Seeing this, do we worship the subject, or praise the artist? The artist—in this case Rublev—intended the former, but in our secular age we are inclined to the latter.**

is in the devotional tradition of personal effacement. Russian icon painters in particular saw their work as a spiritual exercise. As late as the nineteenth century, these artists would embark on a prolonged period of fasting, prayer, and contemplation before beginning their task. The physiological effects of fasting in altering states of consciousness are well known, and are routinely used by most mystical traditions. However, the fact that some creatives use this method to concentrate their minds and to induce a suitably receptive state of consciousness does not lead to the conclusion that fasting is an infallible route to creativity. "Every icon painter should have his own connection with eternity," says modern Russian icon painter Sergei Fyodorov. "Then his icons will give direct experience of it, like a touch of heaven."

CIRCLES AND PATTERNS

The Buddhist and Hindu meditational diagrams called mandalas (circles) or yantras (sacred diagrams) often have the beauty and symmetry of great works of art; but they are also precise descriptions in pictorial form of their divine subject, to be used as a focus and guide for meditation. In Tibetan Buddhist tradition, each mandala is a sacred mansion, the home of a particular deity, who represents and embodies enlightened qualities ranging from compassion to heightened consciousness and bliss. Both the deity residing at the center of the mandala and the mandala itself are recognized as expressions of the Buddha's fully enlightened mind. The seed of enlightenment within each person is nourished by the process of visualizing and contemplating a mandala.

Hindu tantric art is concerned to express the union of cosmic principle (Shiva) with cosmic energy (Shakti), and this is seen most fully in the Sri Yantra with its mesmerizing harmony of interprenetrating triangles denoting male and female principles. From the point of emergence, the *bindu*, there arises the primal centrifugal urge, held within the circle of Shakti, the female essential energy, which is the motive force of the universe it encapsulates.

Tibetan mandalas were often made of sand, each grain of which was ritually blessed. The completed mandala was believed to embody a vast store of spiritual energy, but after a period of time it was dismantled and dispersed—emphasizing the spirit of nonattachment that separates the natural from the religious creative. For Tibetan Buddhists, as for the shaman creators of Huichol sand paintings, the creative product is part of a larger process, a junior partner in the cycle of creation, preservation, and destruction.

COLLECTIVE MANDALAS

Jung found the mandala recurring in his patients' dreams and visions, and this led him to his theory of a collective unconscious shared by everybody and manifested in dreams, visions, mythology, religion, and art. In Jung's Westernized version, the mandala is often perceived as divided into four segments, symbolizing the striving of the Self to achieve wholeness and total unity. In the Eastern tradition, the multifaceted design is centered on an invisible point that is the essence of both the cosmos and the individual. It can be represented in landscape sculpture, as with Native American "medicine wheels," and in architecture such as the enormous monument at Borobudur in Java.

LEFT **The Buddhist mandala is expressive in its symmetry and harmony of the enlightened mind of the Buddha.**

MANTRAS AND YANTRAS

Tantra art uses a variety of extremely rarefied diagrammatic yantras. . . they convey energy-realities which are so inclusive and emotionally exciting as to go far beyond the limits of any ordinary object we can recognize from everyday human experience. The Sri Yantra is the greatest and most complex of these. . . The act of meditating on [the Sri Yantra] is meant to drive the mind to reverse the act of Genesis and stare straight into the continuing act of creation. . . The existence of the world is thought of as a continuous giving birth by the *yoni* (vulva). . . Tantra supposes also that the seed itself generates the *yoni*. The seed [of creation] may be symbolized in the Sri Yantra by a central dot, the original point of energy which has "location but no magnitude," usually depicted as white; it makes its fundamental originating movement in the shape of a female, downward-pointing triangle, which is red. From this original couple, the white and the red, evolves a series of interwoven triangles, four male (upward-pointing) and four more female (downward-pointing). Their interpenetration produces circuits of lesser triangles, which represent the subdividing of the original creative energies into more definite forces. The outer circles and rings of lotus petals symbolize the unfolded reality of the world. All the different phases of the creative process seem to exist at once, since we are looking backward, beyond the flow of passing time.

ABOVE **The Sri Yantra, complex object of meditation, gateway to the beginning of time.**

FROM *THE ART OF TANTRA*,
BY PHILIP RAWSON (1978)

MUSIC AND DANCE

The neurologist Rodolfo Llinás' image of the brain as a musical instrument (see page 149) is not a new one. The Romantics compared the mind to an Aeolian harp, a rectangular box with strings of different thicknesses stretched across the top, all tuned to the same note. Placed where currents of air can set the strings vibrating, this produces overtones which create a strange, unearthly effect. Llinás' model of the brain, although reflecting extensive experimental work, has some resemblance to this image. Whether expressed in terms of neural "bursts of 40Hz oscillation" or of transformers of ethereal energy, both paradigms agree that the mind is visited by energies that demand to be understood. The dreaming brain's need to attribute meaning, or to create meaning from conflicting impressions presented to the dreamer's consciousness, reflects the individual's requirement to maintain psychic balance at all times. Whatever it is that sets off the vibration needs a response. The creative artist's "capacity to imagine new things" is one outcome of that process; the mystic's commitment to entering a greater reality is another.

> Man therefore loves music more than anything else. Music is his nature; it has come from vibrations and he himself is vibration . . . What makes us feel drawn to music is that our whole being is music; our mind and our body, the nature in which we live, the nature which has made us, all that is beneath and around us, it is all music; and we are close to all this music, and live and move and have our being in music . . . Everyone shows harmony or disharmony according to how open he is to the music of the universe.
>
> SUFI INAYAT KHAN

GOOD VIBRATIONS

Many traditions have taught that the origin of the whole of creation is vibration, the Hindu Sound (*nada*) or the Christian Word (*logos*), and this has found corroboration in the scientists' discovery of the primal sound, the vibration of the Big Bang itself. In the Hindu *Sanathana Dharma* or Eternal Religion, "OM" is the sound potential, the first vibration, the center where the worlds of color and of sound are ruled by the same law. "Sound, color, word . . . in their innermost core these methods are wholly identical," wrote Kandinsky. "The final goal (knowledge) is reached through delicate vibrations of the human soul."

Psychic movement and displacement often announce themselves in the form of vibration. The Russian poet Osip Mandelstam experienced a kind of inner rhythm before a poem came to him. Others, such as Nabokov, call it a "throb." Sound underlies both image and speech. Sound and rhythm, music and dance, are basic means of altering consciousness. The beats of the pulse and the heart, the inhaling and exhaling of the breath, are all the work of rhythm. Life is governed by the rhythmic working of the whole mechanism of the body. Sufi mystics believe that among all the arts, the art of music is especially close to the divine because it is a miniature of the law working through the whole universe. The organization of sound becomes music, which is also a language, a form of communication. Its basis is the call and response, forming a connection between speaker and audience.

DANCE AND MOVEMENT

Music and dance are languages that bypass the rational analytic mode. They appear to interpenetrate with all vertebrate activity, and as a result they lead the associationist brain into prehuman and perhaps superhuman resonances. Dance can be art, ritual, or recreation. A rhythmic release of energy, it goes beyond merely functional movement to become an experience that is pleasurable, exciting, or aesthetically valuable. It can also convey emotions, moods, or ideas, tell a story, or serve religious or social needs. The rhythmic movement of dance expresses the powers that the individual feels within the self and in the whole world. Dance allows the release of emotional expression and expresses joys and unhappinesses experienced in life. Needs of the intellect are less important. The relation between emotion and dance is close. Almost all devotional traditions have evolved forms of dance, from the planetary orbiting of Islamic Mevhlevi dancers to the specific performances of shamanic societies all over the world. Dance is the movement of access through the trance state into the other worlds. The Hindu Great God Shiva is seen as dancing eternally in the form of Shiva Nataraja (Lord of the Dance), performing his dance of creation, preservation, destruction, and release, both at the center of the universe and also in the cremation ground of his worshiper's heart, where all desires are burned away.

BELOW **Whirling dervishes. The phrase refers to the ecstatic prayer-dances practiced by Sufis, members of mystical sects within the Islamic world.**

WAKING SLEEP

Hypnosis, an altered state of consciousness involving heightened responsiveness to suggestion, was popularly associated with creative activity in George du Maurier's novel *Trilby* (1895). Hypnotized by the sinister Svengali, the singer Trilby achieves a voice "immense in its softness, richness, freshness." But on Svengali's death her singing reverts to its former wretched level. Some historical credence to the theory that hypnosis might evoke creativity is apparent in the experience of the composer Sergei Rachmaninov (1873–1943), who suffered a three-year sterile period after the failure of his First Symphony in 1897. Following hypnosis treatment, he produced the very successful Second Piano Concerto in 1901, and this inspired a period of creativity that lasted until 1917. However, the most remarkable fact about hypnosis is that it reveals a range of powers within the individual, inaccessible to personal consciousness, but attainable through surrender of the will.

Hypnosis is described as a state of consciousness, dissimilar to either wakefulness or sleep, in which attention is withdrawn from the outside world and is concentrated on mental, sensory, and physiological experiences. When a hypnotist induces a trance, a close relationship or rapport develops between subject and operator. The responses of a subject in the trance state, and his or her objective behavior, reflect what

ABOVE **Sergei Rachmaninov, whose hypnosis helped to restore his creative self-confidence. His doctor for these sessions, Dr. Nikolay Dahl, was himself an accomplished amateur musician.**

is being sought from the experience. A wide range of experiences during hypnotic trance include control of pain, amnesia, dreaming, changes in skin temperature and visual acuity, allergic responses, age regression, and relaxation. In fact, the hypnotized subject is able to exert almost miraculous controls over the body and mind, reminiscent of controls practiced by advanced spiritual adepts—except that all this is at the suggestion of the hypnotist. Nevertheless, hypnotized subjects are able to alter their skin and body temperature like yogis; pain thresholds are massively raised, and memory increased. Hypnosis can also produce a deeper contact with one's emotional life, resulting in some lifting of repressions and exposure of buried fears and conflicts. Whether this is beneficial for creative activity of an orthodox kind is debatable and must depend on a wide range of variables.

ANIMAL MAGNETISM

Franz Mesmer (1734–1815), the Austrian doctor who pioneered hypnotism (Mesmerism), asserted the existence of a power, similar to magnetism, that exercises an extraordinary influence on the human body. This power he called animal magnetism, and effected a number of cures before the practice incurred the disfavor of the medical profession and fell into disrepute. As we have seen, nonfunctioning senses exist

ABOVE **Hypnosis, in a sense, shuts down the governing self so that unconscious aspects of the mind and body come to the fore.**

within the human organism, which are capable, under the right conditions, of receiving information at the pheromonal level. Mesmer's animal magnetism—like the myriad, precisely charted pulses known to acupuncturists—reveals the probability of extensive subsensory (and supersensory) activity within and throughout the body.

Hypnotism returned to popularity at the close of the nineteenth century, when Freud's work on hypnosis and hysteria, under the French physician J. M. Charcot (1825–1893), brought him to the realization of the power of the unconscious. From this he was to elaborate his psychoanalytic theory. However, Freud's recognition of the power of the unconscious was offset by his belief that it embodied only "unacceptable" components, feelings such as fear, aggression, and the like. Modern neuroscience indicates that inner stimulation of relevant cortical centers underlies the division between the conscious and unconscious. This stimulation may arise from a huge

variety of causes, and may well involve Freudian or Jungian processes at some stage. Nevertheless, it is the extent and quality of the unconscious powers that, under certain conditions such as hypnosis, can be truly remarkable, whatever the mechanism. In hypnosis, the "governing self" has abdicated responsibility to another, and that other is able to command powers from the individual that would have been beyond him or her in normal consciousness. Colin Wilson has suggested that the dominance of the left brain in humans, far from being too strong, is not strong enough since it cannot command the powers evoked by the "unconscious governing self" of the hypnotized subject.

Loss of body awareness is a feature of the hypnotic trance, and this too has been induced with interesting though not necessarily "creative" results. In studies using Ganzfeld visual-deprivation techniques, access through altered states to nonfunctioning senses has been recorded in many experiments. Any diminution of the external consciousness, it seems, provides space for nonconscious information of a sometimes unpredictable kind.

My suggestion is that the unconscious senses are operating all the time, whether we know it or not, that we store this information, and that we get at it through a variety of quite natural "acts of attention," which range in a continuous spectrum of innumerable social and personal devices, from the reverie of the fisherman soothed by the ripple and flow of the stream to the frenzy of the gambler and the physical training of the sportsman and the yogi, from the absorbed play of a child with a pet animal or doll, to deep trance "somnambulism," voodoo . . . sleeping on a problem overnight or the . . . sexual embrace itself.

PETER REDGROVE

CREATIVITY
AND CHEMISTRY

Picture yourself in a boat on a river,
with tangerine trees and marmalade skies.

JOHN LENNON

12

CHEMICAL WEDDINGS

Drugs are the time-honored exit route away from ordinary consensual reality. From coffee to cocaine, from aspirin to ecstasy, drugs provide not one but numerous alternatives to external reality. Dissociation from this reality is a necessary (but not a sufficient) condition for creative activity, and drugs certainly provide that dissociation. But this is only part of the creative process, which in its entirety involves bringing something back into external reality, giving form to the imagination. The experience of such dissociation is itself the internal message but it requires translation into external form. By their nature, many impressively mind-altering substances will tend to militate against the processes of ordinary consciousness, for example the processes of concentration, transcription, correction, comparison, and validation required to bring a work of art to completion. However, drugs which work to enhance ordinary consciousness, such as cocaine and the amphetamines, often lack the quality that enables the imagination to reach deep into the unconscious.

Nevertheless, there are arguments suggesting that drugs have helped in the creative process. Puritanism apart, it is generally agreed that art made while on drugs is often less good than art done "cold." However, experience inspired by drugs may often be a valuable resource for the creative to work from. Artists create from the things that they experience and see and hear—if they use drugs, then drugs form part of that experience. Many of the artists associated with drug use were artists before they became heavy users, spending years developing their styles and mediums. Such people are inextricably linked to their creative process. Involvement with drugs will alter their creative process, for better or worse, but will not necessarily determine it.

ABOVE **From the early nineteenth century the notion of the creative artist enjoying trippy, drug-induced visions has become a commonplace**.

THE OPIUM OF THE PEOPLE

In many cases, social and recreational drugs enter a culture through an avant-garde minority primarily interested in the substances' effects on consciousness. This was notably the case in the nineteenth century with opium (De Quincey, Coleridge) and hashish (Gautier, Baudelaire), but coffee, tobacco, and alcohol played a similar role in earlier years. In the twentieth century we have seen a similar process with cannabis and the Beats in the 1950s, the psychedelic revolution and protest a decade later, and even cocaine and the Me generation of the 1980s. Today in the West, the most popular drugs range from coffee and tea to tobacco and alcohol, with marijuana a recent addition. More problematic in social terms are the opiate narcotics such as opium, morphine, and heroin; central stimulants such as cocaine and the amphetamines; the "psychedelic" drugs such as mescaline and LSD; and "designer" drugs such as Ecstasy. The type of drug prevalent in each period reflects and expresses its culture, from the opiates of the Romantic period to today's function-specific drugs designed to enhance particular cortical regions. For many creative artists, however, art is a passion that cannot be replaced by drugs, although it can be extinguished by addiction.

THE SEDUCTIVE POPPY: OPIUM

The Romantic reaction to Enlightenment rationalism inevitably led to experimentation with drugs. The English painter John Martin (1789–1854)—Mad Martin as he was called—set the tone with his vast, phantasmagorical canvases of cosmic scenes and Satanic struggles. These inebriated visions exerted tremendous influence on the Romantic writers, especially Keats and Thomas de Quincey (1785–1859). The latter was the pioneer of modern drug literature, whose *Confessions of an English Opium Eater* (1821) is an autobiography not of one person but of the Romantic imagination, similar to Wordsworth's *Prelude*, but going into more fantastic and secretive areas of experience.

The molecules of opium and its derivatives, such as morphine and heroin (which was discovered in 1898), occupy many of the same nerve-receptor sites and bring on the same analgesic effect as the body's natural painkillers. Within the

> Thou hast the keys of Paradise. Oh just, subtle, and mighty opium!
>
> THOMAS DE QUINCEY

BELOW *Belshazzar's Feast* (1820) by John Martin, one of a series of 16 biblical paintings marked by Martin's fantastical imagination.

opiate-induced cocoon of perfect invulnerability, the individual's strangest unconscious material feels safe to venture out. Opiates first produce a feeling of pleasure and euphoria, but with their continued use the body demands larger amounts to reach the same sense of well-being. The French poet Jean Cocteau (1889–1963) wrote, "With opium, euphoria leads the way to death." Malnutrition, respiratory complications, and low blood pressure are some of the illnesses associated with addiction.

THE OPIUM EATER

In the nineteenth century there were no laws against narcotics. Opium was imported without restriction, and sold in various forms—patent medicines, cordials for putting children to sleep, and general preparations such as laudanum (a mixture of opium and alcohol). Raw opium too was sold in the form of pills and penny sticks. De Quincey himself noted that "the number of amateur opium-eaters (as I may term them) was, at that time, immense" and included people from all walks of life. De Quincey was a member of the Lakeland circle of poets including Samuel Taylor Coleridge, William Wordsworth, and Robert Southey, from 1809 until 1820, when he returned to London and found fame with his vivid description of his own experiences as an opium addict. He found his notoriety as an "opium-eater" embarrassing, but it was also his stock-in-trade. Opium did not in itself make de Quincey a better writer, but it did provide him with the experience and subject matter for his creativity to work on. Opium addiction was the experience around which he could write his autobiography.

ABOVE **Title-illustration for the *Rime of the Ancient Mariner*. The poem predated Coleridge's opium-addiction, but perhaps not his first experience of the drug.**

COLERIDGE, POE, AND COCTEAU

Coleridge had a 40-year love–hate affair with opium, but some authorities believe that the drug helped him more as a philosopher and psychologist than as a poet. The positive effects that opium had on Coleridge could have been the ability to observe changing states of consciousness. Like de Quincey he was interested in dreams and fantasy, the process of falling asleep, changes in perception—opium would have helped him to observe these things more sharply than he would have otherwise. Coleridge had been taking opium for about a year when his most famous poem, "Kubla Khan," came to him as a block of several hundred lines of poetry, of which he could recall (following the celebrated interruption) only about 50. Yet much of his most haunting poetry, notably the *Rime of the Ancient Mariner*, was written long before his addiction. Marek Kohn observed that all his life Coleridge was "pursued by some great dread—a theme most powerfully expressed in 'The Ancient Mariner.' The fact was that Coleridge was always troubled in his mind. Opium was part of his failure to be an ancient mariner—an isolated figure. And it affected the will. 'My case is a species of madness,' he wrote of his addiction, 'only that it is a derangement of the Volition, and not of the intellectual faculties.'"

Edgar Allan Poe (1809–1849) created the popular image of the opium addict—his stories are seen through the confessional eye of the addict. Images associated with opium experience include underground passages, premature burial, hypersensitive perceptual reactions, and so on. His themes and characters indicate that he was acquainted with anxieties—the "morbid acuteness of the senses"—arising from opium addiction. But Poe's derangement clearly extended beyond opium. He was in addition a heavy drinker, and it is clear that he suffered (like so many artists of stature) from manic depression, involving violent mood swings and painful, involuntary alterations of consciousness.

The flowering of the opium culture in France came at the end of the nineteenth century and pervades the creativity of the period, assisted by absinthe (a toxic liqueur distilled from wormwood). But it was not so much the specific effect of the drug that was important as the part it played in "the systematic derangement of the senses" recommended by the leader of the Symbolists, Arthur Rimbaud as the means of achieving a truly visionary art. According to the art historian John Richardson, Picasso's work during his Rose Period at the turn of the century, with its dreamy moods and androgynous figures, is a manifestation of opium. The drug provides a flavor to the work, although there is no direct connection between them.

Picasso moved in a circle of opium takers that included the poet Guillaume Apollinaire (1880–1918) and the mystic and writer Max Jacob (1876–1944), although he later avoided discussion of the subject. However, he did say to Jean Cocteau, "Opium is the least stupid smell in the world" and described it as the greatest invention since the wheel. Cocteau, who depended on opium for most of his life, went much further. It has been suggested that his drawings could not have been achieved without opium enhancement. For Cocteau opium was the means by which he kept in touch with both the real world and the world of the imagination, with his mind released from normal constraints.

> Everything one does in life, even love, occurs in an express train racing toward death. To smoke opium is to get out of the train while it is still moving. It is to concern oneself with something other than life or death.
>
> JEAN COCTEAU

RIGHT **Picasso's *Saltimbanques*. The painter's "Rose Period," 1904–1906, with its feeling of relaxed contentment, may have in part been the result of his opium consumption.**

HASHISH AND MARIJUANA

The psychotropic and medicinal properties of the herb *Cannabis sativa* have been known since prehistoric times. In its resin form of hashish the drug was used in the medieval period by Islamic mendicant saints and ascetics, especially the Islamic Sufis and the Hindu Shaivites, to inspire visions and assist meditation. In its leaf form of marijuana, cannabis is used for these purposes today by Caribbean Rastafarian communities. However, in the West, hashish was believed to have played a part in the murderous activities of a bandit society known as the Hashishins (assassins). At the beginning of the nineteenth century hashish came to France as a result of Napoleon's Egyptian campaign, but it did not make an impact until the 1840s. In 1845 the French writer Théophile Gautier (1811–1872) founded the *Club des Haschischins*, which involved or included the leading lights of French Romanticism, such as Balzac, Dumas, Victor Hugo, Flaubert, Baudelaire, and Gérard de Nerval.

Gautier's account of a meeting of the *Club des Haschischins* (1846) is a classic of drug literature. The overpowering strength of the experiences he and others describe indicates how the effects of a drug may vary according to historic period and social context. The Haschischin experimenters took the drug in the form of a jam, *dawamesk*, administered at a tremendous dosage, and this massive ingestion, together with the ritualistic, deliberately bizarre setting, largely accounts for the violence of the reaction. "After some ten experiments we renounced once and for all this intoxicating drug," Gautier wrote, "not only because it made us physically ill, but also because the true littérateur has need only of natural dreams, and does not wish his thoughts to be influenced by any outside agency."

HASCHISCH

In 1846, Théophile Gautier published his account of a hashish séance at the Hotel Pimodan Paris, where "our circle met to take the 'dawamesk.'"

◎ Not more than half an hour had passed before I succumbed once more to the hashish. . . In an atmosphere of confused light, there fluttered a never-ending swarm of myriads of butterflies, their wings rustling like fans. Giant flowers with crystal cups, enormous hollyhocks, lilies of gold and silver, shot up and spread about me with detonations like those of fireworks. My sense of hearing had become abnormally acute. I could hear the very sounds of the colors. Sounds which were green, red, blue, or yellow, reached my ears in perfectly distinct waves. . . Sound, perfume, and light came to me through multitudes of channels as delicate as hairs through which I could hear the magnetic current whistling. According to my sense of time, this state lasted some three hundred years, for the sensations come in such numbers and so thickly that true appreciation of time was impossible. The attack passed, and I saw that it had lasted a quarter of an hour. ◎

FROM *THE CLUB OF ASSASSINS*,
BY THÉOPHILE GAUTIER (1846)

ALL THAT JAZZ

It seems very likely that cannabis is better suited to music than to words. Most people who have used cannabis report a higher sensitivity to sound. Many of the French *Haschischins* reported the phenomenon of synesthesia, the ability to "hear" colors, "see" sounds. As we have seen, this probably arises from stimulation of the locus ceruleus (see page 72), the funneling mechanism in the midbrain that brings together all types of sensory messages into a general excitation system in the brain. The emphasis on music may be significant. Music and cannabis "have the same frequency," according to some modern musicians. Part of the new music, the new frequencies that have happened in the last 20 years, particularly in so-called techno music, have been stimulated by smoking cannabis. For these musicians, cannabis is the drug of choice.

ABOVE **Louis Armstrong being greeted by fans on his arrival in Germany, 1952. He was a regular cannabis user, but steered clear of harder drugs which had destructive effects on many younger jazz musicians**.

Cannabis played an important part in the rise of jazz from its birthplace in New Orleans in the early years of this century; in fact the first leading musician to have been arrested for cannabis use was the jazz trumpeter Louis Armstrong (1901–1971), in 1930. The drug reached a wider public after World War Two, when it was publicized by the Beat writer Jack Kerouac (1922–1969), particularly in his *On the Road* (1957). This picaresque novel ranges from New York to New Orleans, Chicago, San Francisco, and back again, incorporating mythic elements, operating outside the normal range of experience, and flouting conventions. It is closely involved with jazz. The music that Kerouac particularly admired was bebop, a form of jazz more appreciated by artists than by dancers, and it was his intention to write like a jazz musician, with spontaneous improvisation and free flow.

Kerouac wrote very quickly and used "speed" (amphetamines) as well as marijuana. The poet Allen Ginsberg (1926–1997) declared that his finest works, such as *Dr. Sax,* were "written almost entirely on marijuana," while material written on speed tended to be more ragged. Ginsberg himself used a variety of drugs in his exploration of the "texture of consciousness," writing much of his most famous poem *Howl* under the influence of mescaline (peyote). The effect of the Beat generation of the postwar decades was to establish cannabis as the favorite drug for many musicians and music lovers, particularly in the field of jazz. Milton "Mezz" Mezzrow, the bebopper whose name became a slang synonym for high-quality marijuana, insisted that pot "puts a musician in a real masterly sphere, and that's why so many jazzmen have used it."

THE DOWNSIDE

Meanwhile, the exotic associations of cannabis resurfaced when the American novelist Paul Bowles (b. 1910) moved to Tangier in 1948, thus establishing a bridgehead for Western artists and writers who wished to break free from the stifling social and sexual conventions of the West. The English poet and novelist Christopher Isherwood (1904–1986) records in his diary a harrowing hashish experience with Bowles in 1955. "I'm fairly certain," Isherwood wrote in his diary, "that if I had taken the stuff among real friends, the effect would have been quite different. As it was, I saw myself now as a pretty wretched creature, scared, claustrophobic, utterly insecure . . . It was peculiarly unpleasant to feel my mind racing so fast. It made me horribly tired. And now it became more and more noticeable how slowly time was moving." Interestingly in view of the drug's associations with jazz, Isherwood's one consolation during this unpleasant experience was music, the sound of an Arab flute.

Despite his evident enthusiasm for hashish, even Charles Baudelaire (1821–1867) comes down firmly against it as an aid to creative activity. More eloquent and incisive than Gautier, Baudelaire, in *Les Paradis Artificiels* (1860), gives a graphic but critical description of the drug. "It is the willpower that is attacked," he points out, "and that is the most precious organ. No man who with a spoonful of conserve is able to procure instantly all the treasures of heaven and earth will bother to acquire the thousandth part of it by means of work. The primary task is to live and work." Like Coleridge with opium, Baudelaire identifies hashish as an enemy of the will, and therefore of the artist.

> First of all a kind of preposterous and irresistible hilarity takes possession of you. . . [then] the hallucinations begin. External objects assume monstrous forms... The most singular ambiguities, the most inexplicable transpositions of thought take place. The sounds are colored, the colors heard as music. . . From time to time your personality vanishes. The sense of objectivity that creates certain pantheistical poets and great actors becomes so powerful that you are confounded with external objects. . . Soon the very idea of time will disappear. Occasionally a brief interval of lucidity will supervene... [But] I defy you to cut a pen or sharpen a pencil; that would be a task above your strength.

CHARLES BAUDELAIRE

HEROIN

Among the many artists attracted to Tangier by drugs and gay sex was the American Beat novelist William Burroughs (1914–1997). As postwar uncertainty yielded to the threatening atmosphere of the Cold War, heroin offered a harder alternative reality, and Burroughs was its chief voice. His *Naked Lunch* (1959) is a hymn of disgust, simultaneously violently ugly and irresistibly powerful. "I am trying to write something that will have a life of its own," he told Ginsberg, "something that will put me in real danger—a danger I willingly take on myself." The apocalyptic world described by Burroughs is full of cruelty and sensuality, governed by a series of huge media conspiracies. He depicts a world consisting of those who control and manipulate, and those who submit. Addiction can be a compulsion to submission as well as a compulsion to control. It is addiction itself that is the enemy, and junk is its means of infection.

An important effect of heroin's reduction of anxiety is its separation of the individual from the outside world. The user becomes involved with an absorbing alternative lifestyle that is as much social as pharmacological. It is the social rather than any supposedly creative aspect of heroin that is described so vividly in books such as Irvine Welsh's *Trainspotting*. According to American scholar Avital Ronell, "the addict is the non-renouncer." Paraphrasing Freud, she points out that addicts don't know how to mourn, how to get rid of their feelings. The heroin lifestyle takes over, extending into the ordinary world of speech and communication like Burrough's "evil virus." Heroin doesn't shut down expressive power but narrows it to a self-destructive point where the addiction is defined as the person, not the product. Jung believed that "every form of addiction is bad, no matter whether the narcotic be alcohol or morphine or idealism." Auden made a connection between addiction and the religious concept of sin. "All sin tends to be addictive," he wrote, "and the terminal point of addiction is what is called damnation."

> Specific to heroin is the modern concept of the trash body—something that is excremental, corruptible in its mutability, not idealized, not subservient to a notion of spirit or any sort of superior consciousness.
>
> AVITAL RONELL

> Junk is the mold of monopoly and possession, the ultimate merchandise. No sales talk is necessary. The client will crawl through a sewer and beg to buy. The junk merchant does not sell his product to the consumer, he sells the consumer to the product. He degrades and simplifies the client. Junk yields the basic formula of evil virus.
>
> WILLIAM BURROUGHS

BELOW **William Burroughs (left) with poet and fellow-Beat guru Allen Ginsberg.**

BENDING THE MIND

Psychotropic drugs were of course very familiar to pre-Western shamanic societies. Among the tribal cultures scattered across Siberia, Scandinavia, and Finland, the fly agaric (*Amanita muscaria*) was the sacred fungus that enabled shamans to achieve ecstasy, empowering them to carry out their task of mediating between the human and the supernatural worlds. Can it simply be coincidental that the toadstool inhabited by "little people" that appears in countless traditional fairy tales is always depicted as a red-and-white fly agaric?

ABOVE **Alice, rather shyly: "I know who I was when I got up this morning, but I think I must have been changed several times since then."**

Mushrooms and toadstools have played a creative role in the mythology and folklore of many cultures, from the pre-Christian stories of Grimm to the mushroom of the hookah-smoking caterpillar in Carroll's *Alice in Wonderland*.

MAGIC MUSHROOMS

The Central American cult of *teonanacatl* (the divine mushroom *Psilocybe*) was researched in the 1950s by Gordon and Valentina Wasson, who traced the cult back to 1000 BCE. They described how they were invited by the shaman Maria Sabina to partake of the love feast of the sacred mushrooms, the Nahua "cult of God's flesh." Maria Sabina, who also belonged to the Sisterhood of the Sacred Heart of Jesus, was both Mazatec shaman and Catholic Christian, and she, together with her people, saw "the saint children" as the body and blood of Christ. Wasson introduced Robert Graves to the drug in 1960, and the poet was profoundly moved, claiming that he had "eaten the food of the gods."

Nevertheless, a formidable cultural gulf divides Western people, however well-meaning, from the worldview of shamans like Maria Sabina. "Before Wasson," Sabina said, "I felt that the saint children—elevated me. I don't feel like that anymore. The force has diminished." In the words of her older colleague, Apolonia Terran, "What is terrible is that the sacred mushrooms no longer belong to us. The language has been spoiled and is indecipherable to us . . . Now the mushrooms speak English!"

BELOW **A Mazatec shaman, holding *Psilocybe* mushrooms, which are used in healing rituals as well as being a means of achieving visionary states.**

Huxley's described what he called "the beatific vision," which he saw in a bowl of flowers. It is unlikely that a traditional shaman would have such an experience. "The little mushroom spirits are spirits of the Holy Earth," says a Mexican shaman. "They take me to the ancestors. . . And if I ask them why this man or woman is ill, or whatever it is one wishes to know, the mushroom spirits will tell me."

PEYOTE AND MESCALINE

The cactus peyote with its active ingredient mescaline has been used as a religious communion by shamans, notably those of the North American Huichol people, for centuries. In its synthetic form of mescaline, the drug became known to the West through the work of the English writer Aldous Huxley (1894–1963), especially *The Doors of Perception* (1954). The poor-sighted Huxley's lifelong search for inner vision culminated in the amazing perceptual and spiritual experiences described there. He concluded, in an insight that anticipated modern neuroscience, that the function of the sensory system was to exclude and eliminate material rather than to produce it, and that a much vaster "Mind at Large" had to be funneled through the "reducing valve" of the brain and nervous system. In fact, the active ingredient of peyote, mescaline, affects the neurotransmitter serotonin, enabling the brain to be bombarded with normally excluded visual, tactile, and even auditory input.

ABOVE **The Huichol Indians of central Mexico have long made use of the peyote cactus for its hallucinogenic properties, granting it a religious status.**

[Plato] could never, poor fellow, have seen a bunch of flowers shining with their own inner light and all but quivering under the pressure of the significance with which they were charged; could never have perceived that what rose and iris and carnation so intensely signified was nothing more, and nothing less, than what they were—a transience that was yet eternal life, a perpetual perishing that was at the same time pure Being, a bundle of minute, unique particulars in which, by some unspeakable and yet self-evident paradox, was to be seen the divine source of all existence.

I continued to look at the flowers, and in their living light I seemed to detect the qualitative equivalent of breathing—but of a breathing without returns to a starting point, with no recurrent ebbs but only a repeated flow from beauty to heightened beauty, from deeper to ever deeper meaning.

FROM THE DOORS OF PERCEPTION,
BY ALDOUS HUXLEY (1954)

ACID TRIPPING

Lysergic acid (LSD), a component of the mold of ergot (a fungus that forms on rye grain), was synthesized in Switzerland in 1938 and is probably the most powerful psychotropic drug known to humankind. Huxley encountered acid in 1955, and it was on his advice that the high priest of psychedelics, the American researcher Timothy Leary (1920–1996), first took a trip. Acid was not difficult to manufacture, and very soon reached a much wider public than any previous psychedelic drug. In the 1960s LSD use was widespread among people who sought to alter and intensify their perceptual experience, to achieve insights into the universe and themselves, and to deepen emotional connections with others.

Leary identified phases of the psychedelic experience with the Bardo stages of consciousness outlined in the *Tibetan Book of the Dead*, from "complete transcendence" to "routine game reality," and indeed the arrival of LSD coincided with a surge of interest in mystical and esoteric subjects. The rock world was particularly affected, with such musicians as the Beatles and Santana commanding great influence. For many young people, taking a trip was seen as a way of achieving a "peak experience"—the moment of almost mystical joy and affirmation which the psychologist Abraham Maslow has identified as part of a healthy personality, seeing it as the creative resource recharging the individual's psychic battery. Maslow believed that these experiences of bubbling happiness were not mystical but indicated "higher ceilings of human nature."

ABOVE **Psychedelic guru Timothy Leary in his heyday. He was a clinical psychologist at Harvard, but was fired in 1963.**

BELOW **The Golden Age of the Maharishi: Jane Asher and Mia Farrow, Donovan, assorted Beatles. . . Drugs, music, and meditation, the over-rich cocktail of late sixties culture.**

Despite its power and popularity, LSD's importance for creative activity is problematic. There is no doubt that the 1960s and early 1970s were an immensely productive time in creative terms in the West, fusing mass media and "high" cultural products in a rich banquet, from the novels of Kurt Vonnegut, Jr. to the music of Jimi Hendrix. The acid-fueled multimedia excursions of Ken Kesey and others caught the imagination. There was a feeling that acid was going to energize some creative breakthrough; but it never happened. The acid experience was very different from sitting down for a year to write a novel. When Leary was asked shortly before his death whether LSD could make one creative, he answered, "We have to distinguish between the experience, a new experience—and whether you can communicate the experience. That's where the artistry comes."

BELOW **Jimi Hendrix was one of the demigods of the sixties musical efflorescence which was enhanced, though perhaps not produced, by LSD.**

Whether joyful or dark, the drug vision can be astonishing, but eventually. . . the magic show grows boring. . . Drugs can clear away the past, enhance the present; toward the inner garden, they can only point the way. Lacking the temper of ascetic discipline, the drug vision remains a sort of dream that cannot be brought over into daily life. Old mists may be banished. . . but the alien chemical agent forms another mist, maintaining the separation of the "I" from the true experience of the One.

PETER MATTHIESSEN

TAKING A TRIP

In 1943 Dr. Albert Hofmann, the Swiss chemist who discovered lysergic acid, became the first person to take an LSD trip. In 1996 he summarized his thoughts on the subject.

◎ **With lysergic acid diethylamide (LSD) I hoped to obtain a novel, improved circulatory stimulant. The first synthesis. . . appeared to be pharmacologically uninteresting, and underwent no further tests. Yet five years later, the idea came to me in a strange way, again to synthesize lysergic acid diethylamide for further pharmacological testing. . . At the conclusion of the synthesis, I was overtaken by a very weird state of consciousness, which today one might call "psychedelic." A trace of the substance must accidentally have entered my body, probably during the purification via recrystallization. In order to test this supposition, I made the first planned self-experiment with LSD three days later, on April 19, 1943. . .**

Considering the discovery of LSD in the context of other significant discoveries of our time in the medicinal and technical field, one might arrive at the notion that LSD did not come into the world accidentally, but was rather evoked in the scope of some higher plan. . . LSD might have been predestined by some higher power to arise precisely at the time when the predominance of materialism with all its consequences over the past 100 years was being understood. LSD as an enlightening psychopharmakon along the path to a new, spiritual age! All of which could suggest that my decisions on arriving at the guiding "switch-points" which have led to LSD, were not really undertaken through exercise of free will, but rather steered by the subconscious, through which we are all connected with the universal, transpersonal consciousness. ◎

FROM "LSD: COMPLETELY PERSONAL," A SPEECH DELIVERED TO
THE 1996 WORLDS OF CONSCIOUSNESS CONFERENCE IN HEIDELBERG

LEFT **Ken Kesey and the Merry Pranksters, 1966. Kesey's reputation as a novelist derived from** *One Flew Over the Cuckoo's Nest* **(1962). His later interest in LSD was part of the fun-seeking creative surge of the 1960s.**

LET'S GO FASTER:
COCAINE AND AMPHETAMINES

Cocaine, an alkaloid obtained from leaves of the South American coca plant, was first isolated in 1855. Among the earliest investigators of pure cocaine was Sigmund Freud, who in 1884 had read about the effects of coca leaves on Peruvian Indians. Experimenting with the drug, he discovered the sensations that had been known to South American Indians for millennia: feelings of euphoria, alertness, energy, and lack of appetite for food.

Freud conducted a number of experimental studies on cocaine. His article on the subject observed that "cocaine brings about an exhilaration and lasting euphoria which in no way differs from the normal euphoria of the healthy person... You perceive an increase of self control and possess more vitality and capacity for work... Long intensive mental or physical work is performed without any fatigue... The result is enjoyed without any of the unpleasant aftereffects that follow exhilaration brought about by alcohol."

RIGHT **Sherlock Holmes, famous cocaine addict despite the ministrations of his friend Dr. Watson. Holmes' powers of deduction remained unimpaired.**

Freud's work was enthusiastically received, and cocaine began to be used for a number of applications until its deleterious effects became apparent. As the cases of addiction and paranoid psychosis increased, the medical world turned against Freud and he was harshly criticized. Nevertheless, the effect of cocaine, the empowering sensation which it confers, its ability to enhance faculties needed in everyday life, ensured its clandestine popularity. Sherlock Holmes, the super-detective creation of British author Arthur Conan Doyle (1859–1930), was a frequent user, to the extent that his forearm and wrist were "all dotted and scarred with innumerable puncture marks."

Another known user of cocaine was the American animator Walt Disney (1901–1966). Disney's work has probably reached more people in the West than that of any other artist, though Disney usually acted as the producer and story editor, rather than as an artist. Cocaine may or may not have assisted him in his business decisions, but its contribution to his creativity is not clear.

CHARLIE AND
THE CITY SLICKERS

Cocaine became known as the drug of the 1980s, a not conspicuously creative period. The drug's confidence-boosting, energizing qualities made it the drug of choice for the generation of fashionably selfish young people of the Thatcher-Reagan ascendancy. Writers like Jay McInerney were able to exploit or to celebrate this atmosphere of nihilistic hedonism in such books as *Bright Lights, Big City*, where the intake of "Bolivian marching powder" assumes industrial proportions. Many city users claimed to get the same buzz out of work that they did out of cocaine.

However, it was less popular among creatives than businessmen—who now themselves assumed the title of creativity ("creative accounting" became a popular term at this time). The American

author Robert Stone observed: "It certainly supplies you with a great deal of energy, so you can do a lot of sustained work. It keeps you from wandering off, concentrates the mind." But after a while users begin to lose contact with their lives, a kind of derangement that forces them back to the drug. "The thing is solipsistic," says Stone. "It's about itself. It makes writers verbose and prolix, overloaded and frantic, too long. So I would hope that cocaine hasn't influenced my work at all."

AMPHETAMINES AND DESIGNER DRUGS

After World War Two, amphetamines such as benzedrine became very popular in the West. Synthetic stimulants that act on the central nervous system to increase alertness and lower fatigue, they were traditionally used by students to cram for exams, but soon reached a far wider public. As aids to sustained, concentrated work, they held obvious attraction for creatives of all kinds. Two American writers who used amphetamines heavily in their work were Jack Kerouac and the science fiction writer Philip K. Dick (1928–1982). Dick, whose extraordinary vision is apparent in the film *Blade Runner* (from the short story "Do Androids Dream of Electric Sheep?"), was burdened with financial commitments that necessitated intense productivity, but he clearly enjoyed writing his books fast. The fragmentary, almost expendable nature of his writing could well be an effect of taking speed,

but this "speedy" style, careless and hectic, accurately reflects his subject matter. In Kerouac's case the effect of speed is more clearly harmful. Ginsberg has adversely contrasted *Subterraneans*, a book written mostly on speed, with the "exquisite prose" of the marijuana-driven *Dr. Sax*.

An aid to concentration rather than inspiration, amphetamines are also of interest because they anticipate the modern trend toward the designer drug—chemicals put together for specific psychotropic functions. The most spectacular of these is MDMA, or Ecstasy, which contains amphetamines among other ingredients. According to the American author Bruce Eisner, Ecstasy, which is used by millions, is the first of a new generation of mind-changing substances designed to transform personal relationships and boost self-esteem. The drug is said to open people up to their intuition and feelings, leading to an expanded sense of self-awareness and empathy for others. The phenomenon of techno or rave music, which began in the late 1980s, is closely related to Ecstasy, and the creativity of the movement owes much to the drug. Increasingly assisted by other drugs, Ecstasy enables its users to dance for hours, merging their identities in a larger reality dominated by a range of sounds, rhythms, and pulses that lock them into a shared, joyful unity. This merging of identity in a great dance suggests that Ecstasy is unfavorable to the stubborn individualism of the dedicated creative artist. It seems rather to resonate with the communal creativity of dance and music practiced by earlier societies.

Yet, in another way, Ecstasy too is part of the current compartmentalization and commodification of society. The sense of togetherness is available in tablet form, but only for the duration of the high. Then it's back to work as usual. Designer drugs may be concocted to induce creativity, but induced creativity is not the same as the natural kind.

CREATIVITY NOW

13

Making money is art and working is art and good business is the best art.

ANDY WARHOL

BRAVE NEW WORLD

Recent interest in the concept of creativity among cognitive scientists and psychologists has had its popular counterpart in a spate of books on the subject. Creativity, the ability to use one's imagination to produce something new and valuable, has now become not only a desirable gift, but also a marketable resource that can be developed by reading the right manuals. In such works as Jordan E. Ayan's *Aha!: 10 Ways to Free Your Creative Spirit and Find Your Great Ideas* (1996), creativity is seen as a skill to be cultivated, a source of energy that "fuels innovation and success in every endeavor: business, personal, artistic, communal, and entrepreneurial." Strategies are suggested for harnessing inspiration and assembling the "building blocks of a more creative and rewarding life." Creativity is seen as a technique to be acquired. "The future belongs to those who create it."

Others, such as the author Julia Cameron in her impressive *The Artist's Way* (1991), adopt a more spiritual approach, maintaining that creative expression is the natural direction of life, a constantly emerging self overlaid by limiting beliefs, self-sabotage, inattention, fear, jealousy, guilt, addictions, and other inhibiting forces. Cameron's fundamental technique of "morning pages"—a kind of free-form journal-making to

No one has ever written, painted, sculpted, modeled, built, or invented except literally to get out of hell.

ANTONIN ARTAUD

unravel thoughts and feelings, to focus energy, and to direct action—has proved very effective for many of those who have tried it. Nevertheless, accessing creativity by means of such techniques may seem a brash and problematic approach to something that some secretly believe should remain elusive and mysterious.

But although art involves creativity, creativity does not perhaps involve art. Self-creation, the personal creation of the self, is seen by Jungians and many others as an essential, meaningful, and lifelong vocation. Moreover, as the American art critic Harold Rosenberg wrote, "Whoever undertakes to create soon finds himself engaged in creating himself. Self-transformation and the transformation of others have constituted the radical interest of our century."

On the other hand, while a desire to fulfill one's creative potential is in one sense the purpose of life, the present fascination with "personal" creativity and its development may equally well be seen as a symptom of the fragmentation of society, whereby the individual is simultaneously idealized and disempowered. The Greek author Arianna Stassinopoulos is perhaps right to say, "Our current obsession with creativity is the result of our continued striving for immortality in an era when most people no longer believe in an after-life."

REPLICATION AND DECONSTRUCTION

Imagination bridges inner and outer reality. Open-ended, potential, extending beyond the confines of reason, imagination has long been seen as the key to creative life, on both the personal and the cultural level. But Keats' belief that "what the imagination seizes as beauty must be truth—whether it existed before or not," finds little resonance in the present mass-media age. In fact the concept of imagination itself is under attack in the postmodern Western world, where the creative humanist imagination has been replaced by a depersonalized consumer system of pseudoimages. We live in an age where reality is hard to separate from the image, where the original has been replaced by its imitation, where understanding of the world is preconditioned by the electronically reproducible media of television, cinema, video, and radio. Through these media every live event or performance is capable of being mechanically recorded and retransmitted endlessly. There is no longer a clear-cut distinction between the original and the representation. It is said that superbly executed electronic reproductions of masterpieces adorn the home of Microsoft mogul Bill Gates, the world's richest man.

Originality is one half of the creative equation—the other half being social validation. But in our mass-media age the very notion of originality comes under threat. The idea that the "original work" could be replaceable by the reproducible copy was suggested as long ago as the 1930s by the German critic Walter Benjamin (1892–1940). Benjamin predicted that the new age of mass reproduction and technological communications would threaten the traditional practices of imaginative creation, and our "ability to exchange experiences." In discussing creativity Benjamin distinguished between the "symbol" and the "allegory." The symbol is the original creative object which carries an "aura" of mystery and depth, a humanizing influence that invites us to experience the created object as unique, whole, and original. Allegory, by contrast, may be said to typify the reproducible object, representing a fragmented and impersonalized thing-world where the very idea of the autonomous image is meaningless. The pioneer of postmodernism, Andy Warhol, was unimpressed by the news that Picasso had produced 4,000 paintings in his life. "I can do as many in 24 hours," he said. "Four thousand works which will all be the same work and all of them masterpieces." Thus the idea of a unique imagination producing a unique object degenerates into a play of infinite repetition.

BELOW **Left to right: Joseph Beuys, Andy Warhol, Robert Rauschenberg, a triumvirate of art's Bad Boys, specialists in querying the very nature of art.**

I'LL BE YOUR MIRROR...

Postmodernism deconstructs the modernist worldview to lay bare its constituent parts and fundamental assumptions. It seeks to neutralize the ingredients necessary for this worldview, including God, self, purpose, meaning, a real world, and truth. The postmodern critique dethrones the absolute and

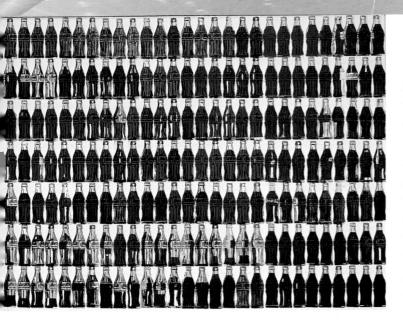

the individual as two Western myths, formulated in the Middle Ages and modernity respectively. Thus expressions of individuality, such as authorship, originality, and innovativeness, are discounted along with those of the absolute, involving ideas of the transcendental, truth, and reality. Originally an architectural movement, postmodernism is now the cultural correlative of our current Age of Information. Postmodernism uses parody and pastiche as basic themes, effacing the dividing line between high culture and mass culture. Postmodernists, according to the critic Fredric Jameson, have been fascinated by this whole "degraded" landscape of kitsch, of TV serials and quiz games, advertising, motels, and airport literature.

ABOVE *210 Coca-Cola Bottles* (1962) by Andy Warhol. Warhol always kept a strong commercial grip on the Muse. "Being good in business is the most fascinating kind of art."

Aesthetic production in our society has become integrated into commodity production generally. Warhol and other Pop artists have stressed this commodification in their work. Their billboard images of Coca-Cola bottles or Campbell's soup cans appear at first sight to be powerful and critical statements. But modern society's commercial culture has shown that it is easily able to neutralize the power of art to subvert and oppose. Thus, while modernist art prided itself on its ability to negate the established view of things, postmodernism seeks to mock it, and perhaps even to celebrate it. Warhol's conflation of art and commerce ("Business art. Art business") led the way for the modern generation of artist-businessmen, ironic entrepreneurs who simultaneously mock and exploit their trade. "How may we ever hope to escape the endless self-parodying of postmodernism, which announces the 'end' of everything but itself?" asks American philosopher Richard Kearney. "And if postmodernism subverts the very opposition between the imaginary and the real, to the point where each dissolves into an empty imitation of the other, can we still speak of imagination at all? . . . Has the very notion of a postmodern imagination become a contradiction in terms?"

In contrast to those who see postmodernism as, in Warhol's phrase, "'a mirror reflecting itself," others stress a more positive aspect. Much postmodern thought is concerned with the possibility that humankind is standing on the threshold of a new age. The postmodern is deliberately elusive as a concept, avoiding as much as possible the modernist desire to classify and thereby delimit, bound, and confine. While modernism seeks closure in form and is concerned with conclusions, postmodernism is open, unbounded, and concerned with process and "becoming." This refusal to acknowledge the old labels and concepts may be a necessary break with the past in order to be open to the future—the first stage in the altered state of creativity. Repetition and reiteration may give rise to new forms, from Mandelbrot fractals to techno music, which point the way forward to a different perception of the world and our place in it. Over time, postmodernism itself may be perceived as a first, inadequate reaction to this aesthetics of repetition.

CREATIVITY AND REPETITION

Repetition significantly affects consciousness. It is routinely used in inducing trance, especially when connected with rhythm. Many traditional styles of music develop repetitively from a simple core beat, with continuously repeated patterns containing an increasing complexity of variations in mood and rhythm. Dancing to sound organized in this way, usually in combination with a variety of drugs, has become the preferred mode of recreation, if not lifestyle, for millions of people in the West—the so-called "House" phenomenon.

Repetition is also found in concert music, for instance in the work of the American composer Philip Glass (b. 1937), which is built around a very few musical phrases repeated over and over with slight changes in pattern and rhythm. Glass' compatriot Steve Reich (b. 1936), one of the pioneers of minimalism, had lessons on the Ghanaian drums and Balinese gamelan in the early 1970s, and these experiences clearly helped shape his distinctive style.

The idea of a seed pattern giving form to an emergent reality through endless repetition recalls the *nada* (sound) and *bindu* (point) of Tantra, especially in the Sri Yantra. It is also the basis of the computer art that is derived from fractals. This consists of putting one or two points on the screen as a seed for a pattern, imposing on the seed a simple set of rules expressed in a few symbols, and just letting the computer run on until a great complexity emerges.

FRACTALS

Fractals are formally defined as geometric figures that have a "broken dimension." They are part of a branch of mathematics concerned with the way extremely complex shapes are generated by rather simple equations. In the 1970s, the Polish-born mathematician Benoit Mandelbrot (b. 1924) discovered that a new geometry could be derived from basic mathematical relationships (fractals), which, when programmed to repeat again and again through the computer, became elaborated into unexpected shapes that have the richness and complexity of natural forms. These have become known as Mandelbrot sets.

Fractals occur in many forms—for instance in the configurations of fluid mechanics—thus affecting even such unconscious processes as the random Action Paintings of Jackson Pollock. Throwing paint at random, Mandelbrot has pointed out, would result in a distribution that followed the fractal-rich rules of turbulence and of fluid mechanics. In fact fractals appear to be relevant to morphogenesis of many kinds, from the growth of plants and animals to the evolution of the universe, and they involve the production of very beautiful, very complex images on computer screens. Euclidean geometry cannot capture the shapes of what we see in nature—trees, clouds, and so on—while fractal geometry can. And therefore it provides a key to nature in a way that no previous geometry has achieved. Very complicated structures can be developed from a very simple formula: multiply, add, and repeat endlessly.

Another important property of fractals is that they are self-similar. This means that the entire fractal is duplicated in itself. A fractal image is obtained from a graphic object to which a certain transformation has been applied that adds an element of complexity; then the same transformation is applied to the new object obtained, which increases its complexity even more, and this iterating process is reproduced to the infinite. The repetitive magic of Islamic tiles is a cogent expression of the power of repetition.

LEFT **Fractal art. Repetition and variation are fundamentals in art, and the development of patterns has endless scope and fascination.**

There is also self-similarity in nature; each part is similar to the whole, the whole is similar to each part of itself. The fractal is therefore reminiscent in its general structure to the structure of the universe, the fabric of the universe which we see around us, and of which we ourselves are part. Mandelbrot's intuition suggests that there is a sameness of structure underlying the world, echoing Blake's vision of "a World in a grain of sand."

The mystery of number colludes with the mystery of nature. An illustration in a medieval Bible shows God as a mathematician, employing familiar geometric shapes but also dealing with what Mandelbrot calls "the wiggles"—natural forms, which are now apparent in Mandelbrot sets. Many mathematicians have been imaginative artists deeply concerned about beauty. But until now the abstract formulas concealed this beauty from nonmathematicians. Fractals present geometry to the senses, making the abstractly beautiful math visible in sensory form. The fiercely reductionist English scientist Peter Atkins has claimed that "these Mandelbrot sets create a resonance between what I see and my inner soul (which I haven't got)."

The art historian Peter Fuller has suggested that the traditional idea of the decorative is somehow deeply involved in our quest to understand and represent ultimate reality. This is exemplified particularly in communal art in traditional societies, but also in the work of Matisse. Decorative art of this kind describes the underlying patterns out of which we and it are made. In the biology of the imagination, the biological basis of art, one can perhaps see a continuity between the decorative images we take delight in and the structures with which we are ourselves constructed, and which have the same kind of "decorative" forms.

CREATIVITY AND THE
INFORMATION REVOLUTION

The tendency of the mass media is to centralize and concentrate, reducing the public to a passive (and paying) audience. However, the emergence of the Internet appears, for the present at least, to suggest a strong counteractive force, a kind of democratization of knowledge. The Internet—a global, online computer network that connects individuals, governments, companies, universities, and many other networks and users—offers electronic mail, conferencing, and chat services, as well as the ability to access remote computers and send and retrieve files. Initiated in 1984, it is estimated that this global "brain" will have 500 million users by the end of the millennium. The wealth of information made freely available on this global electronic network had increased so much by the early 1990s that a host of indexing and search services sprang up to answer user demand, notably the World-Wide Web. The ease of use of the Web has led to a prodigious expansion of the Internet. Its inventor, the English scientist Tim Berners-

BELOW **The virtual realm of cyberspace is the Greek symposium updated to the twenty-first century, bringing all the world together in one place.**

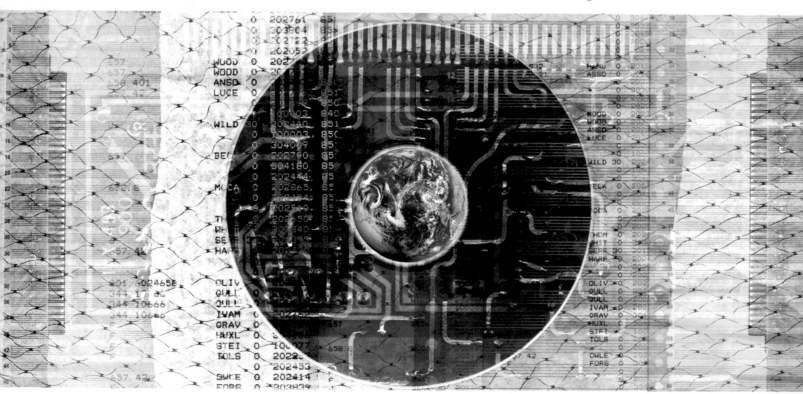

> Now, we will have to find how best to integrate our warm fuzzy right-brain selves into this clearly defined left-brain world. After seeding the semantic Web with specific applications, we must leave it clean and simple so that the next generation can learn its logical concepts along with the alphabet. If we can make something decentralized, out of control, and of great simplicity, we must be prepared to be astonished at whatever might grow out of that new medium... We are forming cells within a global brain and we are excited that we might start to think collectively. What becomes of us still hangs crucially on how we think individually.
>
> TIM BERNERS-LEE

Lee, has said that he wants the Web to be "much more creative than it is at the moment." He has a vision of "inter-creativity"—building things together on the Web. The first phase of the Web is human communication through shared knowledge. The second aspect of the Web, yet to emerge, is that of machine-understandable information, where the day-to-day mechanisms of trade and bureaucracy will be handled by electronic agents, leaving humans to provide the inspiration and the intuition.

It seems inevitable that our consciousness is being modified as contact grows between the human brain and computers, and the virtual spaces generated by them. Many people already prefer to see a football game on television rather than going to the stadium. As virtual reality becomes increasingly sophisticated this trend is likely to increase. Will virtual reality take over, or is neuroscientist Rodolfo Llinás right to say, "At the end the 'real' reality will win, because a virtual meal is not the same thing as a real one!"

As long ago as 1984 the Canadian novelist William Gibson predicted the transformative power of the Internet in his science fiction novel *Neuromancer*, when he created the "consensual hallucination" of Cyberspace, the "place where banks keep their money." Gibson's powerfully conceived vision of the near future, depicting a fragmented, technological dystopia, is both persuasive and unattractive. It assumes world dominance by conglomerates, and the replacement of traditional politics by global mergers between big business, the state, and organized crime (themes that also appear in the original cyberpunk movie, *Blade Runner*). In Gibson's trilogy *Neuromancer*, *Count Zero*, and *Mona Lisa Overdrive*, hackers and data thieves represent the only opposition to informational totalitarianism.

RIGHT **Trapped in the machine? The Internet is either the greatest facilitator of shared creativity ever invented, or the death knell of the social interactions that nourish all art. Take your pick.**

AND IN THE END...

Can a computer be creative? For as long as the characteristics of play and wonder are agreed to be part of the definition of creativity, the answer has to be "No." It is the visceral quality of creativity, its ability to communicate at a level of emotion as well as intelligence, its allegiance to both an inner and outer reality, that make it so important in the continuous evolution of humanity. No doubt, in the narrower definition of creativity as producing something new and useful, computers will play an increasing and probably dominant part in our world. But creativity in its fullest sense involves emotional and irrational operations that no amount of "metadata" can simulate.

Creativity may extend beyond the central nervous system altogether. The study of "muscle memory" concerns the way that, with the acquisition of new abilities such as sports or music, new information is programmed and locked into our muscles as well as in the brain. Some scientists even think that our whole body is part of the memory system, with each cell able to accept information and discard old outdated information. Whether or not this is true, the fact remains that very many different neural systems must deal with a single "seed pattern" of experience, and at very many levels. What distinguishes creatives is the way they deal with this multiple iteration of sometimes conflicting information.

The REM-on neural network that controls dreaming lies in the midbrain, the so-called reptilian brain. Beyond these portals of REM-on and REM-off—like the ancients' dream Gates of Ivory and Gates of Horn—lies a world of experience that the brain struggles to make sense of. This is the nature we share with other animals, and perhaps with the rest of life. The importance of the coyote "trickster" of the shamans' world, the wondrous, ludic force with its transformative powers, was identified both by Carlos Castaneda and Joseph Beuys (see page 22). In its European form of the fox, this most enigmatic of spirit allies also appears as the inspirational power in the work of one of the greatest twentieth-century English poets, Ted Hughes (1930–1998). It was a fox that visited Hughes in a dream-vision when he was a student, confirming him in his poetic vocation. Creative people pay attention to the signals that emanate from this imaginative hinterland, and the more passionate their attention the greater their involvement.

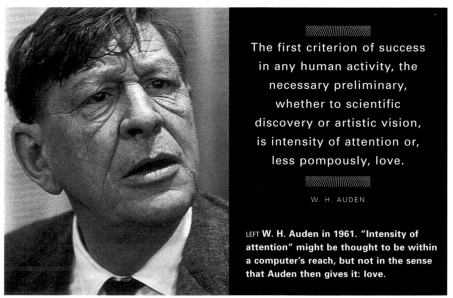

The first criterion of success in any human activity, the necessary preliminary, whether to scientific discovery or artistic vision, is intensity of attention or, less pompously, love.

W. H. AUDEN

LEFT **W. H. Auden in 1961. "Intensity of attention" might be thought to be within a computer's reach, but not in the sense that Auden then gives it: love.**

DREAMING WITH OPEN EYES

Literary critic Al Alvarez wrote in the *Observer* (November 2, 1998) after the death of the poet Ted Hughes:

◎ [Ted Hughes] read English when he went up to Cambridge, then switched to anthropology. . . because of a dream which he told me soon after we first met, wryly, almost as a joke against himself. He was laboring late at night, he said, on his weekly essay—I think it was about Dr. Johnson—bored by it and getting nowhere. Finally he gave up and went to bed. That night, he dreamt a fox came into his college room, went over to his desk, peered at the unfinished essay and shook its head in disgust. Then it placed a paw on the scribbled pages and they burst into flame. The next day, Hughes wrote a poem about the dream—"The Thought-Fox"—and left it on his desk when he went to bed.

The same night, the dream-fox was back. It read the poem, nodded approvingly, and gave the sleeping poet a genial thumbs-up. Hughes took the visitation as a sign. The academic study of literature wasn't for him; it was time to change his life as well as his degree course. Anthropology may not altogether have been what he was after, but at least it concerned itself with more primitive and instinctual societies than our own.

What matters most about the story is that the dream came when he needed it and he was able to listen to what it was telling him. And that is what set Hughes apart from most young poets of his generation: he seemed to have easy, immediate access to his sources of inspiration, a permanently open hotline to his unconscious. ◎

THE THOUGHT-FOX

I imagine this midnight moment's forest:
Something else is alive
Beside the clock's loneliness
And this blank page where my fingers move.

Through the window I see no star:
Something more near
Though deeper within darkness
Is entering the loneliness:

Cold, delicately as the dark snow
Between trees, and warily a lame
Shadow lags by stump and in hollow
Of a body that is bold to come

Across the clearings, an eye,
A widening deepening greenness
Brilliantly, concentratedly,
Coming about its own business

Till, with a sudden sharp hot stink of fox
It enters the dark hole of the head.
The window is starless still; the clock ticks,
The page is printed.

TED HUGHES
SELECTED POEMS (1972)

BIBLIOGRAPHY

Amabile, Teresa M., Mary Ann Collins, Regina Conti, and Elise Phillips. *Creativity in Context: Update to the Social Psychology of Creativity*. Boulder, CO: Westview Press, 1996.

Albunin, Joseph. 'Creativity and Education', in *Journal of Aesthetic Education*, 1981.

Barron, Frank X. *Artists in the Making*. New York: Seminar Press, 1972.

Barron, Frank X., Alfonso Montuori, and Anthea Barron (eds.). *Creators on Creating*. New York: Putnam Publishing, 1997.

Barth, Diane. *Daydreaming: Unlock the Creative Power of Your Mind*. New York: Viking Penguin, 1997.

Baudelaire, Charles. *Les Paradis artificiels: oeuvres complètes de Charles Baudelaire*. Paris, 1928.

Bell, Quentin. *A Biography of Virginia Woolf*. London: Hogarth Press, 1972.

Benjamin, Walter. *Illuminations*. New York: Schocken Books, 1970.

Berger, John. *About Looking*. London: Writers and Readers, 1980.

Bettelheim, Bruno. *Children of the Dream*. London: Thames & Hudson, 1969.

Beyond Reason. Art and Psychosis: Works from the Prinzhorn Collection. Hayward Gallery Catalogue, London, 1997.

Boden, Margaret (ed.). *Dimensions of Creativity*. Cambridge, MA: MIT Press, 1994.

Boorstin, Daniel J. *The Creators: A History of Heroes of the Imagination*. New York: Random House, 1992.

Bowman, Isa. *Lewis Carroll as I Knew Him*. London: Dent, 1899.

Calasso, Roberto. *The Marriage of Cadmus and Harmony*. Trans. Tim Parks. London: Vintage, 1994.

Castaneda, C. *The Teachings of Don Juan*. Berkeley, CA: University of California Press, 1968.

Castaneda, C. *Tales of Power*. New York: Simon & Schuster, 1974.

Cameron, Julia. *The Artist's Way*. London: Souvenir Press, 1992.

Campbell, Joseph. *The Masks of God: Primitive Mythology*. New York: Viking Press, 1972.

Campbell, Joseph (ed.). *Myths, Dreams, and Religion*. New York: Dutton, 1970.

Cocteau, Jean. *Opium*. Paris, 1930.

Coxhead, David, and Susan Hiller. *Dreams: Visions of the Night*. London: Thames & Hudson, 1981.

Csikszentmihalyi, Mihaly. *Creativity: Flow and the Psychology of Discovery and Invention*. New York: HarperCollins, 1997.

De Quincey, Thomas. *Confessions of an English Opium Eater*. London, 1821.

Diamond, Stephen A., and Rollo May. *Anger, Madness and the Daimonic*. Albany, NY: SUNY Press, 1997.

Edwards Betty. *Drawing on the Right Side of the Brain: A Course in Enhancing Creativity*. London: Souvenir Press, 1979.

Eliade, Mircea. *Shamanism: Archaic Techniques of Ecstasy*. New York: Bollingen Foundation, 1964.

Eliade, Mircea. *Myths, Dreams, and Mysteries*. London: Harvill Press, 1960.

Ellmann, Richard. *Oscar Wilde*. London: Penguin, 1987.

Euripides, *Bacchae*. Trans. Gilbert Murray. London: Heinemann, 1911.

Faraday, Ann. *Dream Power*. London: Hodder & Stoughton, 1972.

Fire, John, Lame Deer, and Richard Erdoes. *Lame Deer: Seeker of Visions*. New York: Simon & Schuster, 1972.

Foucault, Michel. *The History of Sexuality: An Introduction*. London: Allen Lane, 1979.

Foucault, Michel. *Madness and Civilization*. London: Tavistock Publications, 1971.

Freeman, Mark. *Finding the Muse: Sociopsychological inquiry into conditions of artistic creativity*. Cambridge: Cambridge University Press, 1994.

Freud, Sigmund. *The Interpretation of Dreams*. London: George Allan & Co., 1913.

Freud, Sigmund. *Civilization and its Discontents*. London, 1930.

Freud, Sigmund. *Leonardo da Vinci*. London: Kegan and Paul, 1922.

Furst, Peter. *Mushrooms: Psychedelic Fungi*. Broomal, PA: Chelsea House Publishing, 1986.

Gardner, Howard. *Creating Minds*. New York: Basic Books, 1993.

Gardner, Howard. *Multiple Intelligences*. New York: Basic Books, 1993.

Gedo, John E. *The Artist and the Emotional World.* New York: Columbia University Press, 1996.

Ghiselin, Brewster (ed.). *The Creative Process: Reflections on the Invention of Art.* Berkeley, CA: University of California Press, 1952.

Graves, Robert. *The White Goddess.* London: Faber & Faber, 1961.

Halifax, Joan. *Shamanic Voices.* New York: Dutton, 1979.

Hobson, Allan. *The Dreaming Brain.* New York: Basic Books, 1988.

Inayat Khan, Sufi. *Music.* London: Barrie & Rockliff, 1962.

Inglis, Brian. *Trance.* London: Grafton, 1989.

Isherwood, Christopher. *Diaries.* London: Methuen, 1996.

Jamison, K. R. *Touched with Fire.* London: Macmillan, 1993.

Jung, Carl Gustav. *Memories, Dreams, Reflections.* London: Routledge and Kegan Paul, 1963.

Kearney, Richard. *The Wake of Imagination: Ideas of Creativity in Western Culture.* London: Hutchinson, 1988.

Khanna, Madhu. *Yantra.* London: Thames & Hudson, 1979.

Kipling, Rudyard. *Something of Myself.* London: Macmillan, 1937.

Koestler, Arthur. *The Act of Creation.* London: Hutchinson, 1964.

Kris, Ernst. *Psychoanalytic Explorations in Art.* London: George Allen & Unwin, 1953.

Leary, Timothy, Ralph Metzner, and Richard Alpert. *The Psychedelic Experience.* New York: University Books, 1964.

Maslow, Abraham. *Towards a Psychology of Being.* New York: John Wiley, 1998.

Miller, John, and Randall Koral (eds.). *White Rabbit: A Psychedelic Reader.* San Francisco: Chronicle, 1995.

Nabokov, Vladimir. *Speak, Memory.* London: Weidenfeld & Nicolson, 1967.

Neihardt, John G. *Black Elk Speaks.* Lincoln, NE: University of Nebraska Press, 1961.

Ornstein, Robert. *The Psychology of Consciousness.* Harmondsworth: Penguin, 1996.

Ornstein, Robert. *Multimind.* London: Macmillan, 1986.

Panter, Barry (ed.). *Creativity and Madness: Psychological Studies of Art and Artists.* Burbank, CA: Aimed, 1995.

Pinker, Steven. *How the Mind Works.* New York: Norton, 1997.

Raine, Kathleen. *William Blake.* London: Thames & Hudson, 1970.

Read, Herbert. *Icon and Idea.* London: Faber & Faber, 1955.

Redgrove, Peter. *The Black Goddess and the Sixth Sense.* London: Bloomsbury, 1987.

Richardson, John. *A Life of Picasso, Vol. I.* London: Cape, 1991.

Rothenberg, A. *The Emerging Goddess: The creative process in art, science and other fields.* Chicago: University of Chicago Press, 1979.

Rothenberg, A. *Creativity and Madness.* Baltimore, MD: Johns Hopkins University Press, 1990.

Rothenberg, A., and B. Greenberg. *The Index of Scientific Writings on Creativity: Creative Men and Women.* New York: Archon Books, 1974.

Sandblom, Philip. *Creativity and Disease: How illness affects literature, art and music.* New York: Boyars, 1992.

Schreiber, Flora. *Sybil.* New York: Warner Books, repr. 1995.

Sternberg, R. J. (ed.). *The Nature of Creativity: Contemporary psychological perspectives.* Cambridge: Cambridge University Press, 1988.

Sternberg, R. J., and Todd I. Lubart. *Defying the Crowd: Cultivating Creativity in a Culture of Conformity.* New York: Free Press, 1995.

Snyder, S. *Drugs and the Brain.* New York: Freeman, 1996.

Storr, Anthony. *The School of Genius.* London: André Deutsch, 1988.

Tart, Charles. *States of Consciousness.* New York: Dutton, 1975.

Tart, Charles (ed.). *Altered States of Consciousness.* New York: John Wiley, 1992.

Tart, Charles (ed.). *Body, Mind, Spirit.* Charlottesville, VA: Hampton Roads Publishing Co., 1997.

Taylor, Rogan. *The Death and Resurrection Show.* London: Anthony Blond, 1985.

Tucker, Michael. *Dreaming with Open Eyes: The Shamanic Spirit in 20th Century Art and Culture.* San Francisco: Aquarian, 1992.

Ullman, Montague, Stanley Krippner, and Alan Vaughan. *Dream Telepathy.* London: Turnstone Books, 1973.

Warhol, Andy. *The Philosophy of Andy Warhol: From A to B and Back Again.* London: Cassell, 1975.

Walker, John A. *Art in the Age of Mass Media.* London: Pluto, 1983.

Wasson, R. Gordon. *The Wondrous Mushroom: Mycolatry in Mesoamerica.* New York: McGraw-Hill, 1980.

Winnicott, D. W. *The Child, the Family, and the Outside World.* Harmondsworth: Penguin Books, 1964.

INDEX

CREDITS

The publishers are grateful to the following for permission to reproduce copyrighted material.

Mrs. Marsha Arnold, Harvard Botanical Library: 169.

Archiv für Kunst und Geschichte, London: 7, 11 (Mr. & Mrs. Leigh B. Block, Chicago), 12 (Fitzwilliam Museum, Cambridge), 22/23, 52, 53 (Private Collection), 54 (Dalí Museum, Beachwood, Ohio), 56/57, 58 (Frankfurt am Freies Dt Hochstift), 61B, 63 (Goethe National Museum), 68 (Kammerhofmuseum, Gmuenden), 72, 78T, 78, 79, 80 (Kunst Handel Berlin), 83, 85T, 91 (National Portrait Gallery), 92/93 (Ca Rezzonico, Venice), 96B, 97 (Whitworth Art Gallery, Manchester), 98 (Mozart Museum, Fort Worth, Texas), 100B, 115 (Versailles Museum), 118, 119 (Fundación Dolores Olmedo Patino A.C.), 120, 124, 126 (Wiener Theater Zeitung), 127, 129, 130B (Tretyakov Gallery, Moscow), 131, 133T, 133BR, 137 (Naturhistorisches Museum), 139 (Private Collection, Monterrey)

AKG London/Paul Almasy: 69T

AKG, London/Erich Lessing: 19 (Musée d'Orsay, Paris), 36, 74 (Musée d'Orsay, Paris), 102 (Den Haag, Mauritshaus), 103, 117 (Musée d'Orsay), 125 (Von der Heydt Museum) 129B (Trinity College, Cambridge), 147, 149 (Musée d'Orsay, Paris), 154 (Tretyakov Gallery, Moscow), 158, 164 (Göteborg Kunstmuseum), 166, 178, 179 (Thomas Amman Fine Art, Zurich)

AKG, London/Niklaus Stauss: 10

The Bridgeman Art Library, London: 19 (Krasnoyarskiy Kraevoy Musey), 28B, 29 (York City Art Gallery), 47TR (ex-Edward James Foundation, Sussex), 30 (Bargello, Florence), 32 (National Gallery, London), 49BR (British Museum), 62 (Prado, Cason del Buen Retiro, Madrid), 66 (Private Collection), 67 (Private Collection), 81 (Norton Simon Collection, Pasadena), 86 (Private Collection), 95 (Fine Art Society), 121T (Prado, Madrid), 138 (Museo e gallerie Nazionali di Capodimonte, Naples)

BAL/Index: 94 (Prado, Madrid)

BAL/Peter Willi: 48 (Private Collection), 90, 143 (Musée Picasso, Paris)

Corbis: 108, 110T, 112T, 172/173

Corbis/Bettman Archive: 113, 123T

e.t. archive: 70, 123B

Hulton-Getty: 71, 85B, 148, 184

Rex Features: 13, 17L, 41, 44, 65, 69B, 135, 144, 168, 171, 171T, 172, 175

Peter T. Furst: 24, 170

Science Photo Library: 18 BM (Vaughan Fleming), 18TR (Carl Schmidt-Luchs), 35 (Sinclair Stammers), 47, 150, 161 (Alfred Pasiekt)

The Tate Gallery, London: 128, 151

Werner Forman Archive: 17R (Sheldon Jackson Museum), 18L (Eugene Chestou Trust), 57T

COPYRIGHT

p. 47TR, Salvador Dali: *Sleep.*
© DACS 1999

p. 48, Georgio de Chirico: *The Purity of a Dream*, 1915.
© DACS 1999

p. 53, Georgio de Chirico: *Il Trovatore.*
© DACS 1999

p. 54, Salvador Dali: *Hallucinogenic Toreador.*
© DACS 1999

p. 66, Willem de Kooning: *Devon*, 1971.
© Willem de Kooning, ARS, NY and DACS, London 1999

p. 67, Joan Miró: *Mythologisation of Landscape*, 1924-25.
© ADAGP, Paris and DACS, London 1999

p. 86, Lucien Freud: *Stephen Spender*, 1940 (charcoal on paper)
© Lucien Freud 1999

p. 90, Pablo Picasso: *Figures on the Seashore.*
© Succession Picasso, DACS, 1999

p. 98, Andy Warhol: *Marilyn.*
© The Andy Warhol Foundation for the Visual Arts, Inc./ARS, NY and DACS, London 1999

p. 117, Henri Matisse: *Luxe, Calme et Volupté*, 1904.
© Succession H. Matisse/DACS, 1999

p. 119, Frida Kahlo: *The Shattered Column.*
© DACS, 1999

p. 125, Max Beckmann: *Self Portrait with Bat and Trumpet.*
© DACS, 1999

p. 128, Marc Rothko: *Black on Maroon.*
© DACS, 1999

p. 139, Frida Kahlo: *Diego and I.*
© DACS, 1999

p. 143, Pablo Picasso: *Minotaur and a Dead Mare in a Front of a Cave.*
© Succession Picasso/DACS, 1999

p. 151, Francis Bacon: *Three Studies for Figures at the Base of a Crucifixion.*
© The Tate Gallery, London

p. 164, Pablo Picasso: *Saltimbanques.*
© DACS, 1999

p. 179, Andy Warhol: *Coca Cola Bottles.*
© The Andy Warhol Foundation for the Visual Arts, Inc./ARS, NY and DACS, London 1999

The publishers are grateful to the following for permission to quote copyright material: *Cahiers d'Art* for an extract from *Conversation avec Picasso* by Christian Zervos (1935), page 79; Faber & Faber Ltd for *The Thought Fox* by Ted Hughes, page 185; Guardian Media Group plc for an extract from Ted Hughes' obituary by Al Alvarez, page 185; The National Trust for Places of Historic Interest or Natural Beauty for an extract from *Something of Myself* by Rudyard Kipling (1937), page 33; Routledge for an extract from *Modern Man in Search of a Soul* by Carl Jung (1933), page 87; Thames and Hudson Ltd for extracts from *The Art of Tantra* by Philip Rawson (1978), page 155, and *Joseph Beuys* by Caroline Tisdall (1979), page 23. Every effort has been made to trace copyright holders and the publishers would be pleased to be informed of any omissions for correction in future editions.